I0817472

ALSO BY MARY HELEN WASHINGTON

The Other Blacklist: The African American Literary and Cultural Left of the 1950s

Memory of Kin: Stories about Family by Black Writers (editor)

Black-Eyed Susans and Midnight Birds: Stories by and about Black Women (editor)

Invented Lives: Narratives of Black Women, 1860–1960 (editor)

Paule Marshall

BLACK LIVES

Yale University Press's Black Lives series seeks to tell the fullest range of stories about notable and overlooked Black figures who profoundly shaped world history. Each book is intended to add a chapter to our larger understanding of the breadth of Black people's experiences as these have unfolded through time. Using a variety of approaches, the books in this series trace the indelible contributions that individuals of African descent have made to their worlds, exploring how their lives embodied and shaped the changing conditions of modernity and challenged definitions of race and practices of racism in their societies.

Paule Marshall

A WRITER'S LIFE

Mary Helen Washington

Black Lives

Yale University Press | New Haven and London

The Black Lives series is supported with a gift from the Germanacos Foundation.

Yale University Press books may be purchased in quantity for educational, business, or promotional use. For information, please e-mail sales.press@yale.edu (U.S. office) or sales@yaleup.co.uk (U.K. office).

Set in FreightText Pro type by IDS Infotech Ltd.
Printed in the United States of America.

Library of Congress Control Number: 2025943109
ISBN 978-0-300-25385-6 (hardcover)

A catalogue record for this book is available from the British Library.

Authorized Representative in the EU: Easy Access System Europe, Mustamäe tee 50, 10621 Tallinn, Estonia, gpsr.requests@easproject.com

10 9 8 7 6 5 4 3 2 1

For Shirley Moody-Turner and Shaun Myers
and in memory of Cheryl A. Wall

CONTENTS

Paule Marshall

INTRODUCTION

IN DECEMBER 2018, I drove to Richmond, Virginia, to visit my eighty-nine-year-old friend Paule Marshall, who was in a nursing home, suffering from dementia. Paule and I had been friends for over forty years, but over the past ten, she had been more and more elusive, not answering the phone and often postponing my visits. I had finally reached her by way of her son Evan Marshall, an award-winning yacht designer living in London, who told me she had been in the Richmond nursing home for several years. I drove to Richmond immediately. Evan was there, and Paule was in a lovely single room. Bookcases lined one wall, with plaques and pictures on each shelf as well as many of her books. This tiny woman seated in a wheelchair, looking unsure of who I was, was not the woman I'd known. It was difficult to talk to her—she would start a sentence and not know how to finish, though she clearly wanted to talk to me. I did most of the talking, naming each of her books, telling her what I liked about each one. When Evan left the room, she struggled to talk more. She knew, however, that I was talking to her diminished self, and, in a moment of clarity, speaking with the insight of a writer, she said, almost defiantly, "You're looking at something that doesn't exist."

I intended to visit her again, but on August 13, 2019, Paule Valenza Burke Marshall died at the age of ninety of "complications due to Alzheimer's disease."

When I left that December day, Evan asked if I would consider writing her biography. He took me to the storage facility where most of Paule's belongings had been packed away, and, offering me three huge laundry tubs containing what looked like a jumble of papers of all kinds—manuscripts, bills, tax receipts—and a few photographs, started me on this awesome task. As I drove back to Silver Spring that night, I realized that in the back seat of my Altima was nearly everything that constitutes the Paule Marshall "archive."

I first encountered Paule Marshall when I asked to include her story "Reena" in my 1975 anthology *Black-Eyed Susans and Midnight Birds: Classic Stories by and about Black Women.* I remember meeting her in person in 1979, when I found out that her novel *Brown Girl, Brownstones* was out of print, and I suggested the book to Florence Howe, the founding editor of the Feminist Press. I met Paule in her New York apartment, 407 Central Park West, and as we talked about the reissue of *Brown Girl,* I saw she had a wonderful oil painting of a young girl by Ernie Crichlow. I suggested that the painting should be the cover of the new edition of *Brown Girl,* and she agreed. I wrote an introduction to that edition in 1981, and her novel became a staple throughout the country in courses on black women writers. In the *Norton Anthology of African American Literature,* literary scholar Cheryl Wall deemed it "the novel that most black feminist critics consider to be the beginning of contemporary African American women's writings."[1] Over the years, Paule invited me to visit her in New York, took me to parties, and once got Broadway tickets for me and Evan to see James Earl Jones in August Wilson's *Fences.* I have one snapshot of me with Paule in a park outside of her condo in

Richmond around 1995. It shows us in deep conversation, as though we are engaged in a fierce intellectual debate— and I am sure we were.

There are precious few documents of Paule's personal life. There was a robbery in the basement storage units of her Richmond apartment when she first moved there, so whatever she might have saved, including photographs from her early Brooklyn life, was lost. As I began to make a more systematic inventory of the laundry tubs I had taken home, I discovered a dozen pages of drafts of uncompleted work, a few snippets of personal anecdotes, teaching notes, IRS records, some important photographs, and a letter from James Baldwin congratulating her on the publication of her second novel. That seemed to be all I had to produce a biography. But on a subsequent visit to the storage facility in Richmond, I discovered two archival jewels. Buried in the mountain of the still unsorted material, at the bottom on a huge packing box, was Paule's iBookG4 computer, where she had begun to write more personally about her life. The device was so ancient it did not require a password. In another box I found the slender, dark green, leather-bound journal Paule kept in 1983, when she was on a writers' tour to China. These are, so far, the only two sources we have of her self-revealed private life.

I began to interview people who knew Paule, including her son, her stepdaughter, her niece, and her friends, who all confirmed that she was a very private person. She was, I discovered, loath to write personal letters, even to her son. So, already hampered by this scant archive, I had the task of writing about a highly reserved and private subject. Paule was cautious, even secretive, in talking about her life; much remained hidden. Her interviews are masterpieces of manipulation and dissimulation, gestures that conceal as much as they reveal, but her fiction can help give a richer sense of this extraordinary woman. She drew from her own life for many of the details and characters in her writing, despite always maintaining that it was not autobiographical.

Although she received many prestigious awards—a Guggenheim (1960), the American Book Award (1984), the John Dos Passos Prize for Literature (1989), and a MacArthur Fellowship (1991),—Paule did not achieve the kind of recognition or attention accorded Ralph Ellison, James Baldwin, Toni Morrison, or Alice Walker. She must have chafed when *Ebony* magazine editors in 1984 finally turned their attention to the new wave of black women writers and ranked them as though conducting a literary contest. The *Ebony* article, "Black Women Novelists: New Generation Raises Provocative Issues," assigned Alice Walker and Toni Morrison first place as "the principal architects of this emerging cadre of Black women novelists," even though Paule had preceded Morrison and Walker with her 1959 novel *Brown Girl, Brownstones* and her 1961 short story collection *Soul Clap Hands and Sing*. *Ebony* gave second and third place to Ntozake Shange and Toni Cade Bambara as writers on "the movement's cutting edge." Paule Marshall, author of three novels and two short story collections, tied for fourth place with the young Gloria Naylor, who had just published her first book.[2]

In a respectful but probing interview in 1991, journalist Jacqueline Trescott noted the lack of commercial acceptance for her work, concluding that Paule "played a part in her periodic invisibility." When Paule responded to Trescott's question about her lack of commercial success and media attention, she filtered her anger through the voices of her faithful readers: "Those who read my work, and love it, are sometimes distressed by what they see as the neglect I've suffered at the hands of the literary establishment. Some of them get downright hot about it." The words Paule chose to describe her situation—*distressed, suffered, downright hot, neglect*—are packed with intensity, and Trescott picked up on the subtle gesture of Paule's withdrawal as she spoke, noting that she "folds her small chestnut-brown hands in her lap, as if she were pulling back from the heat of this talk."[3]

For thirty years, Paule was often her own worst publicist, deflecting attention away from the most challenging and provocative meanings of her fiction. "Television and radio appearances, book parties, public debates, cocktail parties and the like do not appeal to her. She simply refuses to cultivate a marketable image . . . personal interviews such as this one with Trescott unnerve her initially," as Alexis De Veaux noted in a 1979 interview.[4] In another interview, Paule was reluctant to reveal personal details about her life and somewhat defensive about being unwilling to perform publicly:

> The writer has to find ways of becoming a public personality, and I'm not very good at that. I have such a hell of a time to get the words on paper, that is such a struggle for me, that then to take on this other thing which is also a major undertaking is something that I've not been terribly good at. One has to find ways of promoting oneself in the hopes of promoting the work, and my attitude was, look, I've written the book, I've got an agent and the publicity persons in the publishing house, let them go out and sell it . . . but it doesn't happen that way. So one of the reasons for *Brown Girl, Brownstones* not doing very well that first time around was in part that I didn't understand what the whole literary establishment was all about.[5]

Despite the notion that she was responsible for her lack of commercial success, Paule had a contract in 1959 with Random House for her first book *Brown Girl, Brownstones.* Later she was under contract with Atheneum, another major press. She commanded a $100,000 advance for her 1991 novel *Daughters,* a $150,000 advance for her fifth novel *The Fisher King* in 2000, and $75,000 for her 2009 memoir *Triangular Road.* Her notebooks detail all the activity she devoted to publicizing her work, including a relentless travel schedule. Noted scholar Trudier Harris wrote that given her teaching, friendships, writers' workshops, work with women's groups, emergence of book-length studies of her works, and popularity on the lecture circuit, "Marshall's work now exists at a history-making stage." In 2010, when James C. Hall and Heather Hathaway edited and published a collection of her interviews, *Conversations with Paule Marshall,* a complex portrait of Paule and her work was available for the first time.[6] What has not yet been available is a full-length biography that takes the measure of Paule Marshall's entire life, seeing how the parts make a whole.[7]

In calling this "A Writer's Life," I am putting the sparse documentation of Paule's life into dialogue with her imaginative work to reveal more fully the biography of someone whose writing, in many ways, was her life. Despite her aversion to intimate self-portraiture, a biography that traces both the arc and the minute details of her artistic career will bring into focus the magnitude of her achievement and begin to renovate her neglected reputation. In her writing, Paule did what only a few of her contemporaries in black American literature had yet attempted (among them, June Jordan, Audre Lorde, and Toni Cade Bambara): as heir to African American, Caribbean, and African cultures—the Triangular Road—she insisted on viewing black people as part of a world community. She made fierce examinations of colonialism and capitalism, as well as racism and sexism, and powerfully represented resistance to these assaults. She foregrounded nonconforming, nonheterosexual black women, always

Paule Marshall (right) and the author Mary Helen Washington engaged in an intense discussion outside Paule's apartment in Richmond, Virginia, in the summer of 1995.

portraying them as agents in their own lives. For fifty years, from 1959 to 2009, in five novels, two collections of short stories, and her many essays, Paule Marshall set the stage for contemporary black women writers, and she did so with greater authority than any writer before her.

CHAPTER 1

These Is New York Children

IN PAULE MARSHALL'S FIRST NOVEL, *Brown Girl, Brownstones,* the Barbadian mother Silla Boyce warns her women friends to stop using corporal punishment on their children: "You better watch that heavy hand . . . 'cause this is New York and these is New York children." Silla's warning that "the authorities will dash you in jail for [beating] them" is not out of fear of punishment; she is signaling her awareness that these children of the next generation are modern, more privileged than their parents, and aware of their freedom to experiment and explore.[1]

That modern child is visible in the 1936 photograph of Brooklyn-born Pauline Burke, taken when she was six years old. She is seated at a child-size table, her arms placed on a large picture book, her feet primly crossed at the ankle, showing off her white Mary Jane shoes and ankle socks. She wears a billowing white taffeta dress, a white ribbon circling her head and tied in a large bow around the dark Shirley Temple curls that frame her face. It is a picture of a proper black middle-class child, aspiring to and groomed for integration. Only the upward tilt of her head and her pursed lips suggest the defiant character that so annoyed her mother and would become a catalyst for Paule Marshall's writing. Pauline is inquisitive and poised, staring straight at the

Pauline at six years old in a studio photograph, 1936.

camera, but there is also a vulnerability in her expression that is very far from a smile. Born in 1929, one year after the much-duplicated Shirley Temple, she was most certainly not an imitation. She was a new creation of the black modern world, born not into privilege but into a history of black determination and struggle. Her name then was Pauline Valenza Burke; her choice to re-name herself Paule Marshall came later.

Daughter of Adriana Viola Clement Burke and Samuel Burke, both from the small Caribbean island of Barbados, Pauline was born on April 9, 1929. By that time the family had moved from Red Hook to a second-floor apartment over a grocery store at 1061 Fulton Street in Brooklyn, a city in transition. The superstitious Adriana believed that as a result of a dispute with the family downstairs, their neighbor was practicing obeah and had "put something for her" that turned her milk sour, forcing Adriana to wean her daughter abruptly at three months.[2] The Dutch and the English had arrived in Brooklyn in the early 1600s, followed by the Scotch-Irish, Germans, Scandinavians, Jews, Italians, Poles, and Irish. When the West Indians arrived, it was "like a dark sea nudging its way onto a white beach," or, as the poet Gwendolyn Brooks put it, "Where Tea and Father were . . . are dark folk, drinking beer."[3] Pauline came of age in Brooklyn during the short-lived period when both black and white immigrants were forging a path toward economic opportunity. As she nostalgically remembered, "I lived in this wonderful polyglot world in Brooklyn, in the 30s and 40s and early 50s, where you had all these various immigrant groups coming together."[4]

The year 1929 was a good one for a highly gifted black girl from a hustling working-class black immigrant family to be born in Brooklyn, New York. Even if black immigrants and southern migrants were not unaware of the conditional nature of the American promise of a better life, they nonetheless claimed it as their

The second-floor apartment over a grocery store at 1061 Fulton Street in Brooklyn where Pauline was born in 1929.

right, their chance to look for the warmth of other suns.[5] As Adriana was standing on the corner in Brooklyn waiting to be hired by white women for domestic work, she was also "studying the dollar" and working "to buy house." The 1930s and 1940s were decades of fragile integration in the North, when blacks and whites shared the city before it became the "inner" city. During Pauline's early Brooklyn years, the federal programs established by Franklin Roosevelt's Depression-era New Deal influenced everything from education to public works to the arts. Activists of the second generation of the black Left were stirring as early as 1930, creating the American Negro Theatre and the Harlem Artists Guild; and with economic initiatives like the Works Project Administration, new defense industry jobs, and cheap real estate courtesy of the war economy, conditions were favorable for the rise of a black urban middle class, and Pauline was surrounded by those strivers.[6] Upward mobility was not their only goal. The motto of the $6 million Paragon Progressive Federal Union founded in 1941 by immigrants from Barbados was "Not for profit, but for service."

Pauline attended schools with white and black immigrant kids and African Americans, who would take advantage of the free city colleges and libraries in Brooklyn and New York City. As eager as she was to escape what she considered her "provincial" hometown, the Brooklyn she grew up in produced a number of illustrious blacks, including visual artist and fellow Bajan Ernie Crichlow, whose painting graced the cover of Paule's first novel, and Brooklyn-born Bajan Shirley Chisholm, who became the first black woman to run for U.S. president. The prestigious Boys High School in Brooklyn boasted a number of notable black artists, including baritone saxophonist Cecil Payne, drummer Max Roach, pianist Randy Weston, and Paule's first husband, Kenneth Marshall.

Pauline's parents immigrated to the United States in 1922, becoming part of two simultaneous streams of black mobility. The first major wave of West Indian immigration after World War I intersected with the Great Migration of tens of thousands of African Americans leaving the South between 1915 and 1960. Both groups came for many of the same reasons: to escape economic and racial oppression and in search of the jobs that became available during the two world wars. Pauline's mother Adriana Viola Clement, born in 1903, daughter of a cooper, a maker of barrels in which sugar, "the *life blood* of Barbados," was exported, hailed from the hilly district of Barbados called Scotland on the Atlantic. Paule was proud of the energy and determination of both of her parents. In a fictionalized story, she describes Adriana arriving in New York Harbor on the SS *Nerissa,* "awed and overwhelmed seeing New York rise shining and imperial from the sea."[7] She came with "show money," the $50 that Caribbean immigrants had to present to U.S. authorities in order to disembark, sometimes called "Panama money" because it was often supplied by a male relative who worked in the harsh conditions on the Panama Canal and sent money home. In Adriana's case, the money came from one of her brothers who earned it working, and eventually dying, in the swamps and jungles of Panama.[8]

The awe Adriana felt at seeing New York on her first day was soon tempered by her circumstances.[9] Her older brother Winston Carlyle Clement, a hard-working, upwardly climbing Bajan, promptly found her a job as a live-in domestic worker and nursemaid to three children in a ten-room house on Long Island, entitled to Sundays and every other Thursday off; the other nights she spent in her room in the white family's basement. Adriana was then, according to her daughter, an unsophisticated eighteen-year-old so pampered by her older sister Branford Catherine that she was not able to braid her own hair.[10] Paule described the young Adriana as an "overgrown baby," crying her eyes out, her head buried under a pillow, an image that is far from the dominating figure her writer daughter would later contend with.[11]

In contrast to Adriana, Samuel Burke, who was the love of Pauline's life, carried himself as a sophisticated man of the world. Born in 1900 in Barbados, as a young man he made his way to Cuba, where he worked for several years in or near the sugar mill town of Central Hershey near Santa Cruz, which supplied sugar for Hershey's chocolates. Milton Hershey said that he provided for his workers in Cuba just as he did in Hershey, Pennsylvania. He built a town—or "batey"—that he claimed would permit his employees to choose where they would live and provide comfortable homes for rent; good health care; recreational facilities, including a baseball diamond, and golf course, sports club; and a general store. Samuel found himself living in segregated facilities, cutting canes with machetes, the same kind of hard, dangerous plantation work that he would have done in Barbados, but under a hotter sun and without family and friends. When he rose high enough at one point to be allowed to help transport the sugar to the port city of Nuevitas, he encountered Cubans as black as he was and developed a life-long love of Spanish culture—he gave Spanish names to both of his daughters, Anita and Valenza. After his experiences with a world and a culture beyond Barbados, Samuel landed in Brooklyn with a taste for a larger life. Contrary to Paule's memory of her father slipping into the United States as an undocumented stowaway, Samuel Burke's name is listed on the passenger manifest of the SS *Miami* leaving Cuba for New York in 1922, although apparently he never filed for legal papers or became a U.S. citizen.

Two years after Samuel came to the United States, he met Adriana in Brooklyn. In Paule's fictionalized version of their meeting, Sam took a liking to the shy, "sweet-faced Bajan girl," and she to the fast-talking young man who "gets on like somebody raise up in big Bridgetown-self."[12] In Paule's story, Samuel was the "town blade" who seduced the unsophisticated Adriana with his knowing sexual advances, and Adriana was the coy innocent, pretending to resist, all the while enjoying and encouraging the erotic play.[13] Within a few months after their meeting, Samuel and Adriana, already pregnant, were married on September 15, 1924. Their first daughter Anita (called Neat) was born in 1925.

A formal photograph of the young Burke family shortly after Anita's birth was taken at a moment when the family's future must have seemed assured. Adriana wore a 1920s light-colored flapper dress and a long string of pearls as she held baby Anita with obvious pride. Paule's description of Samuel captures his cool pose: "his thick bush of hair parted boldly down the middle . . . a three-piece suit that, although cheap, looks expensive on him. . . . A boulevardier's bow tie [that] complements the bespoke-looking suit, as does the handkerchief and fountain pen in his breast pocket."[14] Some of those items, obviously studio props to suggest their future as a determined, successful, and prosperous American family, belie the fact that the Burke family was living in a cold-water flat in Red Hook, Brooklyn, with the bathtub in the middle of the kitchen.

Anita, whom Paule considered the pretty one, "the perfect child," was four when Pauline was born. Their brother Franklin Edsel, named after the members of two prominent American families, the Roosevelts and the Fords, an indication of the Burke family's desire for Americanness, was born in 1938; an unnamed son, born on June 7, 1941, died one day later. With a brother nine years younger, Pauline was the designated babysitter. Steeped already in the protocols of Bajan respectability, she was resentful and embarrassed when her mother made her take her baby brother in the stroller through the neighborhood. A star student, Pauline feared that she might be taken for an unwed teenage mother, and she was also jealous of her father's great delight in a son.

The dapper Sam Burke believed that he "possessed the ability and talent to be so much more" than a factory worker, but he was never able to secure "a job that didn't call for the overalls and work clothes of a common laborer." He found work in a mattress factory, where he was forced to wear a snood to protect his hair from the lint, "covering his head like a woman."[15] Always entrepreneurial,

Studio portrait of Adriana Burke, baby Anita, and Sam Burke, 1925.

Sam also maintained a side job as a door-to-door salesman after work or on the weekends, walking the streets of black Brooklyn selling cosmetics, stockings, and hair products designed for dark-skinned women that were not available in department stores. The fashion and cosmetic industry in the 1940s and 1950s often made only a single product for "Negro women," presuming the same shade of brown in stockings and cosmetics would suit all black women. For a while, Sam was an enterprising salesman, with an early awareness of the importance of black consumers, whose buying power would become even more obvious with the introduction of pictorial magazines such as *Ebony, Sepia,* and *Our World.* He would pursue all sorts of possible endeavors—radio repair, home study in accounting, trumpet lessons—each abandoned when he lost interest, though he remained optimistic about his next pursuit. Sam was a man who saw the city, as cultural historian Adam Green put it, not only as a place of economic opportunity but "as a site of creativity."[16] For his wife, whom he left in poverty, Sam was a failure, a label she also pinned on her youngest daughter to deter her from her high-minded ambition to be a writer.

The year 1938 was a turning point for the Burke family, especially for Pauline. The grand matriarch of the Clement family, Alberta Jane Sobers Clement, called M'Da-Duh, wife of Prince Albert Clement of Barbados, who had managed to acquire land in Barbados with money sent from her son in Panama, decided to send Adriana the money to sail to Barbados with her two daughters to meet their grandmother. The trip triggered the first of many conflicts between Adriana and Samuel, who called the trip a "harebrained idea" and wanted to invest Alberta's money in a brownstone, "the wise way."[17] Overriding Samuel, Adriana took Anita, thirteen, and Pauline, nine, to spend the year in Barbados, a memory so vivid that Paule captured it in her 1967 short story "To Da-Duh, in Memoriam," which she called the most autobiographical of all her work.

The story served several purposes for Paule in her lifelong struggle to understand the conflicts between her parents and herself. Linked together are several themes that she would rework over the next fifty years: the desire of the child for a self separate from her parents, the triumph of the daughter over a dominant mother, and the oppositional will required for a woman to become an artist.

Adriana tried to enroll Pauline and Anita in school in Barbados, the worst thing she could have done, Paule wrote, "when you know the British system in the colonies."[18] In his 1970 autobiographical novel *In the Castle of My Skin,* George Lamming described schooling in Barbados as an initiation into empire, produced by symbols and holidays. The Union Jack flag was flying everywhere, and the queen's birthday and Empire Day were school holidays. Barbados, Lamming wrote, was truly Little England: "The other islands had changed hands. Now they were French, now they were Spanish. But Little England remained steadfast and constant to Big England. . . . Little England and Big England, God's anointed on earth."[19] Pauline didn't last long in school that year. Corporal punishment was acceptable and routine, and when she was faced with watching children being caned, she told her mother she couldn't take it. She refused to be beaten and "couldn't bear to see others being beaten."[20]

"To Da-Duh, in Memoriam" is narrated by an adult visual artist but captures the perspective of the precocious nine-year-old unnamed daughter and granddaughter, who claims her grandmother Da-Duh as both a kindred spirit and a rival. Granddaughter and grandmother begin to spar as soon as they meet. The girl has the upper hand, however, because the rich vegetation and natural beauty of Barbados—its tall canes and pawpaw, breadfruit, guava, and mango—cannot compare with the industrial and technological might of the United States. The granddaughter boasts about "refrigerators, radios, gas stoves, elevators, trolley cars, wringer washing machines, movies, airplanes, the cyclone at Coney Island, subways, toasters, [and] electric lights," which can be triggered with a mere flip of the wall switch, like "turning on the sun at night."[21] The girl performs the songs and dances of Tin Pan Alley and shows off her Shirley Temple coat, winning over the grandmother, who had previously preferred her "whiter" grandchildren.[22] Da-Duh is amazed and ultimately subdued by this competition. Gloating over the prestige and global status of the United States, the little American granddaughter represents empire. She mails Da-Duh a picture postcard of the Empire State Building, offering further proof of the superior might of the United States. By the time the card arrives, Da-Duh is dead.

Following Da-Duh's death, the narrator's aunt writes from Barbados, telling her of the violence England unleashed on the colony when the workers went on strike. The 1937 labor strikes in the British colonies over labor rights and economic inequality swept through Jamaica, Belize, British Honduras, British Guiana, St. Kitts, and Barbados, eventually leading to independence movements in many Caribbean countries, and also dismantling the illusion of "Little England's" familial relationship to its imperial holdings. First published in 1967, during the Black Arts Movement, the story ends with the adult granddaughter unable to paint distant tropical scenes in imitation of European artists because "the thunderous tread of the machines in the factory below her loft studio jarred the floor beneath my easel."[23] "To Da-Duh" was the beginning of the writer's sense of the importance of the West Indies and initiates another one of Paule's major themes: "America's excessive preoccupation with materialism and the impact of that on its citizens and the rest of the world."[24]

The story triggered a painful conflict for Paule between an elite identity as a U.S. citizen and her Barbadian heritage, or, as she later put it, "the relationship between western civilization and the Third World." When she returned to Brooklyn, Pauline worked hard to erase the signs of Barbadian culture, especially to eliminate the accent she had acquired: "When we went to the West Indies and came back with heavy West Indian accents, the kids used to laugh at us. Right away I got rid of the bangles and I worked assiduously to rid myself of this dirty mark, this Barbadian accent, tried to reject the Afro-West-Indian part of myself."[25] For the rest of her life, she never spoke with a Barbadian accent except in intimate spaces with other West Indians. Pauline had thought of herself as an "Afro-American growing up on the mean streets of Brooklyn," but this trip "reinforce[d] the whole West Indian aspect that was very painful for me because I saw myself belonging to both."[26]

If the Barbados visit exposed Paule's inner conflicts, it also ignited a lifelong desire to unite the two cultures, African American and Caribbean, in her writing and in her life.[27] When she discovered the poetry of Paul Laurence Dunbar at the Macon Street branch of the Brooklyn Public Library and saw the way Dunbar incorporated black vernacular in his poetry, she understood that the Barbados trip could help her bridge the two worlds: "It was only then, for the first time, that I sensed that there were these two things operating for me. . . . I began to see the marvelous gift and the great benefit of that experience."[28] Yet the tension would always remain. Even in 2009, Paule chafed over the memory of a black student at Dartmouth College questioning her presence at a meeting for African Americans.

In the 1940 census, the Burke household consisted of Adriana, thirty-seven; Anita, fifteen; Pauline, eleven; and Frank, ten. Adriana (listed as Viola) is named as head of household, unemployed, and receiving "income other places." The son born in 1941, as well as the reference to Adriana's income from other places, suggest that Samuel was still around in 1940, despite not being listed in the household. When Pauline was about ten years old, Adriana and Samuel combined their salaries from Adriana's domestic work and Samuel's factory salary and were finally able to lease one of the smaller, less impressive brownstones at 501 Hancock Street, "a plain Jane of a brownstone with almost no decorative stone-work on its somber reddish-brown four-story façade," but graced with a single chestnut tree in the front.[29] Unlike the grand brown-stone house Paule enshrined in her novel *Brown Girl, Brownstones,* this one sat alone on a corner next to a commercial street on one side and a small apartment building on the other.

Samuel, however, "in his endless seeking, had found god," and was on his way to abandoning his low-status jobs—his family and the quest to "buy house"—to become a disciple in the mission of Father Divine, whose movement he encountered in Harlem in the early 1940s.[30] He was recruited by Divine to work in Philadelphia, the central site of the movement from 1942 to 1965, and once committed to the Divine movement, he never returned to the family. Pauline was devastated by her father's abandonment and for the rest of her life she would mourn the loss of the father who called his daughters "Lady-folks" and sang, "Rise and shine and give God the glory" each morning to wake them.[31] While Paule would openly celebrate her mother's influence on her writing, Sam would always be there in the margins, a haunting presence in every book she wrote.

Samuel Burke became Brother Burke in the Kingdom of the Reverend Major Jealous Divine (called so because God is jealous of anyone put before him), most likely attracted to this charismatic figure because Father Divine promised a kind of earthly greatness and freedom from the dead-end drudgery of his working-class life. Originally named George Baker, Divine had renamed himself and become one of a series of black cult-like figures who held great power over segments of the black community in the 1930s and 1940s. Divine led his International Peace

Mission from around 1919 through the 1960s, a small community of black followers he started in New York that eventually became multiracial and spread to Los Angeles, Philadelphia, Washington State, and even Europe, Canada, and Australia. Divine attracted black and white followers, men and women, to his integrated banquets, a kind of Eucharist for his followers to dine and commune with God. He preached a combination of conservative and progressive ideas that rejected gender categories, preached against lynching, and prohibited drinking, gambling, or sexual relations—his followers were married to God. Divine instructed his followers to abandon all family ties, refer to one another as "Brother" and "Sister," and consider him their Father. His views on race, gender, and civil rights; rejection of black inferiority; promotion of black entrepreneurship; internationalism; and enshrinement of himself as a divinity were some of the most imaginative experiments of his time. In this Depression-era movement, Divine found jobs for his followers in the restaurants and hotels he established and which they collectively administered and staffed. He inaugurated the first racially integrated hotels in the United States, where his "dark-complected" followers could live inexpensively in simple hotels, called "Heavens," and feel safe from racial discrimination.[32] It was once dubbed the Divine New Deal. Divine was influenced by the New Thought Movement, a kind of self-help program that hitched spiritual ideas to the power of positive thinking. His motto, which his followers repeated on entering and leaving Divine's heavenly mansions, was: "Peace, it's truly wonderful. Father will provide."[33]

Adriana was mystified and angry when her husband left her with three children for what she considered another one of his schemes. But Sam was revising the limited life script he had been given as a black man as well as the insular black Bajan script of relentless upward mobility and clan identification. Like his youngest daughter, he chose an assertion of community and a creative self-construction over mere individualism—and shared identity over clan loyalty.

Facing eviction after Sam deserted the family, the family had to leave the coveted brownstone at 501 Hancock. Adriana and the three children wandered from one walk-up to another, finally able to find cheaper housing in "the cramped third-floor apartment of a brownstone owned by a fellow Bajan," a great humiliation for a proud, striving Barbadian. Adriana spent the next years threatening her daughters "with the dire consequences that awaited us should we become 'little wring-tail concubines caterwauling about the streets looking for men,' " or shame her by coming home "tumbling big with some wild-dog puppy."[34]

With Sam gone, Pauline got her first job when she was twelve, working at a clothing factory "picking threads" earning $25, presumably a week's salary. She lost the job when they discovered at the end of the summer that she was underage. As soon as she turned fourteen, she went back and picked threads every summer. In the winter after school, she painted ceramic figurines in another factory. Her sanctuary was the Macon Street branch of the Brooklyn Public Library, where she discovered literature—most importantly, the poetry of Paul Laurence Dunbar. School was also sanctuary. She was at the head of her class and was named the informal poet laureate at Bushwick High School, one of the best public schools in Brooklyn.

Although we know very little about Sam Burke after he joined Father Divine, we know a lot more about Adriana from Paule's often-told stories of "the poets in the kitchen." Originally entitled "Shaping the World of My Art," an essay in the literary journal *New Letters* in 1973, "the poets in the kitchen" became a kind of ars poetica in which Paule explained how her artistic sense was nurtured as she listened to her mother and her mother's friends spinning tales in the kitchen about their lives: "My mother and her friends would talk about their madams, as they were called then, and in describing them, they taught me about characterization. How you pick up the detail that is striking. I grew up among people to whom language was an art. Art was present in the most ordinary things that they said. They created poetry as they sat around a table talking about poverty, religion, and discrimination in 'this man country.' " In *Brown Girl, Brownstones,* one of Silla's friends stands in awe of her power with words: "'Talk yuh talk, Silla! Be-Jees, in this white-man world you got to take yuh mouth an make a gun." It was poetry as weapon. [35]

Paule described this community of women as politically sophisticated; they discussed the Depression, Roosevelt—"their great savior"—and the war, but much of their political talk was in support of their hero Marcus Garvey and his organization, the Universal Negro Improvement Association (UNIA), which required "Negro blood or African ancestry" for membership. They contributed money to Garvey's Black Star Line. They joined Garvey's Universal Black Cross Nurses Brigade and, dressed in white from cap to shoes, marched every year down Seventh Avenue in the Garvey Day parade. While Sam escaped from the family, Pauline remained "locked in" the kitchen, serving cocoa or tea to her mother and her friends, listening to the women whose oral storytelling was the marvelous literary pageant that made her fall in love with words. The young Pauline learned about the power of words "from [Adriana's] manipulation of language" and "the strong, artistic quality of Black language" "expressed in those areas where we're not censored or oppressed, where we can fully express ourselves."[36]

In the 1973 version of the essay in *New Letters*, the mother-poets appear as consummate storytellers, their freewheeling and robust vernacular voices castigating the white housewives they work for, weaving tales about back home, telling bawdy stories about men unable to perform sexually, obeahs boiling lizard soup to counteract "duppies walking pon the roof at night," and angry recollections of colonial oppression in Barbados: "People having to work for next skin to nothing." Pauline was entranced by these storytelling sessions and the verbal powers of these women, which was one of the reasons she wanted to write: "To see, if, on paper, I couldn't have some of that power."[37] She always credited these women with the skill in the art of oral storytelling that aligned them with what she called "an Ellisonian aesthetic." That is, they were creating what Ralph Ellison insisted on in his art: an expression of the rugged sense of life that transformed black lives and affirmed the worth of black people.[38]

In a 1981 interview, Paule began to unleash her long-simmering anger at her mother, admitting that her mother's influence, although "fundamental and crucial," was also negative: "My mother never directly encouraged me to write. . . . It was her saying to me when I was in Junior High School after I'd won all the medals, saying to me out of her own defeat and failure, that I was a failure. No, the influence was not positive, it was full of problems, stress, and antagonism. She called me a 'force-ripe woman'; 'two head bulls,' she would say, 'can't rein in a flock'; or 'Here you've come to read the burial service over me'; 'Look how I done brought something in the world to whip me.' . . . She wanted me to get a job as a secretary, or at the telephone company, not to go to college," to get along "in a kind of minimal way. . . . Because of all my grand ambitions, she used to call me 'poor great.' "[39]

In this interview Paule spoke candidly about her mother's domination, yet several weeks later, Paule wrote to the interviewer, refusing to allow the interview to be published: "Don't like the way I sound at all in that Boston interview—too garbled and repetitious. Don't want to see that stuff in print anywhere." Later she tried to explain her retraction, saying that she was grappling with the relationship with her mother in spiritual terms and would be more forthcoming in her memoirs: "Also, one of my real breakthroughs since I've started practicing Siddha yoga has been to put to rest some of the painful and negative aspects of my relationship with my mother. I dealt with all that fictionally in *Brown Girl,* and in part in *To Da-duh, in Memoriam,* and that's enough until I write my memoirs and 'let it all hang out.' So just delete the interview part and everything will be fine."[40]

Two years later, in 1983, when Paule repurposed the "poets in the kitchen" essay for the *New York Times,* the mother-poets were significantly diminished. She presented them as a group of ordinary housewives "in shapeless house dresses, dowdy felt hats and long, dark solemn coats," their bawdy vernacular tales rerouted through her own perspective and her voice: "They talked endlessly, passionately, poetically, and with impressive range," she wrote, but their oral stories and voices were eliminated.[41] Their oral art no longer represented an "Ellisonian aesthetic"; it was now a kind of "cheap therapy" that "restored them to themselves and reaffirmed their self-worth." The women were now "the female counterpart" of Ellison's "invisible man," suffering "a triple invisibility, being black, female, and foreigners," not the artists whose expressive magic swept Paule into the orbit of Hardy, Mann, Gide, Conrad, and Wright.[42]

Paule (and her critics) constantly replayed the story of "the poets in the kitchen," rarely acknowledging the contradictory versions of the story and unaware that Paule was eliding the complicated relationship with her mother and the deep and lingering attachment to her absent father. Because her father left the family when she was twelve, and she never saw him engaged in the political and social conversations that so influenced her writing, he seemed to slip from view.[43] Paule almost always repeated the story of his abandonment, which was not only a psychological trauma for her but a financial blow that left the family in extreme poverty and in the shameful position of having to rent rooms in a brownstone owned by a fellow Bajan. She rarely mentioned her father's extramarital affairs, though her memoir notes that Sam often "took to the streets" and that Adriana accused him of having a "keep-miss."[44]

But none of Sam's failures diminished Paule's memory of a charismatic and loving father. When she made the decision to change her name to Paule, about which she tells many different stories, she was following in Sam's footsteps. On a radio program, Jazz90-Cross Talk, in 1990 with host Ernest White, she spoke about her aversion to the name Pauline, which was her mother's choice: "I will not answer to Pauline, which is my original name. My father named me Valenza, but my mother couldn't deal with all that Spanish, you see, so she insisted that I also be called Pauline—Valenza Pauline. My father thoroughly disliked Pauline, and so from very early on, he always called me variations of the name—*Leen-ey, Paulee.* At twelve, I decided to call a halt to the nonsense (The perils of Pauline, and such) and name myself Paule. I especially like the sound of it in French—you can almost hear the 'e.' "[45] The change from Pauline to Paule was both modernizing and masculinizing—she insisted that it be pronounced "Paule—like a man," but she retained the feminized silent "e" at the end—a move toward the gender fluidity and identification with her father that runs through her life and her fiction. Samuel had changed his name to Sam Burke—insisting on having no middle name because "Bajans believe in having too many long, old-time English names. I decided to modernize mine. Sam Burke is all the name I need."[46]

Paule empathized with her father for wanting to surpass his dead-end job prospects and expressed admiration for his daring.

She remembered that he once squandered a week's pay to buy her and her sister U.S. Air Force bomber jackets to show his loyalty to the United States during World War II. One long-overlooked line tucked into her essay about the much-celebrated "mother-poets" is Paule's memory of wanting to write "the story of a girl who could magically transplant herself to wherever she wanted to be in the world—such as Father Divine's kingdom in Harlem."[47] When Paule was interviewed on the *Today Show* in 1990, she told interviewer Deborah Norville that the loss of her father was the great tragedy of her life: "I never stopped missing him."[48] Sam became the luminescent absent father figure, lingering over his daughter's life with a force far greater than the thick, dense, observable figure of the mother.

Paule struggled all of her life to understand her relationship with her parents: "impossible to love [them], impossible not to."[49] By the time she delivered her autobiographical lectures at Harvard in 2006, she was ready to calculate a balance sheet. She confessed to the Harvard audience that on the other side of the love she felt for her father as a child was "an ongoing, unyielding anger," always filtered through her longing to remember the father who cherished her and her sister. She would acknowledge her "helpless" love for Sam Burke, but she also blamed his "antic, endearing, heretical" ways for a lifetime of unwise searching for "replicas" of her father, who appear in her fiction. By 2006, she could acknowledge Sam's failures, but she presented them as a spur to her success: "I might have spent yet another lifetime on the run from the defeat Sam Burke pursued as actively as he did his many ill-fated projects, had I not vowed early on that once I found work that truly engaged me, I would stay the course no matter what." Paule must have felt some discomfort over these recollections about Sam; she deleted them from the published memoir.

Ultimately, Paule would claim that Adriana was the most important influence on her writing, and she dedicated her first novel "To My Mother." Adriana, who berated her for her looks and her ambitions, dead at fifty-three from cancer, the Atlas who held the family together, "refusing to walk away for some never-never kingdom in Philadelphia." It was Adriana's poetic and powerful voice that Paule heard in the kitchen at 501, "without which I might never have come to writing," the "mother-poet" whom she would later excoriate as one of the "thieves" in her life. But a slight shift in focus allows us to see that Sam—the creative, bold, rebellious, and charming father—set the example for Paule of what an artist could be. When the Burke family finally moved into the brownstone house at 501, Paule's father, like Deighton in *Brown Girl, Brownstones,* took the one room in the house that was private—the light-flooded upstairs sun parlor, where he would find repose and recuperation, "a room of his own," an artist's room.

When Pauline enrolled in Bushwick High School in 1942, the Bushwick's student body was a combination of Irish, Italian, Jewish, eastern European, African American, and Caribbean. The school sits on land originally settled by the Dutch, who called it Boswijck, which means "neighborhood in the woods." History books claim that the Dutch "secured a deal from the Lenape Indians," which is undoubtedly a euphemism for the confiscation of the land from the Lenni Lenape Nation of Algonquin people, who had been there "for at least a millennium" before the Europeans descended on them.[50] Pauline and her best friend, an Irish girl named Mary, were the top two students at Bushwick. Pauline was "a bright and compulsive worker" whose devotion to school was greeted dismissively by Adriana: "*Books! Books! Her middle name is books!*"[51]

While the white immigrant kids had not yet achieved the desired degree of white privilege, Pauline discovered that they were already aware of the need to distance themselves from blackness. She and Mary were, she thought, "inseparable." They had the kind of interracial school friendship that in northern cities was infrequent but not out of the ordinary in the 1940s. Pauline took it for granted that she and Mary would march together at graduation, but when the time came to choose partners, Mary began to avoid her: "Mary scarcely speaking to me. Mary ducking her head. No longer studying with me. Graduation when parents and family came out. I took solace. I remember that I had been chosen Salutatorian. Small solace." She called people like Mary who slighted her the "thieves" in her life, and she made a list of them in her unpublished notes: "The speech teacher who discouraged me from thinking of becoming a teacher because I had a hissing 's.' The guidance counsellor who urged me to go to a commercial high school rather than an academic one despite my good grades. Thieves. Thieves who would take from me my sense of worthiness." Later she would add Adriana, who mocked her dreams of becoming a writer, as one of those thieves: "College? Book writing? Look, get from out my eyesight! You ain' hear that the telephone company is starting to hire colored? You best march yourself down there and beg for a job!"[52]

By 1946, when she graduated from Bushwick, where she had contributed to the school newspaper and excelled academically, Paule was having doubts about herself as a writer, and Adriana's disapproval of her career ambitions may have been a factor in her decision to major in anthropology and sociology instead of literature. Adriana wanted to control the iron-willed Paule, but she was also frightened by this talented daughter who openly scorned her mother's desire for materialistic things like a house in the brownstone-filled Brooklyn neighborhood of Crown Heights. Her mother demeaned her high-minded dreams—impractical for a working-class black girl—but Paule knew that since New York city colleges were free, her dream of college was possible even without her mother's help.

Piecing together the battles between mother and daughter from a set of Paule's handwritten notes marked "REBELLION/INDEPENDENCE: NOTES TO BE SAVED," we can see more clearly what fueled their antagonism. In these notes, she catalogued her rebellions, which began at age thirteen with the name change to *Paule* and her refusal to answer to *Pauline.* Her second rebellion was to join the high Episcopal Church, knowing that Adriana had nothing but contempt for religious institutions, no matter what denomination. "I joined the church, sang in the junior choir, knelt and became God's bride at age 13." Adriana "raged and fulminated and almost gave up on me," but stopped short of kicking her out. Even her sister Anita, the "manageable" one, rebelled, and secretly began to smoke at age sixteen, a practice that led to her early death. What perturbed and disoriented Adriana most were Pauline's willful ways, so much like her own: "Own-ways," Adriana called them, feeling the rivalry of a worthy opponent.

Paule's sexual rebellions produced the most serious clashes with Adriana. Curious about the streets and the unknown world, Paule felt she was being denied the privileges Anita enjoyed. None of Adriana's talk of "caterwauling" and "tumbling big" deterred Paule from her adolescent escapes, mainly with her African American friends, who introduced her to the "blue-lights in the basement" parties. Paule says that most of her party-going friends were African American (migrating families, like hers, who had recently arrived in Brooklyn), and that her attraction to those parties was a way of "remaining loyal to my Afr.Am self."[53] Thanks to them she attended her share of blue-light basement parties, which were such a cultural phenomenon that *Blue Lights in the Basement* became the title of a best-selling 1997 record album by Roberta Flack. At these parties, Paule first encountered the Stompers from across town—boys who kept on their hats and coats while dancing the Slow Drag. At first Paule did not understand her friends' references to the "nightstick" until she found herself dancing with "a tall drink of water of a boy with a nightstick of a dick." Still, she wondered, in her "17-year old naivete," how anyone could get excited over a nightstick. "I felt nothing exciting or stimulating . . . Adriana had done her work."

Paule's nightlife included frequent visits to places such as the Paramount Theater, accompanied by a "few West Indians, Most Afr.Am," where they heard singers Sarah Vaughn and Frank Sinatra and pianist Hazel Scott. Staying out all night meant that she "turned up at dawn to a tongue-lashing" from Adriana, but Paule continued to defy her mother until, when she was nineteen, Adriana declared that "two head bulls can't rein in a flock" and gave up the battle. Paule added this final point to Adriana's credit: despite Adriana's "admonitions, punishments, and threats," she never beat us, and she "had an innate faith in me, finally letting me go my own way. I would do nothing to further disgrace her than Sam Burke had already done."

Sam was nowhere around by the time Paule graduated, but Adriana would certainly have attended the Bushwick graduation ceremonies and would have been proud to see her daughter recognized as the second highest student academically in this class of mostly whites. In Paule's formal graduation photograph, there is no sign of the anxiety and self-doubt that would plague her throughout her life, nor of the intrepid writer who would revolutionize the image of black women. She is framed within the conventions of femininity. She wears white elbow-length gloves, a short pearl necklace and pearl earrings, and a full-length white dress with a bodice decorated in so much lace and taffeta that, were it not for the scroll in her left hand, it could be a wedding gown. The photograph seems to suggest that Paule is graduating

Studio portrait of Paule at her Bushwick High School graduation in 1946.

into her mother's bourgeois dreams, but she had already defied her mother and enrolled at Hunter College in Manhattan, one of the city's leading public colleges, and within a few short months she would join the most radical left organization on Hunter's campus.

CHAPTER 2

A Sort of Extraordinary Kind of Person

BETWEEN 1946 AND 1950, Paule entered college twice, the first time somewhat unhappily and the second time more successfully. She overcame a major disease, spent nearly a year in a tuberculosis sanatorium, experienced the exciting new cultural world as well as the casual racism of Manhattan, made her first attempt at a political identity, changed her major from social work to literature, and married her first husband. Between the ages of seventeen and twenty-two, Pauline Burke was inventing Paule Marshall.

The transformation began at Hunter College. One of the free city colleges in New York, Hunter had admitted black women since 1873, when it was known as Normal College, a training school for teachers. As salutatorian of her graduating class at Bushwick High School, Paule was one of only a few black students to get into Hunter. She was admitted to a college with a reputation for attracting a multi-ethnic student body traveling on subways from all over New York City to take advantage of free tuition and Hunter's reputation for academic excellence.

She was elated to be leaving Brooklyn, "in flight from the chaos" of the blight that had overtaken the Bed-Stuy neighborhood where her mother lived, but also fleeing from "the West

Indian 'buy-house' fixation" and the materialism that was so much a part of it." She entered Hunter with both anticipation and trepidation, excited about traveling to the college at 68th and Park Avenue to be a student at the premier college for women in New York. College would get her out of Brooklyn and into the wider cultural and intellectual world of Manhattan.

Although several well-known black women, including actor Ruby Dee, writer Audre Lorde, and theologian Pauli Murray had attended Hunter, they were always a tiny minority of the students. Murray, who graduated from Hunter in 1933 with three other black women, found Hunter stimulating intellectually and made many friends, but Paule never truly felt at home there.[1] She remembered the sound that greeted her in the cafeteria at Hunter as the cackling sounds of laughing female voices. In the 1980s, when she was publishing with Feminist Press, she acknowledged the empathy she felt for those smart college women being slotted into the confined roles designed for women, socialized into ordinariness:

> I did the first two years of my undergraduate work at an all women's, predominantly Jewish, free city college in New York; and practically every day squeals of joy were to be heard in one or another of my classes: somebody else had just gotten engaged. There on a third finger, left hand, would be this outsized diamond, gotten wholesale usually through a relative or family friend who worked or had connections in the diamond center. "I can get it for you wholesale." . . . As young as most of these young women were, they were doomed to become housewives in Brooklyn or Queens—college having been merely the means to raise their stock in the marriage market.[2]

Looking for the least conventional college experience, Paule joined the left-wing American Youth for Democracy (AYD), formerly the Young Communist League. AYD was active even though the college president Harry D. Gideonse declared it "communism in the guise of a youth organization concerned with democracy" and refused to grant it a charter.[3] In November 1946, the group was the subject of an investigation at Hunter and denounced by the Board of Higher Education as subversive. Although the board at Hunter ultimately decided to reject an all-out ban on AYD, it approved the continuation of a Cold War surveillance policy of "recognizing but spotlighting communist groups," and a few years later dismissed four professors for being Communists.[4] Paule would later downplay her association with AYD, calling it "the Communist Party fringe, whose cause I had briefly embraced at age seventeen."[5] Yet it was a clear indication of how early she was drawn to the Left and of her determination even as a young twenty-year-old to fashion a new self and an unconventional life.

Paule's leftist politics were not unusual among African Americans in the 1940s. Louis Burnham, leader of the Southern Negro Youth Council (SNYC), and Paule's longtime friend Ruth Jett were vice chairmen of AYD in New York. Paul Robeson, whom Paule came to deeply admire, was a New York AYD council member.[6] Lorraine Hansberry, who would eventually write the acclaimed play *A Raisin in the Sun,* joined the Communist Party (CPUSA) at the University of Wisconsin. Esther Jackson, co-founder of the leftist Southern Negro Youth Council who lived for a time with Hansberry in New York, joined the party as an undergraduate at Oberlin College in Ohio. African American writer Julian Mayfield joined the CPUSA in the early 1950s, when he was in his early twenties. Mayfield wrote what is perhaps the most compelling statement about the decision of young black intellectuals of his generation to join the party: "The Communist Party, it seemed to young people, offered the best advantage, the sharpest weapon by which to attack society. . . . [So] we joined the most powerful, radical organization we could."[7]

The best clue to Paule's left-wing activities in college is one breezy, offhand remark about AYD in her memoir, where she refers to it as "the Communist fringe" "whose cause I had briefly embraced at age seventeen."[8] More substantive references to her life on the left are in her semi-autobiographical 1962 short story/ essay "Re*e*na," commissioned by *Harper's* magazine for their special issue "The American Female." Paule's story seems out of place in this issue of *Harper's,* which features on its cover the words "The American Female" cut into black-and-white strips and shaped into the curvaceous, reclining body of a smiling young white woman, a large bow atop her head. Harper's cover undercut the political intent of Paule's story.

Each of the three characters, Re*e*na, the radical activist married to Dave, a photographer, and Paulie, the writer who narrates Re*e*na's story, represent some aspect of Paule's own life. Paule called the story a "mixed-bag technically," part story and part essay, a hybrid structure featuring the first of her hybrid characters: Re*e*na's father is from Georgia, her mother from the Caribbean, which allowed Paule to resolve—at least fictionally—the tensions she felt over her African American/Caribbean identity. By blending elements of fact and fiction, Paule felt she could be more openly autobiographical. Paulie and Re*e*na belong to a small group of young black women Paule said she knew best: those from "an urban, working class and lower middle-class, West Indian–American background who, like myself, had attended the free New York City colleges during the late forties and fifties."[9] There are more autobiographical markers throughout: on her twelfth birthday, Re*e*na, like Paule, changes her name from the standard West Indian "Doreen" to the more creative "Re*e*na," insisting on the two e's, the second one in italics. The dark-skinned Re*e*na, one of the few black students in an interracial left-wing group on campus, joins in picketing, demonstrating, leafleting on corners, getting her name on the attorney general's list, and being suspended from school during the McCarthy period. She is also involved in an interracial relationship with a white man until she discovers he is using her to defy his family. She eventually becomes disillusioned and withdraws from the group: " 'I got tired of being "their Negro," their pet. Besides they were just all talk, really. All theories and abstractions. I doubt that, with all their elaborate plans for the Negro and for the workers of the world, any of them had ever been near a factory or up to Harlem.' "[10] Given these autobiographical clues in "Reena," it seems clear that Paule's political activism in college did not yield the friendships or community she hoped for.

At the end of the story, Reena is active in black militant politics, with social action groups focused on protesting conditions in Harlem and imbuing their children with a sense of "their worth and importance as black people": there will be "no white dolls for them." Reena's disillusionment with the radical Left became a feature of the Cold War 1950s, when many blacks broke with the Communist Party partly because of the anxieties of the McCarthy era and partly because a generation of black left-wing radicals, such as Julian Mayfield, Jack O'Dell, and Ossie Davis, moved away from the Left in order to direct their energies and loyalty to black-led struggles in the civil rights and black nationalist movements. Paule would follow the same path.

Paule made no close friends at Hunter, choosing instead to focus on the cultural world of Manhattan. She regularly visited Carnegie Hall, apparently alone, just a few blocks from Hunter in Midtown Manhattan, where she purchased gallery tickets for 75 cents and attended classical concerts and opera. Although Paule's love of opera, classical music, and jazz—Evan says she had a lovely singing voice—never surfaced in any interviews, music was her lifelong passion and is central to several novels, including *Praisesong for the Widow* and her final novel *The Fisher King*. She had a collection of long-playing, multi-disk albums of *Aida*, *Madame Butterfly*, and *Porgy and Bess* featuring her favorite opera star Mary Violet Leontyne Price, the first African American soprano to achieve international acclaim.

Paule's favorite Manhattan hangouts included a hole-in-the-wall deli and coffee shop on Lexington and a cheesecake place called Luna. In a series of impressionistic notes about this period, she wrote: "Observing, Sophistication. Roaming around Manhattan. Felt I was truly a New Yorker. The lunch counter on Lexington Ave. I had just turned 17, my first year at Hunter College. I had escaped B'klyn, which prided itself on being known then as the borough of churches and baby carriages." Like Selina, the protagonist in her first novel, Paule became a flaneur, enjoying a sense of recklessness as she roamed Manhattan: "As part of my getting to know NY, and of escaping B'klyn; NY sophistication. Hadn't Duke Ellington tried to pick me up in Luna—the best place in town for cheesecake." She was also exposed to another side of Manhattan. One afternoon, sitting in the deli, watching the clock and wolfing down her favorite salami and cheese on a bun before she rushed off to class, she became aware of an old man who "looked as if he had spent the day lingering over the single cup of coffee in front of him. And who was repeating now, head still bent over the coffee: 'Nigger.' . . . I had finally reached the City and the broken old man called me quietly over his coffee, nigger. Nigger. So too the old Jewish man in Grand Union on the corner of 90th and B'way. Thieves. Their weapon of choice: the word 'nigger.' The n word. 'Nigger,' people who sought to take from me, to steal from me." That too, she discovered, was part of becoming a New Yorker, the glow of Manhattan "shattered by the bum in the greasy spoon cafeteria."

The trials of Hunter and the excitement of Manhattan came to an abrupt end in 1948 when Pauline was diagnosed with tuberculosis: "I [had] decided to become a social worker, but in the second half of my sophomore year, I became very ill and was forced to leave school."[11] She thought she had contracted the illness from a baby in the family who lived in the downstairs flat of their brownstone, recalling that when she was taking care of the baby, she absentmindedly sucked on his bottle. She had been following a nonstop schedule of sandwiches on the run, a full schedule at Hunter, and an after-school job at the school library, taking catnaps on the long subway ride each day from Brooklyn to Manhattan, which took its toll.

Tuberculosis was considered a ruthless killer of blacks in the first half of the twentieth century, yet an entire industry of sanatoria—hotels, cure cottages, and privately run boardinghouses—existed with a hidden record of racial discrimination. The best institutions, such as the Trudeau Sanatorium in upstate New York, founded by public health pioneer Dr. Edward Livingston Trudeau (great-grandfather of comic strip writer Garry Trudeau), rarely accepted blacks, although painter Henry Osawa Tanner had been treated there in 1876. It is hard to trace the presence of blacks even in the Stony Wold sanatorium, whose stated mission was to serve underprivileged women with TB. There were, however, a few black boardinghouses that cared for TB patients that advertised in black newspapers. One such boardinghouse, run by African American Sylvia Alston, opened in 1917; others opened in 1923 and 1930. In September 1931, the black newspaper *New York Amsterdam News* ran an ad for Hopkins Cottage from a Bermuda-born couple: "Now open for business; overlooking Lake Flower. Vacation, rest and health resort. We take in Tubercular cases."[12]

Pauline stayed in one of these upstate New York facilities for for several months. While there, she wrote letters and "little descriptive things. Vignettes," as she described them to her friends. A Bajan boy from Brooklyn, Rudolph Skeete, "a beau of sorts," who liked them, wrote back that she should think of writing, which prompted her decision to switch her major from social work to English literature when she returned to school.[13] That declaration of her plans to become a writer was fueled in part by her bitterness that Adriana never once visited during her entire six-month stay upstate. These changes in Paule's life parallel

Kenneth Marshall, thirty-five, sits on the marina where he kept his boat, 1960.

those of the character Michel in Andre Gide's 1902 novel *The Immoralist,* which she read later in her Continental Literature class at Brooklyn College. After Michel recovers from tuberculosis, he expresses an intense desire for a new life. The seventeen-year-old Paule was also eager to move past her insular life in the Barbadian community, and her recovery left her with a similar feeling of exhilaration and a need to throw off the conventions of her old life. Michel became the inspiration for her 1961 short story "Brooklyn" and for many of her fictional women who push the boundaries of social and sexual restraints.

When Paule returned from the sanatorium, she did not reapply to Hunter. On September 14, she married Kenneth Marshall, a young sociology student at City College four years older, a magnetic and handsome man with a deep baritone voice. The couple likely met at a local Bajan dance. On their first date, Kenneth took her to a Beethoven concert at Carnegie Hall—and afterward surprised her by taking her to 57th Street to hear Billie Holiday. Paule said she knew then that Kenneth was special, a kind of Renaissance man comfortable with the full spectrum of art, as she was. Since both Paule and Kenneth were still students, they moved into his parents' large multi-unit brownstone building, a kind of family-church compound in Brooklyn, a few houses down from the church at 420 Lafayette Street. Paule's choice not to return to Hunter but to make the short commute from her in-laws' house and their church to Brooklyn College in Flatbush, far from the freedom of Manhattan, was a practical and necessary, if painful, decision. Her marriage complicated her desire for freedom from convention and eventually interfered with her desire to write. Though she changed her major to English literature, she went with convention and changed her last name, from Burke to Marshall.

Paule and Kenneth were both devoted music lovers. Paule loved to sing, and Kenneth played classical piano. Kenneth had graduated from the prestigious Boys High School in Brooklyn, and would go on to Columbia University, and graduate school. Yet while they were both excellent students, Pauline did better than Kenneth academically, and this became one of the tensions in their relationship: "I was getting better grades than he did. He did not have to study but I was hitting the books and studying my butt off. He did not have the motivations and I had to apply myself."

She reflected later about signals he gave on their first date that indicated their marriage might be problematic: "Maybe it was our very first date when I was age seventeen—but anyway, he let me know that he did not want to be married to an ordinary woman. He didn't even want to go out with an ordinary woman! This was age seventeen. . . . My first date with a person! There was on his part the insistence that if I was going to be involved with him, I had to be a sort of extraordinary kind of person because he considered himself that. And he was—very bright and very gifted in his way. And so when we married and I started writing, he was pleased because here was affirmation, confirmation that he hadn't married an ordinary person."[14]

Unlike Paule, whose family was shattered financially by the desertion of her father, Kenneth was raised in a comfortably well-off, conservative, and highly religious Barbadian family that insisted on and supported academic achievement—at least for their two sons. Kenneth's parents were also from Barbados. His mother, Edith Leila Marshall (née Best), arrived in New York in 1914 at the age of fifteen. His father, Evans Marshall, arrived in New York in 1922 at age twenty-two, along with several other relatives. Kenneth was the oldest of four children: Vita was three years younger than he was; Carolena, four years younger; and

Calvin, who became the minister the family hoped for, five years younger.

Brother Evans Marshall was the pastor of the evangelical Lafayette Avenue Church of God in Brooklyn, assisted by his wife. He had been a member of the Church of God in Barbados, which did considerable evangelism in Barbados and other Caribbean islands. Edith, who grew up an orphan and quite poor, had belonged to the Anglican Church in Barbados, but once she met and married Evans in New York they searched together for a strict religious community and found the Church of God. Founded in Cleveland, Tennessee, the Pentecostal Church of God is based on belief in the inerrancy of the Bible, direct experience with the Holy Spirit, and worldwide evangelization to spread the message of Jesus Christ. As the heads of the thriving evangelical Lafayette Avenue Church of God in Brooklyn, Edith and Evans Marshall were able to amass wealth, property, and status, becoming part of the Barbadian aristocracy in Brooklyn. Despite her youthful defiance in joining the Episcopal Church, Paule's working-class family was not religious, and she would remain a religious skeptic her entire life.

By all accounts, Kenneth's father was a gentle man who lived his faith and was more accepting than his wife. Edith, known as Sister Marshall, was a strict, stern, dignified, and judgmental woman who disapproved of the women her sons dated. Sister Marshall's first question to any woman Kenneth brought home was, "What church do your parents go to?" Paule would have had to admit that her family was not religious, and that would have been scandalous to the Marshall family. Paule remembered feeling Sister Marshall's disapproval the first time Kenneth brought her to the house, and later Kenneth told her that his mother had commented: "These women coming in here with their worldly ways. She is a lovely girl, but she is wearing a little too much makeup, and her family are not church folks."[15] Paule was quick to note the hypocrisy: "That was Sister Marshall referring to *my* makeup, while her face was caked with that talcum powder she always wore."[16] Paule and Kenneth's son Evan said later that marrying Paule was another of his father's rebellions: "Rather than finding a girl in the church, he presented the woman he'd been dating and saw that as a chance for both of them to break free of the narrow views of their parents."[17]

In his parents' eyes, Kenneth was the son destined for greatness. Brother and Sister Marshall had always expected their first and favorite son to become a minister, but Kenneth distanced himself from the church and refused to apply to seminary. He threatened to leave home in order to convince his parents to allow him to attend a secular college. Secretly, he was embarrassed by his father's preaching, wincing when Brother Marshall would invent words to sound impressive. Because Kenneth was not allowed to go to the movies, listen to the radio, or socialize in secular settings, he took to boating when he was seventeen, hiding from his parents his purchase of a small starter boat with an outboard motor, which he parked at the Sheepshead Bay Marina.

Paule's mother more than likely approved of her decision to marry a young man from an affluent and respectable Bajan family. Adriana and the Bajan community were aligned with 1950s mainstream culture in pressuring these bright young women to marry and "become housewives in Brooklyn or Queens," and Paule felt the pressure.[18] The photographs of Paule and Kenneth's wedding suggest that these two freethinkers indulged their parents' wishes for a religious ceremony and the traditional Barbadian extravaganza. Paule wore a white gown with a veil and a train, and rode in a long black rented Cadillac limousine to the church. She would always respect the cultural importance of the church, but the large Bajan wedding was her final concession to the Marshall family's religious strictures.

Paule and Kenneth were in many ways kindred spirits: both highly intellectual and highly ambitious, both trying to escape the constrictions of life in tightly knit Barbadian communities. The couple's idea of marriage was far from traditional: "Ours was a mutual apostasy that also rejected traditional marriage, so that while we lived together, slept together, we essentially led independent, unfettered lives." Paule defended their open marriage as part of their youth: "We were only in our early twenties, after all."[19] Their open marriage allowed Paule to express her attraction to women. When her son was a college student, she confided that she had had female lovers even during her marriage to Kenneth.[20] She would soon become aware that her husband's freethinking was limited. His idea of an "extraordinary" wife was not that different from his mother's. He wanted a wife more devoted to him and their homelife than to her career.

As a literature major at Brooklyn College, Paule enrolled in such difficult courses as Shakespeare, History of Philosophy, Classical Drama, Modern American and British Poetry, Modern Continental Drama in Translation, and Early 19th Century Poetry. She was twice exempted from physical education and permanently exempted from swimming, though later, when she was in the Caribbean, she became an excellent swimmer.

In the fall of 1951, Paule took what was considered one of the college's most challenging classes, Continental Novel in Translation, which included twentieth-century writers such as Franz Kafka, Thomas Mann, Marcel Proust, André Gide, and André Malraux. It was taught by the famous and popular Professor Henry Slochower, a German literature specialist, "an outstanding scholar of European literature," and also, in Pauline's view, "a terrible sexual harasser." Slochower, who would have been in his early fifties at the time, offered repeated invitations to Paule to visit his place in the country and made suggestive gestures that made her feel both discomfort and rage: "But I didn't bolt. I stayed on in the course; I needed it to graduate."[21] There was no administrative support or even a term for sexual harassment in the 1950s. "We didn't even think to use the term back in the early fifties. . . . There were no women's groups on campus to which we could take the problem; no notices on the bulletin boards and in the bathrooms with phone numbers to call for help and advice; no sympathetic ear in administration. There was nowhere to turn, no support system of any kind, as I recall. If propositioned, you either cooperated and were sometimes rewarded with an 'A' whether your work deserved it or not; or you refused and ran the risk of getting a 'C' or worse; or you dropped the course."[22]

Paule did, however, acknowledge Slochower's skill as a teacher: "Besides 'old lecher' that he was—'with a love on every wind'—to quote Yeats—he was nonetheless an excellent teacher."[23] She received an A in the course from Slochower, who eventually became the catalyst for her 1961 short story "Brooklyn," one of the few stories she wrote about sexual harassment. She kept her anger over Slochower's sexual invitations in check for nine years until she was ready to write the story.[24]

Pauline received As in most of her classes and graduated cum laude and Phi Beta Kappa in September 1952, but what was most life-changing for her at Brooklyn College was that she was exposed to modernist and European literature—and to a view of the world that would influence her writing, her identity, and her politics. Slochower's course introduced Pauline to the continental writers most critical of bourgeois culture, who challenged moral and puritanical constraints, especially heterosexual norms. Though she never credited Slochower's class in particular, she referred to the European writers she studied in his class as central to her writing. Mann's novel *Buddenbrooks* was the model she used for *Brown Girl, Brownstones*, and Gide's novel *The Immoralist* features prominently in her story "Brooklyn."[25] When she created women characters who struggle against society's constraints in their search for self-fulfillment, she was drawing from a well of ideas first encountered in her engagement with these writers, who gave her both a license and a language to express her increasing dissatisfaction with the culture of the 1950s. She did not mention that many of these writers also embraced homosexual desire as part of their search for fulfillment, and she rarely cited Gide's influence, even though *The Immoralist* was especially compelling for a young woman searching for a way out of Barbadian propriety, female submission, and sexual normativity.

Over the course of the 1970s and 1980s, as Paule both shaped and was shaped by Black Arts Movement aesthetics, she would minimize the influence of these European writers and thinkers on her work. Yet their emancipatory desires modeled for her the freedom to reject sexual conventions and, most profoundly, to embrace a boldness in living that required the courage and daring to see oneself as the sole authority of one's life. As a figure of radical imagination and liberation, Gide served as her model in the 1940s; he would be supplanted by the revolutionary Malcolm X in the 1960s, perhaps a natural progression. In the words of modernism scholar Linda Dittmar, "It would not be impossible to draw a line from Gide to Malcolm X."[26]

Steeped in the grand ideas of modernism, Paule must have found it difficult to return to the traditional Barbadian household of her in-laws. It's hard to know how much pressure was put on the couple to live with the older Marshalls or how deeply this move might have affected Paule, but she got her first taste of how little her "extraordinariness" would count in the Marshall family.

Sister Marshall annoyed the new bride by continuing to attend to her favorite first-born son, cooking his meals on request, and insisting on their attendance at Sunday services, which surely made life intolerable for Paule: "I needed the support and the understanding to be this kind of multidimensional, sort of multitalented person—that I just found it difficult to be the writer, the housewife, the wife, the student because I was still in school at the time. All of it was just so very difficult. And I used to get a little impatient with myself because it seemed to me, why wasn't it manageable? It seemed to me that others had managed it, didn't they? Well, of course they didn't!"[27]

Three years into marriage, Paule expressed her sense of entrapment in her first published story, "The Valley Between," about a young white woman, Cassie, mother of a young child, struggling to return to college against her husband Abe's demands for her to attend to his needs and her motherly duties. Paule too had entered "an early and unwise" marriage when she was barely twenty and still in college, and the story represented her strong need to write about what was happening to her and to "the lives of other women at the time."[28] In order to disguise the similarities to her own life, however, she made the couple white: "I wasn't brave enough back then to deal directly with my unhappiness, or perhaps instinct told me I should try to transform the raw stuff of personal experience into art."[29] For a while Cassie is able to resist Abe's efforts to confine her to "one compressed limited place" as she struggles to stay in the "new world" of books, ideas, words, and images: "Each day she had found a new world before her. And along with the joy of reading had come, with the years, the desire to learn—to have all the muddled ideas made clear, defined in words and images, and thus made a part of her. It was a never-ending search, giving sustained pleasure, making her life, for that moment at least, meaningful."[30]

It is only when her child becomes ill while Cassie is away at school, which Abe blames on her being an absent mother, that she abandons her dreams of college, unable to resist either her husband or the pressures of 1950s domesticity. What Paule captures so perceptively in this story is the posture of self-diminishment that women often adopt in the face of male aggressiveness. In response to Abe's anger, Cassie modulates her voice and behavior: "She timidly opened the bedroom door," or "She watched Abe furtively," or "Her voice was low and wistful" while Abe "stabbed viciously at the prunes." When he "yells," she tries to speak "evenly." Later, when Cassie admits defeat and surrenders her dreams of college, she addresses the larger issue of the power of patriarchy: "I haven't got the strength to defy you anymore—you and your male strength!"[31] Like the story "Brooklyn," "The Valley Between" was Paule's effort to get her feelings of anger, distrust, and powerlessness down on paper. Even later, when she would lay claim to a more politicized, black, feminist, and diasporan aesthetic for her work, her fiction would remain a form of self-reckoning, a way to sort out, tame, and transcend those unmanageable feelings of ordinary life.

CHAPTER 3

An Insane Notion

SOON AFTER PAULINE GRADUATED from Brooklyn College in 1952, she began looking for writing jobs and discovered that mainstream newspapers and magazines in the 1950s were not hiring brilliant young black women English majors with a Phi Beta Kappa key. She was so worried about being young, inexperienced, and a woman that she began using the name Paule instead of Pauline on her job applications, thinking that a male name would make it easier to get an interview. She continued to ward off Adriana, who pressed her to scale down her arty goals and get an ordinary job. She also began work on her first novel and increasingly felt that she needed to be with others who were in the awesome and "terrifying business of trying to be writers."[1] She joined the Harlem Writers Workshop, which was just getting started.

Her friend Rosa Guy, a Trinidadian American writer, introduced her to what became known as the Harlem Writers Guild and to Phillip Bonosky, a Communist activist and writer with dreams of writing for Hollywood until he was blacklisted. Guy had asked Bonosky to start a workshop for black writers because they did not feel comfortable in the left-wing writers' workshop, which attracted mostly whites.[2] From 1951 to 1954, Bonosky kept meticulous notes of the Harlem Writers Workshop in a daily journal, using initials to refer to the participants, although most can be easily identified.

The first meeting of the Harlem workshop took place on October 26, 1951, in a second-floor loft at 125th and Seventh Avenue in Harlem, in the building where Paul Robeson's *Freedom* newspaper was published. After that, the group met at the homes of workshop participants—Alice Childress, John Killens, Walter Christmas, John Henrik Clarke, Julian Mayfield, Rosa Guy, and Paule herself—and agreed to pay Phil $1 per session. At Bonosky's insistence, the meetings started promptly at 8:30 and ended at 11, and soon almost every young black writer of promise in New York became a member, including Audre Lorde, Lonne Elder III, and Douglas Turner Ward (then Roosevelt Ward Jr.), in addition to the original participants. Bonosky wrote wryly of the workshop's left-wing reputation, "Insanity to one side, there was one thing that the anti-Communists were correct about. A white man who met socially with blacks in that desperate period was very likely to be a Communist. Everyone in the workshop was."[3] McCarthyism was on the rise, and with the FBI busy uncovering "suspected" Communists, a Cold War atmosphere prevailed, Bonosky wrote, and "the winds of reaction penetrated our workshop as well."[4]

Aspiring black writers found the Harlem Workshop a congenial and supportive place. Audre Lorde read her first poems in the workshop; Lorraine Hansberry debated James Baldwin on the issue of socially conscious art versus universality, with Baldwin taking the side of universality. Paul Robeson dropped in from time to time and once told Alice Childress, who read from a movie script in progress, that she needed more working-class characters in her plays, to which she replied that she wrote about the middle class because that's what she knew.

Paule read her story "The Valley Between" for the first time on April 8, 1953, at John Killens's house. In his journal entry for that day, Bonosky expressed his exasperation with what he considered the story's bourgeois orientation: "A story by a young woman is read, criticized; she then explains her story, saying that the problem between the wife and the husband has no solution, that the wife's struggle for a degree is a 'symbol' of her rebellion against her life and that she intended neither the husband nor wife to be 'villains.' Very lovely, very young, still you see how influenced she is by the pessimistic moods of the day, the literary decadence of our times."[5] The doctrinaire Bonosky dismissed Paule's feminist story as merely about "interpersonal relation," even as he affirmed her leftist politics: "She was not interested in socially conscious writing. I never understood how she got into these groups, but she was definitely on the left."[6]

Bonosky was also overtly sexist in a later entry, referring to Paule's physical beauty and disparaging her ideas: "P. is a very beautiful, sophisticated young woman, who talks about 'drives' and 'aggressive impulses,' and 'sublimation.' She takes psychology courses in college; her husband is a 'sociology psychiatrist.' They are typical of a certain type of Negro intellectual who has been profoundly influenced by non-class theories (or rather, of course, bourgeois theories), usually with a John Dewey (if it's education) base, or some variety of psychiatry, if it's human behavior. She is able, at one time, to explain the behavior of some Negro men, who violently reacted against racial insults, by saying that their 'aggressive drive' was 'misdirected,' etc."[7]

Bonosky's journal notes about Paule's participation in the workshop not only represent a rare outside view of the young Paule Marshall but also reveal the resistance to gender equality that was prevalent even among radicals in the 1950s. Bonosky reflects what then would have been Marxist orthodoxy: feminism is a bourgeois practice that ignores class divisions among women and favors privileged women; it is liberal and individualistic, a theory based merely on attitudes and feelings, not a confrontation with political power. Bonosky's condescending and sexist attitude toward Paule was out of step with leftist women of the 1950s, including the high-ranking black Communist feminist Claudia Jones and others.[8] There is no evidence that Bonosky openly expressed these views in the workshop, but his dismissal of Paule's story was a harbinger of how her work would be misread over the next thirty years.[9]

"The Valley Between" was published in August 1953 in the left-wing journal *Contemporary Reader*, one of the few journals publishing black writers. Bonosky was a good friend of the editor, Abe (Abraham Lincoln) Polonsky, a blacklisted ex-Communist, and may have helped her get published there. Editor Polonsky called the *Contemporary Reader* "a semi-independent Marxist voice on culture," and Paule would not have been unaware of the journal's left-wing reputation.[10] Its back pages were covered with ads from blacklisted, out-of-work intellectuals offering piano and writing lessons, and writers' credits that included their blacklist record, their "refusal to cooperate with the un-American Activities Committee," and their federal prison sentences.[11] When "The Valley Between" was reprinted by the Feminist Press in 1983 in a collection called *Reena and Other Stories*, Paule did not mention its left-wing debut in *Contemporary Reader*. Considering that many of the people who helped inaugurate and sustain Paule's writing career throughout the 1950s ran the gamut from open Communists to fellow travelers and left-leaning friends, it was a significant erasure.

Paule became dissatisfied with the Harlem workshop and resented the criticisms of the story. She had joined the workshop in order to get the support of other people who shared her ambition, and for a while she did find the community she needed to keep on writing:

> Well, it was wonderful to be in the company of peers, people like myself who were all taking on this terrifying business of trying to be writers. There were even one or two of them, such as John Killens, who had already been published. It offered a community of writers that I desperately needed when I was working on *Brown Girl, Brownstones.* Now, in terms of their criticism of my work, that's another thing we won't go into! I didn't have much patience with their comments! But I needed that group to know there were others out there with this absolutely insane notion of being a fiction writer.[12]

Now, two years out from college graduation, with a husband still trying to finish a degree, she desperately needed to find a job.

Paule's two-year search for a writer's job—she was turned down by *Mademoiselle, Time, Life,* the *Atlantic Monthly,* and all the publishing houses on Madison Avenue—eventually brought her to West 43rd Street between Sixth and Fifth Avenue, where she found herself looking up at "a little obscure, dirty window" [that] advertised *Our World* magazine. Unlike the entertainment and commercial focus of the glossy black magazines such as *Ebony,* founded in 1946 to portray "the happier side of Negro life," *Our World* featured black social and political issues in both national and global contexts, though it still maintained a focus on black success stories and black bathing beauties, and ran such articles as "Secrets Every Bride Should Know."[13] Paule trudged up a narrow, dark flight of stairs to the second floor, where she convinced editor and publisher John Preston Davis, born in 1905 into the Washington, DC, black elite, that she needed the experience. He hired her as a researcher, and within a few months, she was listed on the masthead as a staff writer. Yet there were hints that young Paule and the cocky, hard-driving Davis would not hit it off.

Paule remembered Davis as an exceptional man, but there's no indication that she knew of his life and reputation as one of the notorious Harlem Renaissance firebrands in the 1920s. Along with Langston Hughes, Zora Neale Hurston, Wallace Thurman, Gwendolyn Bennett, Aaron Douglas, and Richard Bruce Nugent, Davis was one of the radicals behind the controversial 1926 Harlem Renaissance publication *Fire!!* Although Paule was still close to the Left when she went to work at *Our World,* she made no mention of Davis as a radical civil rights activist, a man with fire in his heart in the battle for black workers' economic rights.[14]

Davis was a bold thirty-year-old in the 1930s when he infiltrated congressional hearings on New Deal projects and presented such a strong factual case against racial discrimination that he was able to open the doors of FDR's White House to prominent and circumspect black leaders. As the founder and main force behind several militant black labor organizations, including the National Industrial League (NIL), the Joint Committee on National Recovery (JCNR), and the National Negro Congress (NNC), Davis was labeled "Bad Boy Administration Critic" for his persistent and outspoken challenges to the Roosevelt administration.[15]

The many affinities between Paule and Davis should have made them kindred spirits. Davis's political militancy was matched by his deep commitment to black culture. When, as an undergraduate at Bates College, he first traveled abroad, Davis chose to bypass Europe in order "to discover the 'mighty civilization' of Africa which modern Europe and America denied."[16] This is an uncanny foreshadowing of Paule's 1969 novel *The Chosen Place, the Timeless People,* in which the woman Merle Kinbona deliberately bypasses the United States on her way to Africa. At *Our World,* Davis intended to use this knowledge of the black world to draw a new international map of blackness, eliminating the boundaries between U.S. blacks and the rest of the black world, as his future staff writer also dreamed of doing.

Davis also had a reputation for being progressive on gender issues. Once, when the conservative NAACP director Walter White hired a woman to spy on him, she reported that Davis shared all information with her, took her everywhere with him, and took time to explain things to her. Her only complaint was that Davis was such a Victorian that he insisted on paying for her meals when they traveled together, even though she had an expense account. What was even more telling than Davis's ability to charm a secret agent was that, in the ten-year run of *Our World,* he highlighted the achievements of women. "Negro women [are] making great strides in all phases of American life" was typical of the angle on women in *Our World.* An article on black women secretaries showed them in their executive roles at major corporations and government agencies, not as mere appendages to their male bosses. Paule turned in a major two-part article titled "Your Negro Doctor," in which half of the doctors featured were women.

Nonetheless, Paule felt she got little support from the mostly male staff at *Our World,* who, she believed, were waiting for her to fail. Davis recognized her talent but did not always support her decisions. As one of the few women writers, she was immediately tagged to write for the magazine's fashion and food sections. In contrast, when the young Lorraine Hansberry came to New York in the 1950s looking for work, she was embraced by *Freedom* newspaper's left-wing staff, including founder Paul Robeson, editor Louis Burnham, and staff writer Alice Childress, and immediately given major assignments.

Writing for the women's section of *Our World*, Paule straightaway spotted the colorism in the editorial choices and thought it was "a kind of outrage" that Davis, a very light-skinned man born into the elite black society circles of Washington, DC, rejected the dark-skinned models she chose for her fashion stories: "He would make sure that he picked out those that were what you would call the Lena Horne type, and that's why I didn't last very long on the magazine."[17] The treatment of dark-skinned models such as her friend Cicely Tyson—who was featured in a story but not selected as one of its models—was especially disturbing to Paule. "There was this kind of ugliness within the Black community, this non-acceptance of ourselves, this looking towards those within our community who were closest to white in appearance. And, of course, this is one of the reasons the Sixties were so important, that some of the psychological damage was confronted and an effort made to redress it."[18]

Paule also hated the pressures of deadlines and fast-paced writing and was sometimes bitingly critical of the magazine and disparaging of her work there. She described the magazine as "a kind of secondary *Ebony*" and complained, "I was doing these dreadful stories—I can't tell you how awful: 'How many Pairs of Shoes Does This Black Entertainer Have in His or Her Wardrobe?' "[19] She began to be fearful that if she didn't get out of there, "I would end up a hack writer for a third-rate magazine. So in an act of desperation I went home and started writing *Brown Girl, Brownstones.*"[20] As the cultural scholar I. Augustus Durham puts it, Paule couldn't get *Our World* to sign brown-skinned models, so she went home and created her own *brown girl*.[21] Paule was following the trajectory of many black women writers, such as Ann Petry, Andrea Lee, Lorraine Hansberry, and Alice Childress, whose early stints as writers on newspapers, journals, and magazines were incubators—or spurs—for their creative writing.

Despite her complaints, Paule wrote stories that had real import. Her article "Widows Over Fifty" was a catalyst for her novel *Praisesong for the Widow,* and the only one she wrote specifically about women for the magazine. Paule interviewed four black women over fifty, selected by her to cover diverse class and social positions, and presented as creative, socially active, and dynamic community members. The article, which actually says little about their widowhood and almost nothing about their spouses, is crafted with sensitivity toward women trying to earn a living and create satisfying lives without husbands. The tone, ironically, is jubilant. The women featured are a secretary for the pacifist organization Fellowship of Reconciliation; a retired civic activist; a matron of a large New York apartment building; and a disabled former actor. All these widows are depicted as engaged in activities such as giving dinner parties, playing the piano, taking grandchildren on an outing, showing off their art work, meeting with church leaders, and one greeting guests at a benefit for the Department of Corrections. The profiles destroy "the myth that old age is a disease." Yet Paule did not hesitate to show the stark economic differences between white and black women, deliberately unsettling this optimistic picture of black women's lives: "In general, Negro women 45 to 64 are still getting the short end of the stick jobwise. They have to work harder and longer than white women; 65 percent are still in service industries—domestics, cooks, laundry, etc., 80 percent still make less than $1800 a year."[22]

John Davis was confident enough in his fledging writer to send her to Brazil with the seasoned photographer Moneta Sleet, Jr., to cover Brazilian culture. During her time there, from June until November 1955, Paule wrote several articles, including a miniseries on race and culture in Brazil, proving that journalism would become the testing ground for her as a writer. In these six articles, she began to experiment, writing vignettes that use characterization, setting, point of view, flashback, and political commentary to represent this vibrant nation dealing with the complexities and contradictions of its own race prejudice.

Taken together, the six articles—"The Great Otello," "Carnival in Rio," "The Macumba," "A Tale of Two Doctors," "Rio Rebel," and "American in Rio"—presented a microcosm of black Brazilian culture, a finely tuned, though limited, portrait of race and black issues, ranging from articles about black entertainers, the black working class, the black professional class, black political opposition, the culture of voodoo, and black U.S. expatriates in Brazil. Brazil had often been represented as the great melting pot where racial intermixture was acceptable and unremarkable, but a UNESCO report in 1949 produced "a vast documentation of prejudice and discrimination against Brazilian blacks." To Paule's credit, her Brazil series does not mythologize Brazil as free of racial prejudice—or compare Brazil with the United States to show Brazil as more racially progressive. [23]

Although *Our World* rarely assigned bylines, Paule's name appears as the author of the story about carnival in Rio, a tradition begun by enslaved Africans in 1641, which takes place four days before Ash Wednesday. She wrote of an "electrifying" and "mammoth" show, when a "potpourri of races surge into the streets" with bodies "black, brown, and white, and all shades in between." She described the "samba colleges"—the essence of carnival—produced by the darker Brazilians, the day laborers, market vendors, maids, and nurses, who were paid no more than $20 a month but still managed to save $85 for their carnival costume. "This is the day that gives importance and meaning to their lives." Paule reminded the reader what lay behind the scenes of wild abandonment, but she makes her critique by ventriloquizing a condescending and racist voice: "The Brazilian in Rio forgets he is living in an inflation-riddled economy. He seems unconcerned that there are more slums dotting the hills like a cancer than there are the plush, white apartment houses along famed Copacabana. They forget that the cruzeiro (their currency) is practically worthless and that they can sometimes only get water twice a day because of an antiquated system. None of these things matter when carnival comes."[24] As always, Paule notes the injustices of poverty.

However reluctant Paule was to admit it, the *Our World* experience allowed her a period of experimentation, and the characters and ideas she wrote about would eventually populate her fiction. She was beginning to sketch the broad outlines of her lifelong fictional concerns: her interest in the black global world, the histories and power of indigenous cultures, the relationship between racial violence, capitalism, and colonialism, and a concern for "the wretched of the earth." Her article "Widows Over Fifty" was the seed for her 1983 novel about a black middle-aged woman negotiating widowhood, *Praisesong for the Widow.* The series on Brazil inspired her 1961 short story "Brazil" and provided the background for the carnival scenes in *The Chosen Place, the Timeless People.*

It's unfortunate that Paule did not recognize the extent to which Davis's worldview of blackness prefigured her own "triangular road," and that the fictional route she imagined for her characters, from the United States to the Caribbean to Africa, which "shaped the world of her art," was nurtured in the realm of *Our World.*[25] She finally admitted in one interview that she needed to reassess her earlier criticisms of *Our World:* "It wasn't all negative, working at that magazine, it wasn't all negative at all."[26] In her 1960 Guggenheim application, Paule reassessed her work at *Our World* as an exciting and rewarding experience and a powerful preparation for her life as a writer: "Not only did I receive genuine satisfaction from many of the articles I wrote, but I had the oppor-

Paule, twenty-six, on the steps of Brazilian Airlines in 1955, arriving at Rio airport on assignment for *Our World.*

tunity to travel extensively in Brazil and the West Indies on assignment—and this was of immeasurable value in broadening my experience. In some odd way, my work for the magazine served as a release and gave me the necessary confidence to undertake finally my serious writing." In the only photograph of her as an *Our World* writer, a photo she did not remember, a poised and smiling Paule, outfitted in a smart tailored business suit, newspaper in hand and overcoat thrown over one arm, is shown shaking hands with an airline official as she descends the steps of Brazilian Airlines on arrival in Rio. The caption noted that she was bound for Trinidad to cover her next story.[27] International journalist and seasoned world traveler, Paule was only twenty-six years old when she left the magazine. The woman who once described herself as "terrified of life" had crisscrossed the Atlantic Ocean several times and already understood herself as a citizen of the black Atlantic world.

CHAPTER 4

The Girl Can Write

WITH A COMBINATION OF LUCK, swagger, and a six-hundred-page manuscript, an almost completely unknown Paule Marshall got her first book accepted by a major publisher in 1958. While working as a staff writer at *Our World* magazine, Paule had been sharing an untitled manuscript in several writing workshops, including the Harlem Writers Workshop. She began writing the novel to compensate for the kind of "hack" writing she was assigned to do at *Our World.* Not knowing the protocols or procedures for getting published, she simply "looked up 'Publishing Houses' in the yellow pages and took the first name off the list she recognized."[1] Bobbs-Merrill kept the hefty manuscript for six months but eventually rejected it. Undeterred, Paule sent it to Random House, which accepted it, but with editor Hiram Haydn's caveat to revise this "swollen, overwritten baby tome."[2] On signing day, she went to the publisher's offices in the lovely Neo-Renaissance Villard buildings, then on Madison Avenue in the tony East 50s, climbed up the "magnificent, sweeping marble staircase to get to Hiram's office" to sign her contract, and met the founder of the publishing house, Bennett Cerf, who stopped on the stairs to tell his newest author not to get her hopes up because "nothing usually happens with this kind of book."[3]

According to a deflated Paule, Cerf meant these *ethnic* books never do well, confirming her suspicion that the editors did not see *Brown Girl, Brownstones* "as part of American letters."[4] Despite Cerf's condescension, Paule received a $2,500 advance and some helpful advice from Haydn, her "New England Brahmin" editor, to "take my bloated manuscript and go off somewhere and extricate the lovely novel that was buried in the fat."[5]

The advance from Random House provided enough financial support for her to write full-time, so shortly after her manuscript was accepted, Paule quit her job at *Our World* and flew to Barbados, with her manuscript and two cheap Delancey Street suitcases purchased from the outdoor Jewish market on the Lower East Side in tow. With her American dollars, she could live cheaply in Barbados: "I quickly found room and board in a large, newly built manor-style house near the capital, Bridgetown, on the Caribbean or leeward, side of the island."[6] Kenneth made regular visits and enjoyed staying at the "colonial showpiece" of a house, which she rented from Mr. Watson, an elderly Barbadian bachelor who "grudgingly accepted her as a boarder" in return for her help with the upkeep of the place.[7] In return for his miserly treatment, Paule used Mr. Watson as the model for the bitter Mr. Watford in her short story "Barbados" in her 1961 collection *Soul Clap Hands and Sing.*

Paule described the process of revising and trimming three hundred pages from the manuscript as a painful and solitary process, as if she were "a weakling trying to wrestle a sumo-sized opponent."[8] However, being in Barbados also meant that after a long morning of writing and editing, she had the luxury of going for a "sea-bath" in the coral waters and floating away, "arms outstretched, eyes closed, face raised to the sky," unburdened for a few hours from the discipline of the book.[9]

Paule also got to spend time with a group of friends who were part of the pro-independence movement that was just getting started on the island. Many of these people had studied in England and returned home radicalized. They wanted to "tear down all the blasted pictures of the queen" and chase "her kiss-me-ass governor-general out of Government House and run Barbados on we own!"[10] Most of them, including Paule, would not live to see the queen's picture removed. Barbados achieved independence in 1966, but Queen Elizabeth's picture was not removed until 2021, when Barbados became a republic.

When she returned from Barbados after nearly a year, Paule submitted her revised manuscript, and *Brown Girl, Brownstones* was published in May 1959. Although she referred to the novel in her 2009 memoir as a "somewhat standard coming-of-age tale about a girl not unlike myself born and raised in a Brooklyn community that was both African American and West Indian," she was well aware that her own life, as well as that of her main character, Selina Boyce, was anything but "standard."[11] Her depiction of the coming of age of a rebellious, sexually daring, young black intellectual female with a rich interior consciousness and a self-determined future was clearly breaking new ground.

Paule insisted that she was very different from her characters, but much about Selina's life echoed hers: Selina's parents are Barbadian immigrants working and living in the Bed-Stuy neighborhood of Brooklyn and raising two daughters, Selina and Ina. The novel explores Selina's upbringing in a bitterly divided family. As her immigrant parents work in factories and in white homes—her mother striving for upward mobility and the American dream of homeownership—Selina observes the destructive nature of their capitalistic goals. Her father and her friend Suggie are crushed by their dead-end labor in the factory, and even her powerful mother Silla is wrecked by her quest for material success. Except for Selina, the children of these striving communities are shown as docile and conventional, unable to imagine or pursue their own independence. The observant Selina is the hopeful center of this novel—she, like Paule, refuses to take the path of conformity her family and community lay out for her, openly contesting their values but also exploring ways to understand them.

The stark differences between Paule's and Selina's lives are important. What Paule did not reveal until 1991 in an interview with her friend Daryl Dance, is that as a young girl she experienced a date rape, an unwanted pregnancy, and a back-alley abortion.[12] Knowing her secretive and elusive friend, Dance was reluctant to press her further, and Paule never disclosed any more about that experience. What is clear, however, is that Paule wanted an extraordinary life for Selina and would omit anything that would portray her as a victim:

> She is extraordinary for me at least because she doesn't go through all of those terrible things that are supposed to happen to Black people, to young Black women. She is not raped by her father, or her stepfather, or her mother's boyfriend, she does not witness physical brutality between her mother and father, she is not, in other words, a social statistic, she is rather my attempt to create life, the life of a young woman on paper . . . and it is one of the reasons why succeeding generations of young women, Black and White, come to her and find something that says something to them, which is really gratifying for a writer.[13]

Selina had the kind of boldness Paule did not: "She stood up to her mother and at the age of seventeen took a lover. (Something I never would have dreamed of doing!)." Selina's first love affair is with an older man, Clive, an artist, and therefore a disgrace in the eyes of the striving Bajan community, "a man that wun work."[14] Not only does Selina initiate the clandestine affair with someone her mother disapproves of, she manages her college life at the same time and even becomes a star in the college dance company. The text describes the teenaged Selina in the midst of this affair as physically and emotionally radiant, walking home with "an almost irrepressible vitality in her stride, in each cutting swing of her arms. She might at any moment, it seemed, burst into a wild spin or execute another exuberant leap there on the street."[15] For Paule, Selina was a rejection of the 1950s social and cultural protocols for women: she expressed "what all the little repressed West Indian American girls of my generation could not express."[16]

Paule also had a racial agenda: "I determined to make women—especially black women—important characters in my stories when I started writing. To make up for the neglect, the disregard, the distortions, and untruths. I wanted them to be center stage."[17] In creating Selina, Paule created the past she wished she had had—and the future for other young black women that she longed for.

Brown Girl, Brownstones was well received in nearly every mainstream publication, including the *New York Times Literary Supplement*, the *New York Herald Tribune*, the *Saturday Review*, *Esquire*, the *New Yorker*, and the *Manchester Guardian*. The reviews by men, while often favorable, offered little or no analysis of the novel. William Allen in the *Times Literary Supplement* complimented the novel's setting and characters in generalized terms: an era "is carefully observed and characterization is decisive."[18] What seems to have stymied the white male reviewers is what John K. Hutchens in the *New York Herald Tribune* referred to as the "Race Question," which prompted his denunciation of the novel's "studied, polemical patches about the Race Question."[19] Otherwise, Hutchens, who was impressed enough to later recommend Paule for a Guggenheim, concluded, "The book is Mrs. Marshall's triumph, a quiet but assured one."[20] Ted Poston, a fellow Bed-Stuy black writer, wrote a generous review in the *New York Post:* "There is no question that Paule Marshall, like the Selina for whom she must have been the model, has found herself in the fiction field and will undoubtedly be a person there—in her own right."[21]

In *Phylon,* the major black literary journal, John S. Lash labeled the novel a "noteworthy effort" that "comes delicately close to a translation of Negroes into people, whose experience of life is illuminated rather than obscured by the fact that they are immigrant Negroes," conceding that, despite its "imperfections," the novel deserved high marks for producing "a larger and deeper purview of human life."[22] Lash's strange comment about translating "Negroes into people" is a veiled reference to *Phylon*'s racial litmus test for black writers, who, the editors believed—parroting the ideas of white critics—could only achieve "universality" if they avoided or downplayed racial issues. Lash believed that Paule had passed the test by writing about immigrant blacks, as if their immigrant status de-racialized them.

White women reviewers were less agitated about the "Race Question" in the novel, although Dorothy Parker had trouble with the mild hint of race in the title, which she didn't think "worthy" of the novel. Otherwise, Parker's review was glowing. The novel, she wrote, is "so absorbing; the people live and you go with them through the woe and the joy." She concluded that "Mrs. Marshall brings an instinctive understanding, a generosity, and a free humor that combine to form a style remarkable for its courage, its color and its natural control."[23] In the *Saturday Review,* Henrietta Buckmaster, a leftist, understood Selina's double bind—struggling against a "white society" and also "trying to understand the status seeking of her own people."[24] Carol Field's singularly appreciative review in the *New York Herald Tribune* was the only one that tackled the issue of race as central to black lives: "Racial conflict and the anger and frustration it nurtures are part of this tale."[25] But Field also gave equal attention to the importance of Selina's coming of age as a young girl and was the only commentator who noted the importance of the father: Selina "assumes shape and meaning through her experiences with her mother and father, drawn to the mother's 'iron' spirit but much more entranced by her father's 'love of poetry and fantasy, of people and adventure.' "[26]

Reviewers should have been able to place the novel in the context of three other classic coming-of-age novels—Ralph Ellison's *Invisible Man* (1952), Gwendolyn Brooks's *Maud Martha* (1953), and James Baldwin's *Go Tell It on the Mountain* (1953)—all published in the same decade as *Brown Girl*, all semi-autobiographical, all dealing with black identity in a racialized America. Reviewers also ignored an entire tradition of writing by black women from before the 1950s that *Brown Girl* belongs in. A few critics produced the problematic comparison of *Brown Girl* to Betty Smith's 1943 *A Tree Grows in Brooklyn*, a young adult novel about a second-generation Irish Catholic girl growing up in Brooklyn on the eve of World War I, a story of the American melting pot—without blacks.[27] In contrast to the reception of male writers such as Ralph Ellison, whose novel *Invisible Man* was compared to James Joyce's *Ulysses*, William Faulkner's *Light in August*, and Dostoevsky's *Crime and Punishment*, the critical reviews of *Brown Girl* viewed it as unconnected to any prior major literary traditions.

The black male literary establishment also had a hard time trying to contextualize *Brown Girl, Brownstones*, stumbling over gender rather than race. The distinguished educator and cultural critic Nick Aaron Ford was something of a race radical, but less advanced in his gender politics. Ignoring the significant presence of women in Paule's second book, *Soul Clap Hands and Sing*, Ford wrote that he was more comfortable with that collection because it represented "the universal complexities faced by aging *men*." *Brown Girl, Brownstones,* he decreed, "contained no promise as great as this."[28] The editors of *Dark Symphony* sentimentalized the protagonist of *Brown Girl, Brownstones* as "a warm-hearted, second-generation Barbadian girl" who, through her parents, "manages to save her heritage."[29] These critics seemed unable to see the cultural or ideological significance in *Brown Girl* because they could not understand gender as a category of analysis. Black women writers were being inserted into an era defined by male writers such as Richard Wright, Ralph Ellison, and James Baldwin, in texts named *Native Son, Black Boy, Invisible Man, Going to Meet the Man,* and *Notes of a Native Son.* To these critics "the Negro soul" was male. Stories about black women were presumed to be singular, unable to represent the race, the community, or the nation. The important stories were about the conflicts between black fathers and sons or brothers—or between white and black men.

It's important to remember, however, that black writers were walking a tightrope in the Cold War/Jim Crow era, attempting to represent blackness in the conservative literary-racial climate of the 1950s. Black writing was subject to white mainstream acceptance and approval, which meant minimizing racial critique, eliminating any taint of left-wing politics, and avoiding injuring the sensitivities of white readers.[30] To some extent black writers navigated this tightrope by creating transcendent black figures whose complex interiority and struggle for autonomy would be legible to modern readers grappling with their own alienation from community and tradition. Paule's Selina Boyce, Baldwin's John Grimes, Ellison's Invisible, and Brooks's Maud Martha represented the new black modern, asserting individuality over communal bonds, navigating an industrializing world, exposed to new concepts of race, gender, class, and sexuality. When Selina refuses the scholarship from the Barbadian Homeowners' Association—"her final alienation" from a tightknit Bajan community—she becomes the modern figure, aware, for the first time, of "the loneliness coiled fast around her freedom."[31]

While it would take another thirty years for *Brown Girl* to be fully recognized, it immediately attracted the attention of one celebrated and beloved black writer. At a party in a Harlem storefront hosted by Paule's friend and Brooklyn-born visual artist Ernie Crichlow to celebrate the book's publication, Paule was eight months pregnant with her first child and on the verge of divorce. It was there that she would meet poet Langston Hughes, who showed up unannounced just as the party was getting underway, "every wave of his naturally curly hair in place, and his trademark cigarette a permanent fixture between his lips."[32] She wrote to Hughes five days after the party to ask his advice about getting an agent and publicizing the book.

Hughes began to mentor Paule, sending her notes and postcards to congratulate her on every publication, remaining throughout her life one of her most enthusiastic supporters. Hughes called her often, sometimes late at night, scolding her for not writing more: "He wanted me to write more, and faster! 'Paulee, Paulee . . . Do you know that I have a book out for every year you've been alive?' His whole aim was to encourage me, to encourage us."[33] We can see Paule plotting out her writerly life. She channeled Hughes's poetry in much of her own writing, devoted the first section of her memoir as "Homage to Mr. Hughes," and riffed on his poem "I've Known Rivers" by designing her memoir around the interconnecting waters that ran through her life—the James River in Virginia, the Caribbean Sea, the Atlantic Ocean. Over the next few years, she sent Hughes invitations to her book parties, though he was rarely in town long enough to come, and they kept missing each other as both traveled back and forth across the

Atlantic. One of Paule's youngest readers (and a Hughes fan) got a copy of *Brown Girl, Brownstones* from his Barbadian mother when he was only eleven years old. He read it eleven times, then found Paule's name in the Manhattan phone book and called to tell her his mother loved her book. Paule answered the call and was amazed at the precocious young Hilton Als who, like Paule, was already in thrall to the unconventional.[34]

Langston Hughes admired *Brown Girl, Brownstones* for many reasons. It was a departure from the 1950s Ellisonian politics of black invisibility and in sync with Hughes's 1925 manifesto "The Negro Artist and the Racial Mountain," which encouraged black artists to celebrate the beauty of dark faces.[35] The party-going, jazz- and blues-loving Hughes would have appreciated Paule's portrait of the young Selina, drawn to the bohemian life on Fulton Street and Times Square, the jazz, the loud colors, and the wild crowds, and to the sexually advanced Suggie Skeete, who rooms upstairs in the Boyce family's brownstone. Like Hughes, both Paule and Selina struggled against the repressions of family, and all three looked to expand identity by exploring the black Atlantic world.

Both Paule and Langston were similarly inclined to keep their sexual lives hidden. Even though, by 1959, Paule had had both female and male lovers, she never addressed same-gender sexuality in her interviews or speeches— and, in fact, those interviews deflected attention even from the homoerotic relationships in her fiction. In a 1991 interview, when she was asked about "female sexuality" in her stories, she said that she used sexuality as "a metaphor for the kind of bonding that is needed between black men and women."[36]

Although Paule never commented on the homoerotic in her work, it exists in all of her writing, and is the one of the ways she cut a new path for representing black women's lives. Selina's relationships with her young friend Beryl, the upstairs tenant Suggie, and her college dance partner Rachel Fine generate the most erotic language of *Brown Girl.* That sexuality and sensuality unfolds subtly when Selina reads her poetry to Beryl, who falls asleep, pressing Selina closer, "so that they were like the lovers on the slope."[37] Selina also visits Suggie's bedroom, watching Suggie dancing alone, eyes half closed and hips swaying, her robe swinging softly around her hips as though trying to lure an "invisible lover with somnolent eyes and lush arms." Aware of Suggie's bare body beneath the robe, Selina begins to dance with her until, both laughing and sobbing, she feels the room spinning; then Selina drags Suggie over to the bed and they fall, "amid wild shouts and laughter, onto the bed."[38] Note the sequence here and its suggestion of postcoital intimacy: they lie in silence on the bed, gazing out the window until it is completely dark. "The last records dropped," and they hear "the last loud rhythms" of the music, "the soft whir of the turntable," "the laughter and sobs catching in Selina's throat," and the two of them lie "in a pure silence, gazing out the window at the twilight sky and the pale stars embedded there." The scene ends as "together, laughing, their arms circling each other's waists, they crossed the room and opened the door. A wide bar of light from the hall made a path for them and the rich colors of their laughter painted the darkness."[39] The metaphor of a door-opening, path-making, light-filled movement—occurring after intimate scenes between Suggie and Selina—focuses deliberate narrative attention on homoerotic pleasure and confirms Paule's desire to show women's intimacy as a crucial part of Selina's passage to womanhood.[40]

This groundbreaking representation of female eroticism was ignored or misread by the critics, and so was the rich, textured, oppositional blackness that shaped her fiction. Cultural historian Lawrence Jackson rightly calls Paule's fiction "anti-assimilationist" because it refuses the traditional orthodoxies of integration that court assimilation to white America.[41] Paule's intention was to extricate black lives from the white colonizing eye and render them visible as subjects through her own black gaze. That black gaze in Paule's fiction takes pleasure in observing black bodies and black people and fosters intimacy with black characters and communities, a striking counter to the black exclusionist policies of U.S. media culture in the 1950s and the timid literary establishment for whom erasing blackness was the price of "universality." In one scene, Selina imagines watching a family sitting down to dinner, "the children playfully kicking each other under the table as they waited, their small stomachs weak and warm with expectancy as the steam flew up from the pots." As voiced through the narrator, Selina wishes that she could stop time so they could stay safe in those warm rooms, under her watch, "with the eager smiles fixed on their dark faces"—that is, free from the dehumanizing white gaze and the racializing systems that distort black humanity.[42]

When asked about "the black aesthetic" in a 1977 interview with Nigerian poet-activist Molara Ogundipe-Leslie, Paule tapped into the language of 1970s black cultural and political nationalism to name what she had already done ten years earlier:

> Cultural revolution is about how you see yourself. What you think of yourself is part and parcel of other aspects of the revolution, the political revolution. You can't have one without the other. And the black aesthetic, with its emphasis on the celebration of blackness, of seeing beauty in blackness, an emphasis on using some of the traditional forms, rhythms, and imagery in the work and dealing with themes that have to do with black life, is one of the ways of creating this positive image. We are in the process of re-creating ourselves all over the world and it's a fascinating task.[43]

When Selina experiences her first direct encounter with white racism, her shield is not black nationalism; it is the voices of the women and the dispossessed in her life. Mrs. Benton, a white friend's mother, tells her: "You . . . well, dear . . . you don't even act colored. I mean, you speak so well and have such poise. And it's just wonderful how you've taken your race's natural talent for dancing and music and developed it."[44] Selina thinks of those pale eyes as "a well-lighted mirror" in which, for the first time, she sees "with a sharp and shattering clarity—the full meaning of her black skin."[45] The encounter with Benton does not "debase" Selina; this is her baptism into what Du Bois would call "the fraternity of the race." The words of her interior monologue after the racial assault connect her to community: "She was one with Miss Thompson—one with the whores, the flashy men, and the blues; and she was one with them: the mother and the Bajan women—how had the mother endured."[46] For Selina, as with Paule, the two cultures—Afro-West Indian and African American—"merged to become one in me."[47] Following actors such as Abbey Lincoln, Esther Rolle, Diana Sands, and Cicely Tyson, Paule's cultural revolution included wearing her hair in a closely cropped Afro in the 1950s, an expression of blackness radical enough to end a career. When she developed alopecia and lost her hair in her thirties, she wore only Afro wigs.

Paule was taken by surprise when Hollywood came calling. Flush from his success on Broadway and in Hollywood, her friend Sidney Poitier turned up at her apartment and offered her $25,000—roughly equivalent to $200,000 today—to buy the rights to film *Brown Girl.* Paule refused—tragically, according to her son and husband—because she did not want to relinquish her artistic control; but in 1960, when the television network Columbia Broadcasting Station (CBS) approached Paule about producing a television movie of *Brown Girl* for the Television Repertoire Workshop, she readily agreed. The CBS workshop allowed Paule full artistic control as the scriptwriter, and she would also be the casting director, enticing her friends to be a part of the production. She gave a copy of the script to actor and friend Cicely Tyson, suggesting that Tyson play the part of the older daughter, sixteen- or seventeen-year-old Ina. Tyson, who was then thirty-five, wanted the part of Selina, who was about age twelve or thirteen. She cut her hair almost to the scalp and wore it natural, trying to look the part, but Benita Evans, who was twenty, got the role. Ossie Davis, who was also a good friend of Paule's, portrayed the father, Deighton. The off-screen narration was done by Paule. As an adaptation, the one-hour production focused on the conflict in the Boyce family between the parents and covered less than a third of the novel. *Brown Girl* aired on April 24, 1960, and *TV Guide* called it the "best show of the series," urging readers and viewers to "keep an eye on this Miss Marshall. The girl can write."[48]

The year 1959 should have been the moment to celebrate two talented young black female writers: Paule Marshall and Lorraine Hansberry, whose play *A Raisin in the Sun* opened on Broadway a few months before the publication of *Brown Girl.* Paule hoped the play would prove "there was room for an acceptance of a novel by and about a Black woman," but "that didn't prove to be the case."[49] There were stunning similarities between *Brown Girl, Brownstones* and *A Raisin in the Sun.* Both focus on black working-class families and their refusal to stay within the boundaries imposed by white dominance, and both feature a young intellectual daughter who aspires to college and a professional life. There were also distinct differences. The central issue in *Raisin,* by the end of the play, becomes Walter Lee's thwarted desire for masculine power, and the play reaches its highest pitch when his manhood is restored. In contrast, the CBS version of *Brown Girl,* like the novel, is the story of a daughter devastated by her father's abandonment, determined to resist her mother's domination and to forge a path toward her own independence, enabled by the women who mentor her. If *Raisin,* with its focus on a black Chicago family's struggles with housing discrimination, the racial bars to the American dream, and black manhood, was the play for its time, *Brown Girl, Brownstones* was too far ahead of its time.[50] *Brown Girl*'s critique of sexism and sexual and racial violence, its representations of unconventional black women, its expansive female geographical mobility, its open expression of female eroticism, and its linking of U.S. black communities to the diaspora—all this would require another thirty years for recognition and acceptance.

Brown Girl was not a commercially successful novel, partly because Random House did little to promote it, but also because, as Paule notes, "There wasn't the kind of climate within the literary community" for such a book. But she also acknowledges that she refused to make the public gestures to help create a following for her work: "That first time around I didn't understand what the whole literary establishment was all about."[51] She was not interested in television and radio appearances, and she avoided book parties, public debates, and cocktail parties, none of which appealed to her.

In other ways, though, Paule was quite savvy about her career. She applied for and received a prestigious John Simon Guggenheim grant in 1960, with recommendations from Langston Hughes, her editor Hiram Haydn, *New York Herald Tribune* editor John Hutchens, playwrights Loften Mitchell and William Branch, CBS producer Albert McCleery, and Cyrilly Abels, an editor at the upscale women's magazine *Mademoiselle.* She had nearly completed a second book, a collection of four novellas that would be titled *Soul Clap Hands and Sing* and would be published in the fall of 1961 by Atheneum Press. In her application, she wrote that she would use the Guggenheim grant to begin work on her third book, a "comprehensive novel on the West Indies which will focus on a small British island colony during a period of significant social and political change." This would become her epic novel *The Chosen Place, the Timeless People.*

> If I am to realize my full potential as a writer I will need some measure of relief, from time to time, from the exhausting schedule of being a full time mother (I have a year old son), a wife (my husband, Kenneth Marshall, is a sociologist who is presently devoting full time to the completion of his doctoral dissertation in sociology), and housewife. Simply, I need time to work, the chance—now that I am at the beginning of my career—to grow and develop as a writer, the opportunity to

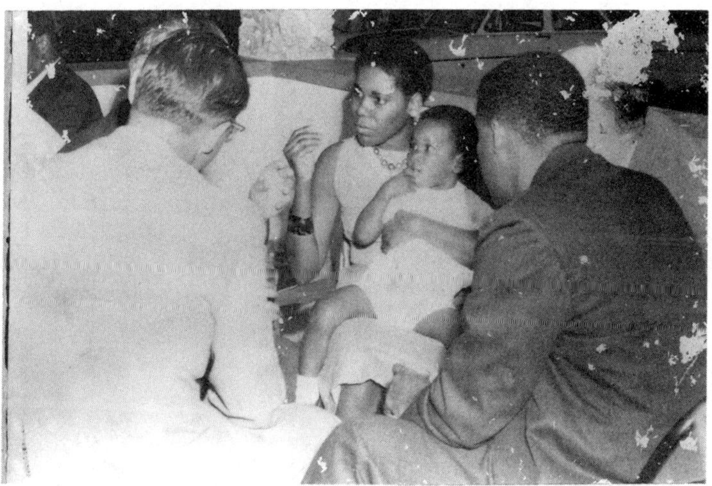

In this 1962 photo, Paule holds Evan, age three, with Errol Barrow (right) who was prime minister of Barbados in the 1980s.

> fashion and perfect my craft. For I am certain that I have something to say. Being a Negro, as well as a peculiar combination of West Indian and American has exposed me to a body of human experience which has not yet found the full literary expression it so deserves.[52]

Guggenheim judges may not have noticed the anger at the edges of Paule's plea for "relief" from being a full-time mother, wife, and housewife, while Kenneth was "presently devoting full time" to his dissertation. What she could not say here is that her determination to be a writer was already creating serious problems in her marriage.

CHAPTER 5

Things Is Different to Before

WHILE PAULE EMBARKED ON a writing and journalism career, Kenneth earned a master's degree in psychology from City College and one in social work from Columbia University. Both were devoted to their careers, their lives and work intersecting in as many ways as they would later diverge. Kenneth began writing about gangs in Harlem and working with an antipoverty program in Paterson, New Jersey, which paid well enough for the couple to move out of the Marshall family compound and into a single-family house in St. Albans, Queens, and may have stimulated Kenneth's long-held desire for domestic bliss with a wife more devoted to him and their homelife than to her career. Kenneth had not bargained for a writer-wife—nor had Paule realized the terms of the bargain she had made.

In early 1959, when they discovered Paule was pregnant and Kenneth had secured a position as a research assistant at Columbia while working on his dissertation, the couple left Queens and moved into the Irvington at 407 Central Park West in Manhattan, a lovely old apartment building overlooking Central Park at 100th Street, where Paule would live, between international travels and visiting professorships, for the next forty years. In September

1902, the Irvington was described in a *New York Times* ad as "the new seven-story apartment structure at 100th Street with large light rooms . . . now ready for inspection. Its suites of seven and eight large rooms *will appeal to particular and exclusive tenants.* Every convenience has been installed, including tiled baths, telephone and all-night elevator service."[1] Those "particular and exclusive" restrictions meant that Central Park West below 100th Street, the dividing line, was off-limits to black people, but by the 1950s when the Marshalls moved in, the eight-room suites had been divided into four-room ones, and several black families were living there.

Their two-bedroom, fourth-floor apartment was sunny and spacious, with high ceilings and a view of Central Park across the street. The prewar building was not prestigious enough to have a doorman, but the city's control over how much a landlord could raise the rent meant that the Marshalls were paying only $350 a month—even as late as 1989. Paule had potted plants everywhere and one tall tree that almost reached the ceiling. Over time, she purchased a grand piano, and the paintings and prints that adorned the walls, one by Ernie Crichlow that became the cover of the 1981 Feminist Press edition of *Brown Girl, Brownstones.* Paule also had etchings of scenes of the West Indies that hung in the hallway. The Marshalls befriended and collected art by the emerging black artists of the 1960s and 1970s: Romare Bearden, Ernie Crichlow, Norman Lewis, and Elizabeth Catlett.

Paule's affair with 407 was, however, a kind of love/hate relationship because the elevator would regularly break down, the boiler would conk out, and the landlord tried every ruse to get them out because he knew how valuable the building would be if he could get rid of the long-standing low-paying renters and turn the Irvington into a market rate co-op. The great location was marred by one other thing: the A-train, which ran from 59th to

125th Street, vibrated underneath it every ten minutes. To relax, Paule rode her fold-up bike on the weekends when Central Park was closed to cars, sometimes with Evan in tow. She walked and jogged in the park and did a fair amount of entertaining. Yet her discontent with 407 continued, heightened by the tension she felt with Kenneth over the new book of short stories she had begun.

Evan Marshall was born in 1959, shortly after *Brown Girl* was published. Moments after she delivered the baby, still groggy from hours of labor, Paule heard her elated husband calling to her, "Paule, Paule, you've come through for me. We have a son."[2] The "for me" was telling. Once Evan was born, there was even more insistence that Paule fulfill her role as a homemaker. In silent rebellion, she used the money she earned from *Brown Girl* to hire a nanny for her son and went to a friend's apartment in the afternoons to begin writing her second book. "I went off to a friend's apartment and worked every day on *Soul Clap Hands and Sing*, and there was strong objection to that. Yet I went ahead and did it."[3] While Kenneth liked the idea of having a famous writer-wife, he couldn't face up to the reality of the hard work writing required.

Their private discord was papered over by their public image. In the early 1960s, as Paule was emerging as a new voice in American fiction, she and Kenneth became something of a power couple. Their friends were politically engaged progressives fighting for liberal causes and comfortably middle class, the New York black cultural elite: Maya Angelou, Langston Hughes, Ernie Crichlow, Abbey Lincoln, Max Roach, Louise Meriwether, Rosa Guy, James Baldwin, Ossie Davis, and Ruby Dee. Paule's closest white friend was Connie Sutton, a well-known left-wing anthropologist, whom she met in Barbados in 1958 when Connie was on a research trip and Paule was researching and writing *Brown Girl*. Connie and her first husband Sam attended parties at the Marshalls' apartment, and their sons, Evan and David, were nearly the same age, so their families became very close. The Marshalls were also close friends with several black professionals: Ruby Nottage, a teacher and school principal, and her husband Wally Nottage, a child psychologist, and their daughter Lynn, who later became a renowned playwright; physician Calvin Sinnette, his wife, teacher and principal Elinor Jennings, and their daughter Caleen Sinnette Jennings, who also became a noted playwright.

Kenneth was particularly close to leftist labor activist Jim Haughton, a Princeton grad and probably the most militant of their friends. Haughton's first wife Eleanor Happy Leacock, whose father was the famous academic Kenneth Burke, was an esteemed anthropologist. Evan remembers that "this was for them a very exciting period, with very intelligent people who saw a new dawn coming in terms of civil rights and for career women like my mother and my godmother Connie."[4] However, Paule was particularly sensitive to the subtle racism directed at the black middle class. She remembered Leacock eyeing but not commenting on the Phi Beta Kappa ring she wore around her neck.

These were also deeply political times—the murder of Emmett Till, the March on Washington, the Montgomery bus boycott, the desegregation of Little Rock High School. Paule was involved in the Association of Artists for Freedom (AAF), which Paule felt filled the urgent need for a northern front of the civil rights movement.[5] After the killing of Addie Mae Collins, Cynthia Wesley, Denise McNair, and Carole Robertson and injury to scores of others at the 16th Street Baptist Church in Birmingham, Alabama, she joined Ossie Davis, Ruby Dee, Odetta, John O. Killens, and James Baldwin in the AAF's fight for a Christmas boycott in 1963—which failed because it was not supported by major civil rights organizations. But these protests were the signs of change and new visions of freedom in the air.

Paule got the idea for *Soul Clap Hands and Sing* while she was in Barbados in 1957 and 1958 finishing the manuscript for *Brown Girl.* Published in 1961, this second book was a collection of four short stories that launched Paule into international waters. Its focus on men and masculinity, which allowed her to "deal with aspects of my own personal history," may have foreshadowed her own marriage crisis.[6] Each story is set in a place in the diaspora—Barbados, Brooklyn, British Guiana, and Brazil—the alliteration a sign of their common threads. Each features an elderly or aging black man as the central character. In three of them—"Barbados," "Brooklyn," and "Brazil"—heterosexual masculinity is tied to dominance and violence. In the fourth, "British Guiana," homosexuality is represented as a dangerous choice but also a potential source of freedom. This ground-breaking collection also inaugurates the diasporan turn in Paule's fiction by portraying a global blackness as also gendered, queered, and in tension with sexual desire.

Paule offered many different motivations for *Soul Clap Hands,* as if she were testing out its appeal to diverse audiences. She first said that she wrote the stories in response to criticism, "to see if I could write convincingly of men."[7] But she also said she had been deeply influenced by the Black Arts Movement and wanted to try "to sort out what was happening to black and colored peoples throughout the world" as they dealt with "the new colonialism."[8] Further, she described *Soul Clap Hands* as an extended debate with herself over living a meaningful life, which entailed a commitment to her writing. "Writing *Soul Clap Hands* was one of my ways, through these characters, to ease some of the tension of what I was feeling—how was I going to order my life; how was

I really going to commit myself to being a writer and all that entails."[9] In her notes, she was forthright about the autobiographical element of her work: "This is an imp. aspect of my work: the work is autobiographical in the sense that I use it—the stories & novels—to answer questions I'm putting to myself; to resolve conflicts, to effect reconciliations, to put to rest old angers and hurt, to forgive and make peace once & for all, to bless and release." The one thing Paule does not include in this list of motivations for *Soul Clap Hands* is her growing realization that in order to safeguard her freedom as a writer, in order to sail "to the holy city of Byzantium," she needed to separate from Kenneth's demands and attend to her art.[10]

The first story, "Barbados," recalls Paule's time there while writing *Brown Girl* when she rented a room in a house in Bridgetown owned by Mr. Watson, a solitary bachelor, who "grudgingly accepted her as a boarder" in his "colonial showpiece" of a house in return for help with upkeep, though, she recalls, "he scarcely said two words to me the whole time I was there."[11] Watson becomes Mr. Watford in the story, an elderly man who has accrued property and money during his exile in the United States, returned home to his gated Colonial American–style house, and kept himself separate from the poor he disdained. When a local teenaged boy collects coconuts from Watford's trees to sell at the market, Watford admonishes him for wearing a button in support of the new Barbados People's Party, pursuing politics instead of learning a trade and accepting his colonial status. The young unnamed servant girl Watford hires is at first docile and acquiescent, until she becomes romantically involved with the teenaged boy, who gives her his political button. When Watford catches sight of the button, he violently confronts her about her sexual affair with the boy, which seems to him "as if it was a new power which would steady and protect her." A local shopkeeper gently warns Watford that these two young people represent the end of colonialism and the inevitability of an independent Barbados: "Things is different to before. They not so frighten for the white people as we was."[12]

In "British Guiana," Paule wrote the central figure of Gerald Ramsdeen Motley as an ethnic mixture of white, East Indian, Chinese, Creole or high-colored, from a once-wealthy family and alienated by both class and sexual desire from any communal bonds. After a brilliant school career in England, Motley returns to take his place among the high-coloreds, enjoying his privileged but empty life alone in the large colonial house, "sharing his class's indifference to the colony's troubles."[13] Although he denies his sexual feelings for a young working-class man, Motley once experienced an ecstatic erotic vision on a trip into the deep interior of the Amazon rainforest that the narrative presents in metaphors of threat, terror, and pleasure:

> Slowly, as he had moved over the thick underbrush, parting the tangled branches and looped vines which hung like a portiere before him, he sensed it. The bush had reared around him like the landscape of a dream, grand and gloomy, profuse and impenetrable, hoarding, he knew, gold and fecund soils, and yet somehow, still ravenous. So that the branches clawed at him, the vines wound his arms, roots sprang like traps around his feet and the silence—dark from the vast shadow, brooding upon the centuries lost—wolfed down the sound of his breathing. He had felt a terror that had been the most exquisite of pleasures and at his awed cry the bush had closed around him, becoming another dimension of himself, the self he had long sought. For the first time this self was within his grasp. If he pursued this dark way long enough he would find it hanging like a jeweled pendant on the trees—and it would either shape his life by giving him the right answer to Orly's offer or destroy him.[14]

Paule set this experience—enticing but threatening—as a turning point for Motley. To choose a homosexual identity Motley would have to relinquish the economic and social advantages of the high-colored elite and brave their disapproval and perhaps even violence. Motley turns away from this "dark way," gradually giving in to the seductions of a conventional and comfortable life that would be deadly to his soul. Paule understood the danger of the path Motley contemplates. Her good friend Cliff Lashley, a Jamaican poet and scholar, a "bright, gay man with a tongue that could do untold damage," was killed brutally in 1993 in Jamaica by his lover, who "bit off the head and the tongue that housed it." This account of her friendship with Lashley trails off with this unfinished final line: "What he didn't understand, what I barely understood myself at the time was that . . ." What didn't Paule and Lashley understand? Perhaps it was the extent of the brutal hostility toward gay people in that land so well known as a tourist paradise, which may have cautioned her not to allow Motley to take that path.

In "Brooklyn," the only story in the collection that is set in the United States, the protagonist, Miss Williams, a Howard University graduate from a middle-class black family, now teaching in Richmond, Virginia, is studying French literature at Brooklyn College during the summer in a class taught by the womanizing Professor Berman. In the introduction to the 1983 edition issued by the Feminist Press, Paule revealed for the first time that "Brooklyn" was based on a personal incident of sexual harassment by her professor at Brooklyn College, who offered repeated invitations to Paule to visit his place in the country and made suggestive gestures that made her feel both discomfort and rage but also powerless to act.[15]

"Brooklyn" is especially important as a model for reading all of Marshall's work, which makes great demands on the reader, and exposed the limitations and biases of Paule's male critics. While Berman's gaze and point of view appear to dominate the story, a close reading shows that the narrative undercuts Berman's sexualizing views at every turn, requiring the reader to attend to the small, seemingly insignificant gestures—haptic and aural—that signal Miss Williams's resistant interiority. As soon as Miss Williams enters the classroom, Professor Berman entertains plans to seduce her, first suggesting a visit to his office to discuss her thesis on André Gide's 1902 novel *The Immoralist,* and then inviting her to his summer place in the country. Throughout their brief conversations, Berman is aware of her skin, "like a rich, fine-textured cloth," and her "disturbing, dangerous, but fascinating" appeal, and of his desire to possess not only this one black woman but "the host of black women whose bodies had been despoiled to make her."[16]

Gradually, Berman becomes aware of Miss Williams's "*startling forcefulness.*" When he tries to assign sinfulness to the Gide novel, she is not listening: "But she had not heard this; *her mind had already leaped ahead.*" Berman tries to make a joke: "*And his playful tone went unnoticed.*" When Berman speaks as the wise professor, Williams drops her voice, and "*he had to lean close now to hear her* (my emphasis)." In contrast to his "twitching" and/or "pulsing" eyelid, which occasionally makes him appear to be winking, her "abstracted gaze" is either "disturbing and dangerous" or a "clear, cold gaze," through which he reads her disgust and/or her pity. Berman now knows how *she* sees him: "He sensed that she glimpsed a legion of old men with sere flesh and lonely eyes flanking him: 'old lechers with a love on every wind.' " Miss Williams's first reaction to Berman's sexual invitations is not submissiveness or fear but "mute, paralyzing rage." He "had not expected so subtle and complex a force beneath her mild exterior. . . . It was like a strong and restless seed that had taken root in the darkness there and was straining now toward the light."[17] Berman finally recognizes that this woman cannot be contained or subordinated within his gaze. Given Berman's impotence, we are led to wonder what Paule was up to in this story ostensibly about male sexual dominance.

Keep in mind that Paule stages the swim scene at Berman's country home in the same lyrical and pastoral language of Gide's *The Immoralist,* suggesting that Miss Williams and Gide's protagonist Michel experienced a similar transformation. In one of Michel's last days in the southern Italian town of Ravello, he discovers a spring of clear water, and under the glow of shimmering sunlight, he plunges into the spring and comes out "numb with cold" but now "without any more shame, with joy. I judge myself not yet strong, but capable of strength, harmonious, sensual, almost beautiful." Critics understand this scene as the one that frees Michel to experience his homosexuality, although those encounters are never fully dramatized. The novel ends as the sister of the Arab boy Ali accuses Michel of preferring the boy to her, and Michel answers, ambiguously, in the final unfinished line of the novel: "There may be some truth in what she says . . ."[18]

When Miss Williams walks with Berman to the lake at his country home and stands beside him, preparing to enter the water, she also is described as plunging deep into the water, as Michel does at the spring in Ravello. When she finally emerges, her white swim cap is "the sign of her purity," and her arms "a pale, flashing gold in the sunlit water," while Berman's skin, "bled white and flaccid with the veins like angry blue penciling—marked the final barrier."[19] Literary scholar Shirley Parry was the first to argue that Miss Williams's symbolic plunge into the physical lake, a "shadowy underwater place," marks "the final barrier" to Berman's sexual fantasies, and can be understood as the moment in the story when "the heterosexual/heteronormative narrative is effectively dropped," and another, transgressive sexual story emerges.[20] However ambiguous this ending, Paule made sure that it would track closely with *The Immoralist,* and she clearly meant for "Brooklyn" to be decoded through Gide's novel. Like Michel, Miss Williams is now empowered to undertake a journey to recover and accept, however tentatively, a new, perhaps queer, self.

Critics may have missed the transgressive sexuality in *Soul Clap Hands,* but its critique of masculinity set off some reviewers. Karl Sealy, writing in 1962 in the Barbadian magazine *BIM,* was so outraged that he claimed the stories represented a personal animus toward men. "Women," Sealy opined, "add more to the misery of men whom they attract or to whom they are attracted than they do to their happiness."[21] The treatment of men in *Soul* was for Sealy a vicious, unpitying attack that "hurls revilement and contempt" and "quiet, controlled scorn" at men; thus, Sealy concludes, the servant girl in "Barbados" encouraged Mr. Watford and therefore deserved to be attacked: "And, yet, would not Mr. Watford have been content to drift his lonely way to his grave with his doves, if this girl had not imposed herself upon him, and if she herself had not tacitly suggested and expected the advances which she so brutally repels?"[22] Sealy interprets Berman's sexual advances in "Brooklyn" as "misconduct," deserving "no more check than does the cruelty of children."[23] Unexpectedly, Sealy backtracked at the end of his review, praising Paule for her originality and for tales that "throb with the reality of a heated pulse." He predicted that "*Soul Clap Hands and Sing* will hardly ever need dusting among the haunts of those who read."[24]

Other male reviewers, slightly less misogynistic than Sealy, simply misread the stories and, in some cases, defended the lecherous professor. It took more than twenty-five years for the esteemed African American scholar Darwin Turner to reverse his original sympathetic view of the sexually predatory professor in "Brooklyn." Turner first viewed the white professor "who loses his job because of McCarthy's zealous search for Communists" as the real victim.[25] In an extended introduction to *Soul Clap Hands*, written more than twenty-five years later in 1988, Turner recognized that when he first reviewed these stories as "a young male professional," he had been "haunted" that he might be one of these tragic men who missed their chance for love and companionship. But now, in his mid-fifties, having witnessed such a fate in the lives of his friends and colleagues, though not in his own, Turner was ready to admit Paule's perceptiveness about these men.[26] In *Phylon*, Nick Aaron Ford sympathized with Professor Berman, viewing his threatening and unwanted sexual advances toward his student as an attempt to seek "fulfillment of his identity in an affair with Miss Williams."[27] Ford's positive spin on Berman's motives discounted Williams's revulsion toward Berman's advances and ignored the fact that his desire for Miss Williams is triggered by his sense of her vulnerability as a black woman.

Many mainstream critics did recognize Paule's enlarged world vision in *Soul Clap Hands*. In the *New York Times*, Henrietta Buckmaster pointed out that the black subject in Paule's collection "is undergoing a considerable sea-change, acquiring new fictional dimensions and associations." Buckmaster notes that Paule moves from an examination of the outer "social pressures on the Negro" to a subtle and evocative examination of "inner tensions."[28] The *Kirkus Review* commented that Paule had "expanded a private sense of race and color into an enormously wide almost mystic sense of the chiaroscuro of life itself in its mixed moods and human dimensions."[29] Others noted that Paule's vision encompassed a larger part of the colored world, and was therefore moving beyond a limited national view of black life and culture.

As a result of the impressive sales of the edition of *Brown Girl, Brownstones,* the press asked Paule to collect her female-centered stories, and Paule agreed. Two of the stories from *Soul Clap Hands,* "Barbados" and "Brooklyn," were included in Paule's short story collection *Reena & Other Stories,* published by the Feminist Press in 1981. It was a carefully calculated move that established Paule in the feminist community and garnered the first real attention to her work. The feminist value of "Brooklyn" was hardly noticed until it was rediscovered in the 2000s by the #MeToo Movement.[30]

On September 10, 1961, Paule's friend James Baldwin sent her a postcard from Tel Aviv on his way to Africa, in admiration for *Soul Clap Hands:*

> Dear Paule: This is a very belated Thank You for your book—
> and a very rushed & inadequate suggestion of how much I
> admired it—admire you—for all that grace & courage & clarity.
> It's very beautiful, Paule, although the situations are horrible.
> Please don't stop now—not that you can. I'm enroute for
> Africa via Israel—hadn't planned it that way, but it throws a
> very valuable light over everything. See you this winter.
> Best.—Jim Baldwin[31]

When Paule applied for a John Simon Guggenheim Foundation grant in 1960, she was already at work on *Soul Clap Hands.* With the Guggenheim money—"those checks in the thousands of dollars that regularly arrived from New York"—Paule tucked her three-year-old son under her arm and went to Grenada for a year to write her next novel.[32] In contrast to her spare accommodations in Barbados, she was able to rent an old-style Creole country house with a separate study for writing, and hire a housekeeper, a gardener, a cook, a laundress, and a nursemaid for Evan.

She also had access to a beautiful beach nearby for her "sea-baths."[33] Although Kenneth was not "an island person," his son provided an incentive to visit occasionally. On one visit, Kenneth brought Evan an expensive electric battery–powered Stutz-Bearcat car, which his son rode to his delight around the veranda. Kenneth always carried his eight-millimeter silent movie camera, taking photos of Evan and Paule on their way to the beach or Paule having a cocktail on the veranda. Paule fell in love with Grenada, enchanted with the "small but gloriously variegated volcanic beauty of cratered mountains, shapely green hills, waterfalls, rivers, rainforests and valleys replete with every kind of tropical tree, foliage and vegetation imaginable."[34] The beauty of Grenada became the backdrop for her next novel, *The Chosen Place, the Timeless People.*

Paule had outlined in detail in her Guggenheim application the novel she planned to write. It would take place during the period following Home Rule, as the people of a fictional Caribbean country experiment with self-governance. The constellation of people would include the masses of agricultural workers on the vast sugarcane estates, the black middle class, especially "the bright young men" who returned from the United States and England with their progressive ideas, and the white merchant class who maintained economic control. Paule added three U.S. anthropologists into the mix, modeled on a field work team she met in Barbados, which included her friend Connie Sutton. In her application, Paule wrote to the Guggenheim committee that she wanted to avoid the label of protest literature, conceiving of black people in "the larger dimension of [their] humanity," enabling that understanding "which is so crucial to the solution of racial intolerance," a nod to Ralph Ellison. But the final line of her application was an unambiguous expression of black solidarity, saying her purpose was "to have a fruitful dialogue with my people that would extend their vision of life." Paule also meant for this novel to be a corrective to such novels as the 1955 *Island in the Sun* by white British novelist Alec Waugh (the older brother of Evelyn), which she described as reinforcing touristy images of the Caribbean as "places of calypso ditties, waving palm trees, sun-whitened beaches," and sensationalized interracial romances. *Island in the Sun* was made into a 1957 film starring Harry Belafonte, who wrote the title song with Irving Burgie, helping to produce this vision of an idyllic island.

Paule finally had everything she needed to write: a perfect location, time, solitude, money, help with housekeeping. Yet once she settled in to begin work, the excitement she felt about the book disappeared. As soon as she put out her writing materials—a new Royal typewriter, a new desk, her steno pads, and all her research material—she experienced the worst writer's block of her life. Why? she wondered. Perhaps the money and the lack of accountability had produced a sense of "paralysis and impotence."[35] Maybe she was dogged by guilt over being away from "the Struggle."[36] Why wasn't she back in the United States helping with the voter registration drive in the South or raising money for Artists for Freedom? She churned out page after page that ended up in the wastebasket.

Paule's editor Hiram Haydn wrote in his memoir that hers was the most striking writer's block he had ever witnessed. Her ambition and demands on herself as a writer were formidable, as she was a woman with an iron, inflexible will: "She wants, with every ounce of her powerful, proud, stubborn, flamboyant nature, to write a novel that takes life by the throat, squeezes it till its tongue hangs out, and then flings it in the face of the white world, crying out, 'There! That's what I mean, you idiots!' "[37] Haydn found her somewhat frightening: "I cannot count the people, who, after first meeting her, have said to me, 'Formidable! Tremendous! She's beautiful, but she scares me.' At times I admire myself for being both her editor and her friend."[38] Haydn also witnessed Paule's desperation and self-doubt. "She wailed, groaned, cursed and then refused to speak altogether. She had dried up, she couldn't write, what she had written was meaningless weak trash, she would never write again, she was through."[39]

Then something miraculous happened. She abandoned her study and took Evan on beach trips. One morning, when she saw a crowd of the mostly poor supporters of the chief minister Eric Matthew Gairy packed together on a rickety and overcrowded lorry going to an all-day rally to support Gairy's reelection as Grenada's chief minister, she spontaneously set out on foot to join them—leaving Evan with the nanny—and escaping the torture of yet another unproductive workday.

Although there were many figures in the pro-independence movements that Paule admired—one was Errol Barrow, activist and the first prime minister of Barbados—Gairy was not one of them. Paule watched Gairy's impoverished supporters roar their approval as he entered the Grand Anse harbor on the deck of a "stately white, flushed-deck sailboat," dressed all in white, his hands spread out against the mast in the pose of the crucifixion as he exhorted the crowd to vote for him.[40] Paule was incensed at this manipulative scene ("All that was missing were the crown of thorns and the stigmata on his open palms"), especially because no provisions had been made to feed the massive crowd, which had stood waiting for hours in the mid-afternoon heat.[41] In Paule's view, Gairy was "a minor figure in the unfortunately long and disheartening list of postcolonial leaders who misused, disappointed and failed their own."[42] Although Gairy's quest to be prime minister was short-lived, he lived on as the model for her critical portraits of all the neocolonial figures in her novels.[43]

The excursion to Gairy's political rally was followed by another event during her time in Grenada that spurred Paule's return to the excitement and purpose of her work. She was invited by an English woman, a literature teacher at a school in St. George's who was passionate about the Big Drum/Nation Dance, to accompany her to the celebration on the tiny satellite island of Carriacou, less than two hours away by the local schooner. Paule joined her "schoolmarm friend," along with the Carriacou people living in Grenada, for the annual event.[44] She was taken with the rituals and the history, which traced their lineage back to what they considered their "true-true nation": Manding, Arada, Cromanti, Congo, Yoruba, Igbo, Chamba. She joined the circle of dancers on a dusty dance floor and, like the middle-aged Avey in her 1983 novel *Praisesong for the Widow,* she experienced a transformation that she would understand only decades later. When she returned from Carriacou, the curse had lifted, "the paralysis broken," and she began to work on the new novel with renewed energy.[45] The inflexibility, determination, and fury Haydn recognized allowed her to begin again working on *The Chosen Place, the Timeless People.*

Unexpectedly in 1961, Paule had to leave Grenada for New York to accept the $2,000 Richard and Hilda Rosenthal Foundation Award (worth about $22,000 today) for *Soul Clap Hands and Sing,* an award given for a fiction work of "considerable literary achievement." The award was presented at the American Academy of Arts and Letters in the majestic neoclassical series of buildings in Washington Heights, where she went "unwillingly," because she was "struggling mightily" to get her new book under way. Ralph Ellison was at the ceremony. He assumed his place, she recalled, as "an indisputable member of the pantheon" seated among the literary patriarchs. William Faulkner, who received the

Academy's Gold Medal just months before his death, was there, along with writers Robert Penn Warren and Aldous Huxley.

Paule remembered Ellison, "ensconced among the giants," as "profoundly unapproachable, aloof, inaccessible. Could be talkative and witty," she noted, "but to the company in general." She shook Ellison's hand that night, telling him what an honor it was to meet him, but "I felt the distance, the chasm, the remoteness, the unbridgeable distance." What struck Paule as absurd and even menacing was Ellison's refusal to take off the London Fog trench coat he was wearing, "the uniform of those who monitor our every word, to be added to our dossiers in Washington." On the other hand, she granted, "it was understandable, a form of self-protection," maybe from the young militants like Paule, who noted his absence from the civil rights movement. Paule's relationship to Ellison stands in for her vexed relationship to the mainstream literary establishment and the constrained space of black authors—especially black women—within it. Thirty years later, in her unpublished typewritten notes, Ellison's shabby treatment of her when she was a newly published writer in the 1960s and he an esteemed member of the literary establishment still rankled: "*He cut me dead every time we've been in the same room.*"

Back in Grenada, Paule's year-long stay was the turning point in her marriage.[46] By 1962, their thirteen-year-old marriage was essentially over, partly the result of Kenneth's objections to her writing career and partly because of his affairs with other women. In Kenneth's dissertation, "The Fighting Gang in Transition: A Study of the Structure and Functions of the Urban Adolescent Fighting Gang and An Analysis of Functionally Equivalent Deviant Group Modes," which details his relationships with the black youth he worked with in Harlem, he candidly admits that even the boys in these gangs suspected his infidelity. The boys knew Paule, and they did not tolerate

Kenneth joking about any extramarital dealings. "They knew and liked my wife, and they wanted to see mine as an ideal marriage."[47] Once, when Kenneth was joking about his plan to dance with the attractive advisor of the girls' group, one of the young men threatened to tell Paule: " 'You know, Kenny, if your wife should be getting a little letter in a couple of days, you'll know what it's about.' "[48] It was not the first time the boys threatened to inform on him.

When Paule returned from Grenada, Kenneth was involved with one of his graduate students, whom he later married, a very smart woman according to Evan. While Evan does not remember his father as a violent man, he exercised a kind of dominance over the women in his life. Evan overheard an argument between Kenneth and his second wife Jonni over the dress she wanted to wear for their evening out. "I can hear my dad saying, 'You are not wearing that dress.' And I remember distinctly the sound of the dress being ripped up. He had ripped up the dress, and that is not something my mother would have tolerated."[49]

Evan speculated that after Paule published *Brown Girl, Brownstones* in 1959, Kenneth hoped she would "settle down and be a mother, maybe teach or something."[50] Yet as Paule settled into writing rather than domesticity, the divorce became inevitable. Recalling his mother's exasperation with Kenneth's objections to her work, Evan readily defends her: "In the long run, my mother would say he was still this pampered West Indian boy whose mother put his meals on the table religiously and that's what he wanted, someone who would put his meals on the table and would recognize him as the head of the family."[51] Paule felt she had to remain "stubbornly determined" to keep writing, even though she knew that it was hard on her son "being the child of a mother who writes."[52]

She would feel this guilt all of her life, yet she remained firm: "I think this is something women have to acknowledge about themselves—their right to fulfill themselves."[53] Motherhood was "exhausting" because Paule was trying to tend to a child, write a book, and defend against her husband's objections to her writing, but she was more direct about the demands of motherhood than about the strains in her marriage.

Paule's struggles with 1950s conventions of marriage and motherhood are foreshadowed in three texts: her 1953 story "The Valley Between," *Brown Girl, Brownstones,* and most clearly her 1962 story "Reena," part essay and part fiction, published a year before her divorce. This hybrid form provided the distance Paule needed to represent a woman like herself, a wife, mother, and artist seeking autonomy and a way out of marriage. Paulie, the first-person narrator, is the author of two published books, as Paule was in 1962. She sits in the background listening to and retelling Re*e*na's life story. Re*e*na, the left-wing political activist, had, like Paule, changed her name from the standard West Indian Doreen to the more sophisticated Re*e*na, adding an italicized "e." Re*e*na's husband Dave, a photographer, most clearly represents Paule's own artistic conflicts. He works for a small "Negro" magazine doing the unimaginative work of photographing the black bourgeoisie and successful celebrities, as Paule did as a writer at *Our World.* Because of his "fatal diffidence," Dave remains at the magazine, unwilling to take the risks he needs to succeed as a photographer. Re*e*na pushes him to open his own studio, and he begins to achieve a modest success, as Paule did—some awards, a few exhibits, a little money. Still he is unsatisfied because what he really wants but cannot make himself try for is the "gaudy, commercial success that would dazzle and confound that white world downtown and force it to *see* him."[54] Re*e*na and Dave divorce because his struggles overwhelm her. Was Paule exposing her own fears about promoting herself, concealing, under the cover of a male persona, her own desire for greater commercial success and recognition? Was it more acceptable for a man to demand greater self-expression as an artist, to claim his right to the kind of autonomy women are taught to fear and conceal, to allow his ambitions to roil a marriage? At the end of the story, all three figures vanish—intangible and enigmatic—but what is left is a diagram of a complex inner life, a black woman artist's split self.[55]

If Paule was full of anxieties and self-doubt, Evan's father, as his son described him, was not. Evan remembers Kenneth as "a laid-back man, with a cigar in one hand and a Scotch and soda in the other." He never saw his father nervous or anxious and attributed that to Kenneth's doting parents, who inspired a lot of confidence in him. Proud of his biting wit, "my dad nicknamed himself 'Fat Daddy.' " He was piloting his own boat and driving sports cars when very few blacks could, but that kind of swagger had another side. Once, when he and Paule were on their way to a party in his red Austin Healy 3000, they were pulled over by a white policeman in Brooklyn. When the officer saw the car, he began deliberately taunting Kenneth, calling him by his first name: "Kenneth, you were speeding. Kenneth, I'm going to have to give you a ticket." At the party, Kenneth was still seething from the encounter and ended a conversation with a white man by punching him in the face, knocking him into the refrigerator so hard it broke. Other moments presaged trouble. Without consulting Paule, Kenneth took money they had saved together and bought his second boat, a twenty-six-foot Trojan cabin cruiser that cost $2,000. Evan said later that his father "might have assumed that that my mother would understand how important it was, despite the fact that my mother was seasick every time she stepped on a boat."[56]

Over the years when Paule was asked about the marriage, she made few comments on its happier periods or on Kenneth's admiration and respect for her work. In one tender memory she recalled that Kenneth had named her first book, which was finished and had been accepted and still had no title. "Husband at the time came to the rescue. 'Look,' he said, 'it's about a girl, right, who's black or dark brown, and it's about these old brownstone houses these West Indians are working three and four jobs, killing themselves to buy.' The title *Brown Girl, Brownstones* was his contribution." Evan remembered that his father said he was so moved that he wept after he finished reading *Brown Girl.* And when Kenneth first saw a copy of *The Chosen Place, the Timeless People,* he was genuinely proud of Paule's accomplishments: "Here's a picture of your mother on the cover with her Afro wig. Look how glamorous your mom looks."[57] Yet the compliment thins in view of Kenneth's inability to supply the emotional support for the "extraordinary" woman he said in 1950 he wanted to marry.

Paule divorced Kenneth Marshall in Juarez, Chihuahua, on August 6, 1963. As part of the settlement Kenneth took the more valuable artwork from their Central Park West apartment. Paule kept only the Caribbean etchings that adorned the hall.

CHAPTER 6

Black Is to Seek a New Way

IN 1964, PAULE was thirty-five years old and newly divorced. Evan spent the week with her at 407 Central Park West and the weekends at 470 Lenox Terrace in Harlem with Kenneth, the relaxed parent in charge of the fun times. Evan also would spend time in Brooklyn with his grandparents, but he'd often escape to Paule's sister's (Anita, called Aunt Neat) house and hang out after church to escape the strict religious Marshall household, where Christian programs played on the radio nonstop. Anita, who had married a Barbadian named Wesley Wharton, was also divorced. She and her son Leslie lived in a one-bedroom apartment in Brooklyn, a short walk from the Marshall family compound. Paule and Evan would often see Anita and Leslie, and whenever they were in Barbados and Grenada, Paule would send for Leslie to come and spend time with them. Anita was the family's great cook of Barbadian dishes—fried fishcakes and souse—and always wore an armful of bangles. She was a seamstress and eventually the foreperson of her team at a company in Manhattan, although she could afford only a small apartment on the eighteenth floor of a Brooklyn building. Leslie slept on a fold-out sofa. Anita had a modest life, and even though Paule was a very inclusive person and very close to her sister, Anita often felt out of place in her sister's intellectual and social circles. The hint of a rivalry between the sisters surfaces fictionally in *Brown Girl, Brownstones* when Selina describes her sister Ina as conventional and destined to a dead-end marriage, and also briefly when Paule describes Anita in her Harvard lectures as the "manageable" one.

Paule favored public school for Evan but was overruled when civil rights activist James Farmer, whose daughter Tammy was enrolled at the private Bank Street School in Greenwich Village, encouraged Kenneth to send Evan there. Located at 69 Bank Street in 1964, the school was designed to expose children to new academic, physical, social, and political environments, sponsoring trips to different locations around New York to "expand their concept of human geography." Kenneth was sure that race would not be as much of a factor at the progressive Bank Street as it would be at the nearby PS 46.

Paule spent part of her days squiring five-year-old Evan to the school bus, packing healthy lunch boxes for field trips, and running interference with issues of racism at the Bank Street School, which occurred despite Kenneth's assurances that they wouldn't. When Evan and his friend Gary, the other black boy at Bank Street, were chosen to play monkeys in the school play, "my mother was indignant: 'You're not playing any monkeys.' "[1] Overruling Evan, Paule called the teacher—and, whoever ended up playing the monkeys, they were not black. Even when Evan was as young as five or six, Paule talked to him about race, preparing him for the inevitable racism he would face. "Nothing really caught me off guard, so when a little girl told me we could be boyfriend and girlfriend if I weren't black, I was prepared," Evan said. "My mother was always communicating this with me—to be aware of how white America can treat you, never forget that racism is so deep in the bone that you may think of someone as your friend, and on some level they might be, but be on guard. You cannot let them define who you are."[2] Paule lost the battle on elementary school, but she won the college battle. Evan went to Hampton University, a historically black college in Virginia where there was an excellent architecture program. After graduation, when he decided to study at the Yacht Design Institute in Maine instead of one of the prestigious Ivy Leagues, Paule was fully supportive. She was determined for Evan to feel both independent and a part of black communities.

There was continuity between Paule's domestic lessons on racism and her public life. Throughout the 1960s, she was embroiled in the politics of black nationalism and, like many black intellectuals, questioned the aims of integration. After what Ossie Davis called "ten years of quiet disciplined orderly protest" that did not secure black freedom or black rights, many black activists and intellectuals, following figures like Malcolm X, continued to press for radical alternatives that connected them to international movements such as those in Cuba and Africa.[3] African American intellectuals Julian Mayfield, Maya Angelou, W.E.B. Du Bois, and Shirley Graham left the United States to live in Ghana.[4] Paule did not expatriate to Africa; she helped shape a radical black politics through public witness at home. She joined black activist groups such as the Association of Artists for Freedom (AAF); presented her first public black nationalist statement; participated in protest marches; began formulating a black feminist politics; and earned her own FBI dossier. In her 1969 novel, *The Chosen Place, the Timeless People*, she captured the revolutionary importance of the Cuban Revolution and African and Caribbean independence movements by creating the "triangular road," which would take her fictional characters on a reverse Middle Passage from North America to the Caribbean to Africa.

In June 1964, a moment of rising racial tensions in the United States, Paule was invited to be a speaker at the Town Hall Forum at West 43rd in Manhattan, called "The Black Revolution and the White Backlash—Who Speaks for the Negro . . . and Who Listens?" Paule's speech that night might have been the primer for the Black Arts Movement, though it would never be cited as such by those considered the founders of that movement. The event was sponsored by the Association of Artists for Freedom to discuss the role of the white liberal in an era of increased black militancy or, as the moderator put it, "one of the final attempts at communication between the races."[5] Paule was joined by several other black artists and AAF members, including actors Ruby Dee and Ossie Davis; poet LeRoi Jones; novelist John O. Killens; journalist Louis Lomax; and playwright Lorraine Hansberry. There were three well-known white panelists: David Susskind, television commentator; James Wechsler, editor of the *New York Post*; and Charles Silberman, journalist and editor of *Fortune* magazine and author of the 1964 book *Crisis in Black and White*.

Silberman was one of the liberal whites who understood that black disillusionment with the slow pace of civil rights progress was on a collision course with white fears of black militancy: "When the struggle for Negro rights moves into the streets, the majority of liberals are reluctant to move along with it."[6] *Crisis in Black and White* garnered accolades from whites as well as from black leaders; Ralph Abernathy, Whitney Young, and even Malcolm X endorsed it. Yet despite its support for black progress and its indictment of white racism, Silberman's book leveled some patently racist claims of its own. For Silberman, there were "unpleasant facts" that had to be acknowledged: "Negroes *do* display less ambition than whites . . . Negroes *do* have 'looser morals' . . . they *do* care less for family."[7] These problems, he believed, were firmly rooted in U. S. culture and therefore "cannot be exorcised that easily."[8] Running through Silberman's professed belief in black equality was a distrust of black militancy and a conviction that it was the "Negro problem" that had to be solved rather than white racism. If Silberman was considered the progressive white voice on racial issues, it would not be hard to predict the inevitable conflicts at the Town Hall Forum or the ones that exploded in the streets of the country.[9]

The barely suppressed anger of the black speakers at Town Hall was matched by their eloquence. Lorraine Hansberry, the celebrity of the moment after the Broadway success of *A Raisin in the Sun*, argued that John Brown had modeled a tradition of white radicalism and urged the white panelists "to stop being a liberal and become an American radical."[10] Ruby Dee reminded the audience of the failure of nonviolence when the South African police murdered unarmed people in Sharpeville in 1960. Like all of the black panelists, Ossie Davis and John Killens pointed to the deeper structural problems of racism that could not be solved by interracial liberalism. LeRoi Jones came late and spoke last, but he did not disappoint; he dismissed the forum as essentially wrongheaded for putting black artists in dialogue with people from *Fortune* magazine and the *New York Post*—the same people, Jones declared, who are "sitting on everybody, black and white, that's being sat on."[11] After Paule's contribution, it was clear that the white panelists could offer no real defense against the rising tide of black nationalism.

Paule was the only speaker who did not direct her remarks toward "the white liberal." Instead, she called for a "dynamic dialogue with those at the bottom of the heap" because one of the most insidious features of society is that "it has made for economic and social separations within the Negro community."[12] She outlined a black nationalist statement, calling for "independent black organizations" and, in the words of Frantz Fanon, "the rise through revolutionary struggle of the darker peoples of the world."[13] She began by redefining the terms *black* and *white*:

> I would like to begin by saying something about the two words which form the poles of our discussion this evening—*black* and *white*—and how, in my mind, they have become less important as a description of a man's color and more important as the description of an essential attitude of mind and heart. *White* has begun to suggest more and more to me a moral callousness and timidity, a kind of rigidity and blindness, a childish belief that if you close your eyes tightly enough the bad man will disappear. *White* is wealth without wisdom and an incredible innocence, which is matched only by arrogance. In a word, it is a force in the world today that is opposed to change even when that change is necessary for survival.[14]

Reversing the assimilationist logic of the integrationist camp, Paule offered a new definition of "black" that could be read as an invitation to white people to embrace blackness: "At the same time the word *black* has also expanded in meaning. It has come to stand for that force that recognizes change—social and political change and movement and struggle—are essential realities of human existence. It is the willingness to question and reject the old established institutions once they have proven obsolete and unjust. *Black* is to seek a new way."[15] Paule showed her prescience in defining the terms *black* and *white* as representations of their relationship to power. Whiteness, as she explained it, is both willful blindness and opposition to change. Black is not only a color but a force for change, the ability to question and to demand equality.

Paule was ready with specific action plans. In solidarity with the civil rights movement in the South, she advocated expanding the voter registration program, "which SNCC [the Student Nonviolent Coordinating Committee] is conducting so admirably in Mississippi and Alabama . . . the right to vote is critical if we are to gain our rightful place in this our country."[16] Beyond the electoral political process, she counseled "carefully planned boycotts and other means of economic protests."[17] Toward the end of her speech, Paule turned to examining systems and structures: "There is a need to start exposing the many faces of the man downtown. For some reason, there has been a failure even on the part of the most radical groups in this country to spell out in clear terms, in clear language, just how this system conspires to deprive the Negro of his basic rights."[18] And finally, as the only one on the panel who expressed a Pan-African viewpoint, Paule called for expanding the limited nationalist view of black struggle, channeling Malcolm X's revolutionary imperative that black Americans should seek help "from our brothers throughout the world who have already achieved the first step of their revolution."[19] When nationalists such as Amiri Baraka (formerly LeRoi Jones) and Larry Neal wrote their black nationalist manifestoes, they would never mention Paule Marshall nor cite her speech at Town Hall in 1964.

That night Paule kept a lookout for the "men in regulation tan trench coats, positioned at the rear of the hall, notebooks out, busy taking down the names not only of the speakers," and recognized that Malcolm X was seated a few rows from the stage. When Paule looked up from her typed statement that night and scanned the audience, his was the face she was looking for. She saw him there "smiling up at me, approvingly." Just back from his transformative hajj to Mecca, Malcolm was undoubtedly hearing the echoes of his own speeches and writings in her call for "a worldwide struggle for human rights" and the revolutionary struggle of black people against racism and colonialism.

The furor at Town Hall raised a ruckus in the *Village Voice,* beginning with an article by journalist Jack Newfield, "Mugging the White Liberal," which called the event a "fratricidal Armageddon" and the white panelists "goldfish dropped into a tank of sharks."[20] Jazz critic and historian Nat Hentoff listened to the tape of the proceedings and disagreed in a *Village Voice* article that slammed Newfield's response as "hysteria." Hentoff argued that the white panel members were "estranged from Negro reality" and "simply did not have the capacity to really listen to what was being said."[21] He found no outrageous attack on whites but rather a careful, emotional response to the events of 1964—in Alabama, Mississippi, and Chicago—that called for the powerful movement for change voiced by the black speakers at the forum. Hentoff mentioned Hansberry once, but his multiple references to Paule signaled that her analysis deserved the most attention and was the most effective one of the evening.

When Evan listened to the tape of his mother speaking at the forum for the first time in 2020, he was taken aback by the power of her voice. Later he recognized that he had known this person all his life: "My mother never held back on what she believed. Although she expressed herself in understated elegance, not pounding the podium, the fierceness of her beliefs always shone through. She never worried about how blacks would get ticked off or that white liberals would think badly if she got on their case. I've always admired her for that. She never sugar-coated her beliefs or held back on what she thought needed to be said. She had that steeliness from the time she was very young."[22]

Paule left the Town Hall event that night contemplating joining Malcolm X's new movement, the Organization for Afro-American Unity (OAAU). At some point in the early 1960s, she had met and become friends with Malcolm X, who had become part of a small cohort of the radical New York community. Paule and Malcolm visited each other's apartments, but much of their contact was by phone, when Malcolm would call Paule late at night to chat. For her part, those chats helped to ease the guilt, "the sense of futility and self-indulgence" she felt about being a writer "instead of out on the barricades."[23] Malcolm assured her that the commitment to the struggle "is fought on many fronts and literature is certainly one of those fronts."[24] He insisted that her efforts "focused on the struggles of people of color throughout the world" was important to the cause. Their telephone calls were invariably followed by a silent caller who never spoke, and she suspected that government spies were sending a warning: "Big Brother [was] listening."

Paule saw Malcolm for the last time on December 31, 1964, three months before his assassination. She invited him and his wife Betty to a New Year's Eve party at her apartment, playfully warning him, "I am doing this disgraceful thing of having a New Year's Eve party."[25] Though she worried that the Muslim Malcolm would disapprove of her serving the traditional Barbadian souse made from "the cleft feet, oversize ear lobes and snout of the pig" and black-eyed peas flavored with pork, she was relieved when his look of disapproval was followed by a forgiving smile "that seemed to crack open the whole of his stern, long-jawed face and introduce an innocence." He spent the entire evening with his back against a wall by the window where he could observe whoever came in or out of the front entrance. He was the center of attention, and for once, Paule said, the guests did not drift in and out and no one left early. She wondered later if he would have survived assassination had he eaten some pork for good luck.

Not long after the forum, Paule published a sensitive story about youth violence and urban poverty that reflected her growing identification with the Black Arts Movement and also her interest in the work her husband was doing in the 1960s with the gangs in Harlem. It centers on Hezzy, a vulnerable boy who is accidently shot by someone in his own gang. "Some Get Wasted" appeared in an anthology edited by historian and professor John Henrik

Clarke. The story is a northern urban black woman's revision of Richard Wright's 1938 story "Big Boy Leaves Home," which had depicted white violence against black boys in a pastoral southern rural scene. Like Big Boy, Hezzy's tough exterior hides his frailty. The kid who wets the bed the night before the attack also tries to blank out the memory of his mother holding him in bed as a child. The imagery of innocence and threat in Wright's story is reprised in the scene of Hezzy and his Brooklyn gang drinking wine and tussling with each other to prepare for the fight: "The wine coupled with the sun unleashed a wildness in them after a time and they fell upon each other, tussling and rolling in a heap, savagely kneeing each other and sending the grass and the bits of loosened sod flying up around them. And then just as abruptly they fell apart and lay sprawled and panting under the dome of leaves."[26] The southern white mob in Wright's story is replaced by northern black gangs targeting one another, a destructive internecine violence. Hezzy dies thinking of his rivals as "still his People."

In 1970, when editor Clarke revised the anthology, he used his introduction to define the black literary postwar period as "the Ralph Ellison–James Baldwin era," excluding Ann Petry, Gwendolyn Brooks, Alice Childress, Dorothy West, and Paule Marshall, the postwar women writers included in the anthology. This erasure is a crucial postscript to the activist period in Paule's life and a foreshadowing of the way she and other black women artists would be excluded from or marginalized in Black Arts canons.

Ahead of all the black literary manifestoes that would appear in the 1970s, Paule was defining her own black aesthetic during the 1960s, putting black women at the center in speeches and articles that might be labeled the forgotten documents of Black Arts feminism. Paule was one of the speakers at a three-day conference, "The Negro Writer's Vision of America," organized by John O. Killens at the New School for Social Research in

April 1965. Speaking on a panel called "The Negro Woman and American Literature," which turned out to be the standout panel of the conference, she was supported by writers Alice Childress and Sarah E. Wright, and singer Abbey Lincoln. The conference was dedicated to Lorraine Hansberry, who had died in January of pancreatic cancer, but her memory did not translate into an equal participation of women and men speakers. The keynote address was given by James Baldwin, the plenary speaker was Killens, and, in the five panels over three days on such topics as black drama, poetry, mass media, publishing, and the black literary tradition, only seven of the thirty-three participants were women.[27]

As chair of the panel, leftist activist and author of the memorable 1969 novel *This Child's Gonna Live,* Sarah E. Wright set the tone of feminist opposition with her opening statement: "A virtual wilderness of the human mind exists with respect to what it is to be a woman, a mother, a responsible-minded citizen, a creator of significant and humanly meaningful work, a thoughtful person."[28] Wright's introduction of Paule was special. She spoke of Paule's Guggenheim Award for *The Chosen Place, the Timeless People,* her Rosenthal Award for *Soul Clap Hands and Sing,* and a Ford Foundation grant for her current novel, and then concluded with what she considered an equally impressive award for Paule: "Winner of the affection of the artistic community for her diligence as a worker at the business of making art, for her faith in the future, her motherhood."[29]

Paule began by challenging the narrow and damaging images of black women in works by white writers, specifically Thomas Nelson Page, Gertrude Stein, Carson McCullers, Margaret Mitchell, and William Faulkner. She chastised some early black writers for replicating the stereotypes created by white writers and perpetuating some of their own, naming William Wells Brown, whose 1853 novel *Clotel* featured the "star-crossed mulatto," and Jessie Fauset, whose

1924 novel *There Is Confusion* produced what she called the black respectable elite in nineteenth- and early twentieth-century fiction. She was not shy about criticizing W.E.B. Du Bois for the "dark, sensuous, primitive, dancing half-naked" Zora in *The Quest of the Silver Fleece,* who must then be reborn as a respectable woman. Paule believed that the creation of the modern black woman character began with black writers, citing Dorothy West's novel *The Living Is Easy,* Alice Childress's *Like One of the Family,* Gwendolyn Brooks's *Maud Martha,* John Williams's *Sissie,* and the women in Baldwin's *Go Tell It on the Mountain* as examples of works that captured the complexity of women. (It is not clear why she did not mention the character of Lutie Johnson in Ann Petry's important protest novel *The Street.*) Paule devoted only six lines to her own *Brown Girl, Brownstones,* reserving her fullest attention for *Maud Martha,* a remarkable choice, considering that the literary establishment had never embraced it—but perhaps that's why Paule felt so strongly it should be recognized. Paule showcased Brooks's novel for taking the simple domestic life of a working-class black woman and representing "the Negro woman as a full and interesting fictional character."[30] Toni Cade Bambara's 1970 landmark anthology *The Black Woman* made no mention of the panel, even though the transcript was published in 1966 in the journal *Freedomways.*[31]

Another remarkable and almost forgotten document shows that black women in the Black Arts era were thinking about other black women. In her article "Problems of the Negro Woman Intellectual: Liberated from Pall of Mediocrity" in the August 1966 issue of *Ebony* magazine, pathbreaking journalist Ponchitta Pierce asked the Pulitzer Prize–winning author Gwendolyn Brooks to name the black women she considered intellectuals. Brooks dismissed such obvious qualities as "bright, brilliant, productive, effective, intelligent, creative, eminent, discerning and/or distinguished," which she claimed did not automatically entitle one to the "security" of the title *intellectual*.[32] In a jab at sexism as a deterrent to women's intellectual life, Brooks said sardonically that intelligence in a woman "is often an unpalatable, sometimes a frightening and infuriating distraction" and "the brain-owner, herself, is steadily interrupted by demands on other parts of her body."[33] Brooks defined the woman intellectual as "a tough, risk-taking, disciplined adventurer in the realm of the mind and the spirit: She must be willing to deliberate. She must be willing to risk being wrong. She must be willing to tear herself to pieces and put herself together again. An intellectual is one who observes and/or claws out facts and ideas, worries them, turns them inside out, assembles them, relates them, and—on the *highest* level—enhances or nourishes them."[34] There were, in Brooks's estimation, only five women who qualified for the "golden title": Lorraine Hansberry, Era Bell Thompson, Margaret Walker, Margaret Just Butcher—and Paule Marshall.

Seven years after John Henrik Clarke proclaimed the James Baldwin–Ralph Ellison era, black feminist Barbara Smith's landmark essay "Toward a Black Feminist Criticism" announced a new era. Smith was the necessary angry voice protesting the lack of a feminist analysis of black women's writings, especially the absence of attention to lesbian writers.[35] Smith shone a spotlight on the critical landscape that had made black women's literary work invisible: white women critics, ill-equipped to deal with racial politics, ignored black women's literary work; black male critics, hampered by their inability "to comprehend Black women's experience," dismissed black women's literature and ignored sexual politics; black lesbian writers were not even on the literary map. Smith declared that no segment of the literary world was aware of black women writers before 1977, a claim that overlooked the black women writers who had been doing that work as far back as Gwendolyn Brooks's 1945 *A Street in Bronzeville.* A brief catalogue would include Brooks's 1953 novel *Maud Martha;* Paule's 1962 story "Reena"; the 1965 "Negro Woman and American Literature" panel at the New School in New York; Paule's 1973 essay "Shaping the World of My Art"; Toni Cade's 1970 anthology *The Black Woman;* the 1974 issue of *Black World* focused on "Black Women Image Makers"; Alice Walker's 1972 essay "In Search of Our Mothers' Gardens"; Walker's 1976 review of Ann Allen Shockley's *Loving Her* in *Ms.*; and the 1970s literary anthologies, which constituted an archive of the early black feminist writings of Alexis De Veaux, Ntozake Shange, Octavia Butler, Paulette Childress, Sherley Anne Williams, Gwendolyn Brooks, Toni Morrison, Toni Cade Bambara, Paule Marshall, Alice Walker, and Gayl Jones.[36]

In May 1965, four months after the assassination of her friend and mentor Malcolm X, Paule discovered that the State Department had assembled a dossier on her, filled with "a list of each rally, protest meeting, demonstration and march I had participated in, including the first-ever joint Civil Rights–Anti-Vietnam march, which had taken place that past winter in Times Square."[37] The dossier surfaced because Paule had been invited by Langston Hughes to accompany him on a month-long U.S. State Department cultural tour of Europe. She was summoned to Washington for a briefing before being given official permission to go on the tour. Paule was panicked. Her outspoken critiques of U.S. racial politics were a hallmark of her life and her fiction, and she was well aware that the State Department tours were designed to protect the image of the United States and, for the Europeans, to shore up U.S. support for programs like the Fulbright lectureships that brought American scholars to European universities. At a time when U.S. racial violence had been televised across the world, badly damaging the nation's image abroad, she knew the tour was a means of inserting her into the "global ideological warfare"—on the side of the United States. On March 7, 1965, "Bloody Sunday" in Selma, Alabama, six hundred unarmed peaceful protestors led by twenty-five-year-old John Lewis were violently attacked, beaten, and tear-gassed by state troopers and deputies as they tried to cross the Edmund Pettus Bridge.[38] With these images fresh in her memory, Paule intended to speak her mind about the U.S. government when asked, even if her freedom to criticize might be interpreted as a sign of American freedom: "With my decidedly black skin and uncovered mouth I would be a visible and vocal proof of the country's commitment to First Amendment rights." Like Silla, she would take her mouth and make a gun.

Paule was interviewed by a State Department official who proceeded to chat amiably before pointedly placing her hand on the extensive dossier on her desk and delivering the white-gloved warning: " 'It seems you've been fairly active.' "[39] If Paule ever obtained the dossier, she never revealed what was in it, but despite it, she was approved for the tour with Hughes to Copenhagen, Paris, and London.

The tour was grueling, with lots of rain and a nonstop schedule of talks, meetings, and hastily eaten meals, which disturbed Langston more than Paule and William Melvin Kelley, the other black writer Hughes invited. They stayed at Langston's favorite, the Hotel California, down the street from the Sorbonne and across the street from a Moroccan hostel and the office of the influential magazine *Présence Africaine.* Langston complained, " 'Paule-e, these State Department folks in Paris are messing with us. Here, they got us singing for our supper morning, noon and night only to come up short every time on the supper, the main meal of the day.' "[40] In a black-and-white photograph of the tour group, Paule and Langston are standing and Kelley, author of the novel *A Different Drummer* and a short story collection *Dancer on the Shore,* is seated in the front row. They are pictured with the entire cultural entourage of more than fifty participants outside the Royaumont, a thirteenth-century former Cistercian abbey north of Paris converted into a conference center. All are dressed formally in shirt and tie or tailored suits and dresses; at least ten of them appear to be black. Within the Gothic stone halls of the Royaumont, the three held a seminar on African American literature for teachers and graduate students in American literature.[41]

After Kelley left early for a possible job in the States, Langston and Paule went on to Denmark, where they were invited, "without advice from Washington," to appear at the Students' Association and at the Danish-American Discussion Club. Their Danish hosts expected Hughes to present a favorable impression of the United States, "despite a past record of militancy in the race question."[42] The State Department's USIS (U.S. Information Service) cultural exchange files between the United States and Copenhagen indicate that as far back as 1955, U.S. racial segregation was sharply condemned by the Danish: one circular reported that "the Danish press was still obsessed with the Autherine Lucy case and the problem of desegregation."[43] On the other hand, the Danish government wanted to hold on to their valuable Fulbright program, expressly designed to "favorably [affect] Danish attitudes towards the United States."[44] The progressive-minded young Danish graduate students and scholars repeatedly asked Hughes and Marshall about the U.S. civil rights movement, which encouraged Paule to step in and, to Hughes's dismay, eagerly detail for this audience "the deep and lingering racist nature of American society" and the racial violence against young civil rights workers in the South, which, she stressed, could be traced back to U.S. government policies.

Expressing deep anxiety about offending their American supporters, the Danish contingent wrote to USIS apologetically that the two writers had left the image of the United States "bloody and tattered"—although to the "immense delight" of the students in the audience. To their great relief, the Danes reported, such a "mopping-up operation like that of Hughes and Marshall is rare."[45] The Copenhagen incident was not the end of Paule's critique. At a press conference at the American embassy, the *Pittsburgh Courier* reported that when Arthur Spingarn, eighty-seven, president of the National Association for the Advancement of Colored People since 1940, claimed that there had been civil rights progress, since " 'brutality is only found largely in a few of the Southern states,' " Paule replied acidly, " 'Whether you string up a man on a rope—as has been done in the South—or you refuse him admittance to a job as the case in New York, is to me only two different kinds of brutality.' "[46] However explosive these encounters in Copenhagen—the files from Paris and London were apparently lost—Paule's recollection in her memoir is so brief and restrained that it obscures the diplomatic firestorm she and Kelley (and to a certain extent Hughes) had ignited.

Paule never published her Town Hall speech and would not mention her rebellion on the State Department tour until her memoir in 2000. Her 1960s activism was written into her next novel, *The Chosen Place, the Timeless People.* Written between 1961 and 1968, the novel incorporated the complexities and urgencies of the issues that emerged in a decade that had spiraled from the guarded optimism of the 1963 March on Washington to black rebellions across the country. *Chosen Place* took Paule seven years to write and would cause her as much trouble after its publication as it did to write it. Paule said explicitly that she was concerned with the larger issue of exposing "the horrendous colonialism we have all undergone, and she wanted to imagine black people struggling against that domination and control."[47]

Paule's critique of U.S. imperialism is represented in a set of images that run throughout the novel: the United Corporation of America (Unicor), with offices in Philadelphia and giant commercial enterprises of steel, oil, and banking crisscrossing the world; Cane Vale sugar factory, the Anglo-American sugar refinery that vandalizes the economy of the fictional Caribbean island of Bourne and impoverishes the workers. The U.S. military is signified by the drunken colonel in full uniform who commands the island's "missile-tracking stations," and sits in the American-owned "barracoon-turned-nightclub" called Sugar's where young black women and men are made available for white tourists.[48] By setting the novel in fictional Bourne—comprised of the modernized, politically corrupt New Bristol and the poor section, Bournehills—Paule imagined a microcosm that would have a "larger application and meaning" for her black diasporan vision. This was, she said, "not just a West Indian novel," and she called on her readers not to spend time trying to identify the place but to see its larger meaning about what is happening in the third world.[49]

In this tightly woven allegory about colonialism, neocolonialism, and the problems of independence, Paule put a woman, Merle Kinbona—a name meaning "good kin"—at the center of a small cast that includes the anthropology team of Saul, a Jew who works for the Center for Applied Social Research in Philadelphia; his WASP wife Harriet, whose family was deeply involved in the slave trade; Allen, a young, white, closeted-gay anthropologist on his second field trip to Bournehills; and Vere, a young Bournehills man recently returned from picking fruit in Florida and New Jersey who dreams of fast cars and the fast life. Other main characters of the novel are the workers: the cane cutters and the factory workers employed in the Cane Vale Sugar Refining Factory of Bournehills who exist in conditions only marginally better than slavery. Described in imagery recalling the Middle Passage, the sugarcane factory resembles the "deep hold of a ship"; the loud roar of the rollers that crush the juice from the canes is an "almost human wail"; and the workers "might have been from some long sea voyage taken centuries ago."[50] Paule is making a deliberate and caustic comment on the literary and cinematic versions of the Caribbean that reduced colonized spaces to tourist playgrounds, including the one starring Harry Belafonte, *Island in the Sun.*

At the other end of the economic spectrum on the island are the educated blacks who have studied abroad and returned home to take their places as the neocolonial elite, most prominently represented by the barrister Lyle Hutson. Paule describes the pretentions of these professional men—doctors, civil servants, and lawyers—as they greet the anthropology team at Merle's party: "And they were very much of a type. They were all, to a man almost, drinking imported whiskey, scorning as a matter of status the local rum, which was excellent; all wearing dark-tones, conservative, heavy English suits in spite of the hot night. Some, like the pale, austere permanent secretary, had on matching vests, and a few wore their old school ties."[51] Lyle taunts Merle and Saul for holding onto romantic ideas about socialism: "You make me feel young again, girl, you and the doctor here, talking all that socialist nonsense they used to serve up to us at LSE [London School of Economics]."[52] Merle is disdainful of men like Lyle who have cut ties with the ordinary and the poor of their country, accumulating the status symbols of colonial power in a desperate desire to feel secure in a world that has granted them only provisional status. Lyle admits that he is in full support of the European and American investors' plans to turn the island into a hotel and gambling site for tourists, boasting that "we shall be selling the island as the newest vacation paradise in the Caribbean."[53] Lyle is the model of Fanon's depraved bourgeoisie: those who will "take on the role of manager for Western enterprise, and will in practice set up its country as the brothel of Europe."[54]

As in all of Paule's fiction, the black middle class is charged with the moral and political choice of aligning themselves with colonial or racist systems or remaining close to the people "at the bottom of the heap."[55] The daughter of a wealthy landowner and his black servant and the great-great granddaughter of a white slaveholder, Merle knows she too is part of the colonial system. She wears the jangling bracelets on her arms as a reminder of slave chains. Educated in England, Merle returns to Bournehills a broken woman, prone to depression and catatonic episodes after her African husband Ketu, on discovering her lesbian affair with a white British woman, leaves her and takes their daughter. As a beloved member of the Bournehills community, however, Merle is passionate about helping to change their condition. When Merle's father dies and leaves her an estate, she keeps only the house, selling or giving away the rest of the land in small plots to the people in the village. Paule called Merle "a Third World revolutionary spirit" who, like Ghandi, continues to exhort the poor and oppressed "to resist, to organize, to rise up against the condition of their lives."[56]

Of all the Black Arts manifestos produced during the 1960s, none has the scenic power of Paule's novel. One example in *Chosen Place* is the annual island-wide celebration when the Bournehills people reenact a commemoration of the history of the nineteenth-century slave revolt under the slave leader Cuffee Ned. In a brilliant juxtaposition of images, the steel band marchers in the parade name their band the Twenty-Sixth of July Guerrilla Band, linking them to the guerrilla movement in Cuba that gave rise to the 1959 Cuban Revolution, a revolution Paule fully supported. With toy guns and machetes, the steel band marchers sport the trademark attire of Fidel Castro and Che Guevara: "A large contingent of the Guerrilla Band made up entirely of young people from the Heights joined forces with Bournehills. Dressed in olive fatigues, heavy combat boots and helmets camouflaged with leaves, the young men sporting beards and puffing cigars and all of them, even the women, brandishing cardboard machetes and grenades, the members of the guerrilla band came charging toward Queen Street and the Bournehills troupe, singing the praises of Cuffee Ned and firing toy machine guns and pistols."[57]

Carnival's symbolic reenactment of historical memory and collective power has a real-world effect when the sugar-grinding machines at Cane Vale break down and the workers at the factory are forced to gather together to save their crops from ruin by hand. Working until exhausted, the Bournehills community gather and haul their crops the longer distance to the New Bristol mill for grinding, working as a collective for the first time. Without the machine, they nonetheless save their crop.

In a sign of her own private transformation, Merle summons the courage to return to Africa to find her daughter and confront her husband. She removes the bracelets that signal her internal discord and no longer straightens her hair, leaving it "in a small rough forest around her face."[58] She tells Saul that on her journey back, she is going to bypass the United States, "the damn place you're from . . . where they treat the black people, the very ones who made the bloody country rich in the first place, so badly . . . where, every time you look around, they're warring against some poor, half-hungry country somewhere in the world."[59] In solidarity with the Bournehills workers investing in their own labor and the Carnival marchers reenacting revolution, Merle refuses to take the usual and much shorter route to Africa through London via New York; instead she intends to follow the route of the Atlantic slave trade, "going south to Trinidad, then on to Recife in

Brazil, and from Recife, where the great arm of the hemisphere reaches out toward the massive shoulder of Africa as though yearning to be joined to it as it had surely been in the beginning." From Brazil, she plans to fly to Dakar, and from there she will take the long cross-continent journey to Kampala, Uganda.[60] This arduous journey, adding thousands of miles so as not to touch U.S. soil, represents a critique of U.S. racial and imperial violence but, more important, it suggests how *Chosen Place* envisages the scope of resistance as a transnational vision of historic renovation across the Global South.

The reviews of *Chosen Place* in the mainstream press were complimentary, if not substantive. Thomas Lask in the *New York Times* recognized Paule's convincing understanding of human weakness, but said little about the novel's larger political critique of colonialism and slavery.[61] In the *New York Times Book Review,* Robert Bone, one of the white critics in black literary studies, commented on the "brilliance" of the Carnival chapter, which plays out the mythic theme of "the timeless people" "reenacting the revolt of Cuffee Ned, which allowed the Bournehills people to find sustenance for the future from the brutal past."[62] However, Bone could not seem to place the novel in an international context or compare it to other works that addressed the problem of colonialism. While Paule named Joseph Conrad's novel *The Heart of Darkness* as a precursor text—she sent the young anthropologists in the novel on psychological journeys that reveal to themselves something of their true and "darker" selves—Bone could see the novel only in terms of race. *Chosen Place,* he wrote, is "the best novel to be written by an American black woman, one of the two important black novels of the 1960s, and one of the four or five most impressive novels ever written by a black American. Marshall belongs in the front rank of Afro-American novelists."[63]

The Chosen Place was published during the heat of the Black Arts Movement from 1965 to 1975.[64] The turmoil of the 1960s, including the failure of the civil rights movement to lead to real political and social change and the urban rebellions that spread across the country, helped to produce the political and creative responses that came to be called the Black Arts Movement (BAM), more aptly described as a series of debates over the meaning of black culture. Those changes could be seen in the formation of black journals, black studies in the universities, black bookstores, and black publishing houses. Literary historians trace the formation of the BAM to the Black Arts Repertory Theater, opened in Harlem by writer and activist Amiri Baraka (then LeRoi Jones), and to the manifesto by Larry Neal entitled "The Black Arts Movement," published in 1968.

These and other efforts of BAM writers to define a black aesthetic sparked debate from the beginning, but at its simplest, it meant a nationalist aesthetic that would celebrate black culture, speak to black communities, privilege black vernacular culture, and critique and/or reject the domination of Eurocentric culture and norms. There were always fundamental disagreements over how to define a black aesthetic and fierce critiques of the Black Arts Movement for its masculinist orientation, its affirmation of the heterosexual family as central to black community, its view of homosexuality as a form of deviance, and its absolutist claims about who or what could be considered authentically "black."[65]

Having just produced what she called a battle for the black psyche in the most revolutionary terms and images possible, Paule could not have been prepared for the harsh critiques of her novel by black militants, especially two Black Arts Movement women. Jean Carey Bond, a Black Arts militant reviewing *Chosen Place* in the influential black left-wing journal *Freedomways*, was particularly irate about what she considered the novel's violations of Black Arts protocols. Bond praised Paule's carefully crafted plot, her complex characterizations, her critique of colonialism, and her use of West Indian dialect in her characters, but judged Paule's novel as straying from the new sensibility in art created by the new black artists "from Johannesburg to L.A."[66] Bond accused Paule of being one of the "Rembrandts in black face" for writing in standard English.[67] For Bond, Paule had failed the "new standards based on a black ethos," which required a distinctive, recognizably "black," formal style.[68] Paule should have been "liberating and vandalizing" the King's English, because that is "the only meaningful thrust in the black arts today."[69] To that end, Bond demanded that all of the narration of *Chosen Place,* not only the speech of the characters, should have been in dialect, thereby producing a style commensurate with a truly black vision.[70]

Bond was not the only one to object to the novel on grounds of black nationalist aesthetics. "The black intelligentsia," as Paule called them, were highly indignant about the novel's love affair between a black woman and a Jewish man, which Paule defended as "this marvelous flowering."[71] Some black activists, including Larry Neal, said that the novel was "a betrayal": "That there was an interracial relationship in the book was just insupportable to them, so they didn't even deal with the real meaning of the novel."[72]

Black nationalist poet Nikki Giovanni reviewed *Chosen Place* in the January 1970 issue of *Negro Digest,* oscillating between admiration for an "expert" writer and exasperation over the novel's interracialism. Speaking for "we Black people in America," Giovanni distrusted what she considered Paule's incomprehensible foreignness and sexual deviance.[73] For Giovanni, the character Merle was a tainted woman—"fucked by the white woman and the white man."[74] Even more problematic for Giovanni, the novel's geographical setting in the Caribbean consigned the novel and this Brooklyn-born author to the realm of the foreign and exotic. Giovanni called the novel "a new strange wine brewed by a mysterious West Indian princess."[75] In her essay "A Race for Theory," scholar Barbara Christian, a native of the Virgin Islands, pointed out that she came from the West Indies and "was amazed by the narrowness of [Giovanni's] vision."[76] Marking Paule as a betrayer, a "mysterious West Indian princess," and a "Rembrandt in blackface," Neal, Giovanni, and Bond assumed that Paule's extension of blackness beyond national boundaries and her violation of Black Arts protocols confirmed her outsiderness to the black literary tradition.

The negative portrayals of homosexuality in *Chosen Place,* especially the depiction of Merle's lesbian affair with an English woman, suggest that Paule was not immune to Black Arts orthodoxy. As Merle explains this affair to Saul, she passes herself off as an innocent victim, a "brainwashed West Indian" who fell in with the "ringleader of a wild crowd," a much older, upper-class English woman, who used her money to buy, and, presumably debase, "foolish people like me."[77] In Paule's depiction of sex tourism in Sugar's nightclub, the narrative focus is mainly on the white gay male tourists preying on the young Bournehills men, with little note of heterosexual male predators.

It is important, however, to measure these clearly homophobic scenes against a subtle shift that occurs near the end of the novel when Merle's beloved friend Allen tries to reveal his homosexuality to her, and she proposes that he only needs to find a "nice girl, get married and have some chil—."[78] Noting Allen's scathing look, Merle cuts herself off before finishing the sentence. Allen's reproach is a judgment on the cultural domination of heteronormativity that muscles all others to the fringes of or outside acceptability: "It's impossible for people like you who've always been out there *in the center* to understand my kind."[79] That Paule highlights Allen's critique of Merle's homophobia prefigures her own changing views of sexuality. Even as late as 1983, Paule struggled with her guilty feelings about being attracted to women and the need to conceal these relationships. It would take her three more novels to gradually chip away at negative representations of homosexuality in her work.[80]

The *Chosen Place, the Timeless People* eluded its Black Arts critics because Paule was equally elusive. As literary historian James Hall put it, she was uncategorizable, "at once always possibly, but never only, protofeminist, post- or anticolonialist, anticapitalist, nationalist, internationalist, Pan-Africanist, and American."[81] Cultural historian Kimberly Benston wonderfully defended *Chosen Place* as "too complex in its intersections and complications to be easily assimilated into existing frameworks, and so can be paradoxically underappreciated precisely in its nonconformity and elusivity."[82] Paule's forward-looking work would begin to find its audience in the feminist 1970s and in the post–black nationalist aesthetics of the twenty-first century, defined by cultural critic Margo Crawford as "Black Post-Blackness," and by Black Arts historian GerShun Avilez as "aesthetic radicalism," both of whom offered a more expansive understanding of Black Arts culture.[83]

Contrary to the claim that there was no definitive "Black Arts Novel," *The Chosen Place, the Timeless People* was the most impressive Black Arts novel of the 1970s.[84] Paule used her unique political vision to explore, experiment with, and transform the blackness of the Black Arts Movement—to push it into a more transnational, queerer, woman-centered place. James Baldwin understood Paule's vision and wrote to her from Istanbul on December 1, 1969, after reading the galleys of *Chosen Place:*

> You have taken the most difficult of situations with one strong hand and told us something about it which we knew, but never

> knew like this: that island in the sun. I realize that I am being incoherent; presently, I will try to pull myself together, and say learned professional things. But it's been a very long time since any book, even books I admire, have stirred me so, and so surprised me, and made me so rejoice: girl, you have really started something. What can I say? I'm sorry, I meant to sound intelligent, and I've fucked it all up. Merle—especially—is a great creation, and she has no precedent. But enough. I just wanted you to know that you've made all of it worthwhile again, thank you, Paule, really, and I do thank God.[85]

Another writer who understood Paule's special gift was the poet June Jordan, who wrote to Paule from the artist colony Yaddo to thank her for sending her *Chosen Place*, this "monumental and singular and unforgettable and beautiful, huge work—now we have this vision."[86]

CHAPTER 7

In-Betweenness

After the eight years of struggling to finish *Chosen Place*, Paule confided to Langston Hughes in the spring of 1967 that she was "somewhat at a low because of certain setbacks of an amorous nature," adding, "A good man is hard to find, somebody said, and it's no lie." The summer of '67 brought happier prospects. Taking the advice of Virginia Woolf, she decided "to travel and idle" for a while, and she chose Haiti as the last in the chain of Caribbean islands that she hadn't visited. Leaving Evan in the States with his father, she took a small tour bus with a group of French Canadians up to Petionville, the hilltop aerie of the Haitian rich called Cap-Haïtien (aka Le Cap, Cap, Okap, and Little Paris), and rented a room in a guesthouse set on a small inlet. On her first evening there, she and her companion/tour guide Danielle were joined by the only other boarder, Nourry Menard, a businessman and lay historian deeply steeped in the history and politics of Haiti. Nourry was impressed that Paule was a writer: " 'C'est vrai!? Un ecrivain! Un romancier!' " Paule was equally smitten with Nourry. He began visiting her in Port-au-Prince and, after she returned to the States, he traveled to New York to see her. "My French," she said, "steadily improved." Evan, about eight or nine at the time, liked him immediately. "He was

Paule's husband Nourry Menard at their home in Cap-Haïtien, Haiti, in the 1970s.

a tall, dark-brown, handsome man, very nice, quite regal, very interesting. And I was kind of happy about it because my father had long since remarried. I never had any issues about it."[1]

Paule admired Nourry on many levels: his knowledge of history, his political shrewdness, and his textbook-perfect French. She was also taken with him physically: "his prominent forehead that belonged on a scholar and made him appear taller than his average height; the formality of his tone and gestures. As for his eyes, which were oddly hazel against his blackness, and his careful smile, they were both too complex to read. Eyes, I discovered, that were the molten dark-honey brown of the tupelo honey you poured for yourself in the health food store. Sweetness I could taste on my tongue whenever he turned toward a light." Danielle pronounced him "*Un homme de bien,* a man of worth, a gentleman." With some hesitancy, Paule decided to take her chances: "Knowing the dangers, Yes, I married him."

In 1970, Paule, forty-one, and Nourry, forty-two, both divorced, were married in Elton County, Cecil, Maryland, and began a ten-year transcontinental marriage, planning to divide their time equally between Haiti and New York. Nourry owned an ice-making company in Port-au-Prince that did quite well, since many people without refrigerators went to the ice factory. In the same ice-making complex, Nourry started making a sugary cola called Cola-Nectar. Early on in their relationship, Paule, Nourry, and Evan visited a factory in Buffalo, New York, that made a bottling machine that would upgrade his old ones. With the help of a $5,000 loan from Paule, the machine was installed in Nourry's factory within a few months.

Haiti was a fascinating and beautiful island, and Paule steeped herself in its history and culture, which impressed Nourry. The island's poverty did not go unnoticed, but for Paule "the breathtaking mountains and green, bountiful valleys," "the Pearl of the Antilles," as Napoleon had called it, were extraordinary. She was also aware of the corrupt politics of the dictator François "Papa Doc" Duvalier, who was followed by his son "Baby Doc," and the Tonton Macoute secret police, a special operations unit within the Haitian paramilitary force known for brutality, still active, targeting opponents of the regime. As Paule would soon learn firsthand, Haiti was a quasi-police state where the Tonton Macoute could come at any time to anyone's house. During the 1960s, Nourry had been head of the Haitian Consulate in Dominica, and like many affluent Haitians and academics, he saw the harm being done to the country. While Nourry was not particularly wealthy and no longer had any political influence, he was still in the crosshairs of the Duvalier government. His oldest sister's husband had been taken by the Tonton Macoute, and the family never saw him again. Once when Duvalier came to Cap-Haïtien and there weren't enough vehicles for the entourage, the police commandeered wealthy Haitians' cars, and soon that would include Nourry's Jeep, which they returned, damaged, a few days later.[2]

Nourry and Paule rented a standard American-designed suburban tract house in Bel-Air, built by a U.S. research team, just above the city of Cap-Haïtien in the lower foothills of the mountains. Built for middle-class Haitians, theirs was the second to last house up the mountain at the end of the road, surrounded by orchards and gardens with a huge mango tree in the front. In one photo, Paule is sitting on the veranda, holding a vase of flowers, overlooking the hills. In another, she is standing in front of the Citadel, a nineteenth-century military fort designed and built by the tyrannical Henri Christophe to stop the French from invading the country they once colonized.

To get to the house in Cap-Haïtien, Paule and Evan would fly into Port-au-Prince and stay in a small hotel. Nourry would pick up his daughters, who lived nearby with their mother, and then they would all drive or fly to Cap-Haïtien. The eight-hour drive would take them through winding mountainous roads passing through local villages. Sometimes the entire family flew to Cap-Haïtien in an old, battered propeller plane, most likely bought from the U.S. Army—taking their lives in their hands, according to Paule. On the landing strip, the airfield crew would have to run out to get the protective barrels away from the runway, set there because Papa Doc was fearful of a coup d'état.

Driving from Nourry's factory to the house, which was almost at the crest of the mountain, Evan noted the villages, very poor, and people living in small huts with wallpaper made of newspaper, through which you could see small fires burning at night. To

Paule, circa 1973, at home on the patio in Cap-Haïtien, wearing a white headwrap that matches a white and lavender caftan.

Paule, who admired the majesty of the locals and their cultural pride, these were the timeless people she had written about in *Chosen Place*. Paule read the expression in their eyes as their refusal to engage the present with its defeats, "but rather focusing their gaze backward on past events" until the promise of the past could be fulfilled, just as the workers did in *The Chosen Place, the Timeless People*. It was a look "that might well have been more about my longing than anything else."

Paule became a beloved stepmother to Nourry's two daughters, Rosemonde and Nancy, and Tante Paule to her new niece Chantal. Twelve-year-old Evan, who now had two stepsisters close to his age, remembers their time in Haiti as blissful: "For me and the girls it was a great location for hiking. While Nourry was working, my mom would organize day trips to local hotels where we would go for a swim and spend the day. I remember it was very pleasant being there."[3] Nourry escorted Paule and Evan to nice places for dinner and took them to see all the beautiful sights, such as the upscale suburb of Petionville, where the writer Rosa Guy lived for a few years. When he had to work he would hire a driver to take Paule and the children around.

Rosemonde remembers Paule as the perfect stepmother: "All of my memories of her influence are positive. She was very, very good to us. I never had the experience of the evil stepmother syndrome."[4] The twelve-year-old Rosemonde knew very little English, but Paule devoted two or three hours a day to teaching her and would not speak French until her stepdaughter became proficient in English. Later Nourry sent her to Rosarian Academy, a Catholic boarding school in West Palm Beach, Florida, where one of the nuns assessed her strengths in English and told her, "You were very privileged to have such a teacher."[5]

Nourry was proud of Paule's accomplishments, her intellect and her elegance, and both of them seemed sure that their transatlantic marriage could work. Nourry, an independent businessman, would spend half the year in New York, and Paule would be in Haiti the second half, which would allow Evan to be in the U.S. during school vacations. Nourry liked New York and was always willing to come to spend time with Paule. According to their niece Chantal, when Paule discovered she was pregnant, both she and Nourry were excited about the baby, and both were saddened by the loss when she miscarried.[6] Nourry developed a close relationship with his stepson, with whom he was affectionate and playful. Paule became more fluent in French, so all their conversations were in that language. Evan remembers that they never allowed any fighting between them in front of the children.

During her half years in Haiti, Paule wanted to drink in the culture of what was becoming her second home. Once she told Nourry she wanted to experience an authentic voodoo ceremony. She had discovered that Madame Noelsine Baptiste, the woman who did their laundry, was a devotee of a Vodoun sanctuary, a *hounfor*, and Paule asked to accompany her to one of their rituals so that she could compare Vodoun with the Big Drum/Nation dance ceremony she had witnessed in Carriacou. For Paule, this was a Haitian ritual derived from the African religious tradition, and she was eager to experience something authentic, beyond the touristy version the hotels provided. When Nourry objected to her going, Paule teased him that "he was as bourgeois, conservative, and hopelessly Catholic as his hero Toussaint, a devout Catholic raised in the church, [who] had also disapproved of Vodoun." Softening somewhat, Nourry offered his large flashlight, and Paule followed Madame Baptiste and her own mind down the mountain through a tunnel of trees, bushes, and rocks, with Madame Baptiste carrying upside down on her head a three-legged stool for Paule. The thatched-roof shelter on the bare ground, open on all sides, was the "poorest sanctuary" Paule had ever seen, but Madame Baptiste transformed the place with the cornmeal designs she drew on the floor. Soon a mass of people, all dressed completely in white, began to dance and sing, and "even the most starved-out face among them" seemed "lit from within by the fervor of their belief." As Paule observed a young

Paule in front of the Citadel, the nineteenth-century fort at Cap-Haïtien, circa 1973.

man become possessed by a *loa,* or spirit, she remembered Zora Neale Hurston's portrayal of Vodoun in *Tell My Horse.* In tribute to Zora, Paule took to her feet and joined the dancers. After the ceremony she walked back down the path, carrying the three-legged stool, humbly following Madame Baptiste, "the artist whose day job was washing our clothes."

A year into Paule's marriage to Nourry, while she was just beginning her academic stint at Yale, Kenneth Marshall died at age forty-six in an accident while cruising on a friend's boat. At around 10 p.m., as the boat came into the dock, Kenneth went up on the foredeck to jump off to tie the line but slipped, hit his head, and fell into the water. His wife Jonni, whom he'd married in 1964, dived in after him when she heard the splash, but he was unconscious and sank before she could retrieve him.

The death of his father may have strengthened Evan's attachment to Nourry, and he enjoyed playful teasing and horseplay with his stepfather. But at twelve he was also in the early stages of teenage conflict with his mother, and once, when Paule was probing him about his moods, relentlessly trying to find out what was bothering him, Evan finally blamed it on Nourry's teasing, "just to get her off my back. I said he's touching me too much, but I didn't really mean it. I just thought she would leave me alone." Later Evan couldn't actually remember much about the horseplay. "I was never open with her," he recalled of his teenage relationship with his mother. He disliked her constant questioning, though he came to accept that probing was in her nature. "She was a writer. She was so aware and wanting to understand." Paule's relentless questions and worries were a burden Evan learned to live with. He wanted some privacy and he saw a paradox in Paule's efforts to get him to open up with her, considering, he said, that "one of the themes in her life is how much she concealed about herself."[7]

Throughout the entire decade of the 1970s, the years of her marriage to Nourry and her half life in Haiti, we can document Paule's professional life, but the story of her marriage to Nourry is almost a blank page. In the index to *Conversations with Paule Marshall*, an extensive collection of fifteen interviews with Paule published in 2010, there is no entry for her first husband Kenneth Marshall, or Nourry Menard, or Haiti. In these interviews Paule spoke briefly about her first marriage to Kenneth (always referred to as her "first husband") and the obstacles that marriage posed to her writing, but there is no mention of Nourry or her second marriage. Her 2009 memoir *Triangular Road* makes no comment about either husband. Paule must have announced her second marriage publicly because Toni Morrison sent a thank-you letter on May 12, 1972, to "Paule Marshall Menard" in Cap-Haïtien wishing Paule "a splendid and fruitful stay in Haiti."[8] We know that Paule intended to end her silence about her marriage to Nourry. On the desktop of her computer she left in storage, she included a forty-one-page account of the end of her marriage, and even though it is deliberately elusive, it is an intimate and self-reflective account.

Although Nourry had hopes that Paule would come to live full-time in Haiti, the chances of that faded as her career began to take off. She still felt the pull of the security and comfort of her anchor at 407 Central Park West as well as the excitement of Manhattan. And there was yet another development in her life, one that perhaps compensated for the shunning of *Chosen Place* by the hard-liners in the Black Arts Movement. Black studies as an interdisciplinary academic field was then in its formative period, just beginning to expand. Scholars in the arts, humanities, and social sciences were forming a collaborative black intellectual community that was forging new paths in African American and pan-African research. In 1970, the same year she married Nourry,

Paule was offered her first university appointment, as visiting lecturer in the inaugural African American Studies Department at Yale, which was at the forefront of institutionalizing black studies as a field following a wave of black student activism. It was a significant recognition of her work, which had been ignored or undervalued elsewhere. Her Yale salary was $20,000, equivalent to $150,000 in today's market. Ironically, while her writing had finally elevated her status, teaching would leave her little time to write.

Paule's colleagues included historian John W. Blassingame; art historian Sylvia Boone, who taught a course called The Black Woman—Yesterday and Today; Mervyn Alleyne, a specialist in Caribbean Creole languages who taught Black Literature of French Expression; and the esteemed Arna Bontemps, who taught the Harlem Renaissance course, a period he lived through and had helped to create. As eminent as this cohort of black scholars was, they also had to put up with being patronized. A future star in African American studies, Houston Baker, then a student at Yale, observed firsthand the attitude of some white Yale professors about the university's new black directions. Baker overheard two professors boasting that, in contrast to the salary offered newly hired white professors, they were able to get Bontemps "cheap."[9]

Paule was assigned to teach Themes in African American Letters and a prose writers' workshop and immediately encountered the problem that would always plague her as a teacher: she did not like being in front of a classroom, especially a large one. Instead of her preference for a creative writing course in a small intimate setting, she had been assigned a large survey course that was so comprehensive she snidely called it "The Black Experience From the Year One," or "the monster." Paule was expected to handle the literature section of "the monster": "It did no good for me to point out that this wasn't in my contract or that I wasn't a scholar or an academic but a storyteller." She found herself in a huge lecture hall facing more than a hundred "fiercely bright, fiercely articulate little Yalies." Paule was aware of the constant critique that black students "should be addressing themselves to technical knowledge" and was therefore heartened by the number of black biology majors who had never heard of Frederick Douglass or W.E.B. Du Bois filling up her classroom to take a liberal arts course on black biography.[10]

As she settled into academic life at Yale, Paule became active on campus, speaking along with writer and activist Julius Lester in April at the Leadership Banquet and Symposium, a cultural festival that also featured a performance by LeRoi Jones's Drama Troupe. She drew on her contacts with the black artistic community in New York, and on one occasion invited her friend the avant-garde saxophonist Archie Shepp, a professor of black music at the University of Massachusetts, Amherst, to lecture in her class. But when the Yale conference "The Black Women" was held in December 1970, organized by African studies professor Sylvia Wynter, the invited speakers were Maya Angelou, Gwendolyn Brooks, and historian John Henrik Clarke. Paule was not there. She and Nourry had been married for only five months, and she was on her way to Haiti for the winter break.

Paule decided to begin the large survey course with Olaudah Equiano's 1789 slave autobiography, *The Interesting Narrative of Olaudah Equiano,* which details his life from Africa to slavery and eventual freedom in America. Paule was drawn to Equiano because of his love of the sea and his presentation of self, not as a victim or a racialized other but as an African and a warrior, "Olaudah of the Loud Voice." Her deep appreciation for Equiano's art would have been infectious for any student of literature, and apparently many were captivated. There was another positive side of teaching for Paule. Equiano's *Narrative* became the inspiration for her next novel, *Praisesong for the Widow,* which was "critical to my thinking and development as a novelist." Paule sends Avey, the central character in *Praisesong,* on a voyage from America to the West Indies in what she viewed as a symbolic reversal of Equiano's forced voyage from West Africa.

Before Paule could begin work on *Praisesong,* she had a score to settle. Her novel *The Chosen Place, the Timeless People,* which should have fit comfortably in a Black Arts canon, was instead disparaged—or misread or not read at all. Strategically, in 1973 she placed her first major essay, "Shaping the World of My Art," in the literary journal *New Letters,* which in 1971, under its new editor David Ray, had opened its pages to a range of black writers, beginning with an entire issue on the new and unpublished work of Richard Wright. The journal published a diverse set of black writers, such as Amiri Baraka, Owen Dodson, Cyrus Colter, Michael Harper, Margaret Walker Alexander, and Paule Marshall. Several issues posted full-page advertisements for the publications of the Detroit-based Broadside Press and included photos of black nationalists Baraka, Haki Madhubuti, and Sonia Sanchez.[11] Cosmopolitan, interracial, diasporic, and progressive, *New Letters* was the ideal forum for skewering the Black Arts contingent that had belittled *The Chosen Place, the Timeless People.*

Paule smoothed the sharp edges of her critique in *New Letters* by connecting her own storytelling artistry with that of her mother and her friends, the poets in the kitchen. Surely their familiarity with obeah, juju, Vodoun, white racism, the Middle Passage, colonial oppression, and Marcus Garvey, an artistry she had inherited from them, answered Black Arts critic Larry Neal's call for an aesthetic based on "Race Memory." Paule allowed that Baraka and Neal were right about black music having direct and dynamic links to black communities, but these women artists, she asserted, were carrying on communal traditions "as ancient as Africa." Rejecting Neal's contention that the novel was an irrelevant form for black people, Paule defended the traditional novel as an extension of the African-based storytelling of these women poets in the kitchen, a tradition that could not be simply dismissed as a "white" Western product, as Neal had claimed. Like the blues, Paule countered, literary work "transformed our suffering into art." She cited Esther Jackson, the radical editor of *Freedomways,* who agreed with her that "music, dance, painting and the like can transmit something of the emotional tone of our lives both past and present," but "they cannot really communicate that content which must be interpreted in words."[12] Paule was articulating a defense of her own independent black, feminist, diasporan aesthetic as a basis for a Black Arts novel—most notably the one she had just published.

One way to sort out the mystery of Paule's liminal status is to understand her "in-betweenness" as a sign of what Bill Mullen calls her uniquely independent intellect, a writer who could work "comfortably across such contested terrain" as black feminism, Black Arts nationalism, civil rights, transnationality, and left-wing radicalism.[13] In addition to the essay in *New Letters,* she published essays in the 1970s designed to work that expanded terrain. Her tribute to Fannie Lou Hamer in *Vogue,* "Fannie Lou Hamer: Hunger Has No Color Line," extended the profile of the fifty-two-year-old southern civil rights activist beyond civil rights activism. She presented Hamer as a "political strategist" and "social engineer" for initiating such antipoverty programs as the Freedom Farm Cooperative and Head Start. Paule noted that Hamer's travel to Africa had allowed her to think beyond national borders, and she quoted Hamer: "We've got to hook up with all the other non-white peoples of the world. We need them if we're going to make it." In another mainstream women's magazine, *Mademoiselle*, Paule reviewed Ralph Ellison's collection of essays *Shadow and Act* in 1974, again risking the disapproval of the Black Arts folks, whose antipathy to Ellison was mutual. Paule had been snubbed by Ellison, but she thought he deserved credit for his essays celebrating the resilience of black culture, as she had done in her work.

Paule suffered a kind of "critical banishment" for her nonconformity. Unwilling to line up behind any one camp, Paule's black nationalism was tempered by her commitments to black feminism and to a diasporan focus; as a leftist and anti-capitalist, she supported the civil rights movement but questioned its liberalism; her feminism was qualified by her insistence on unity between black men and women. She was rarely cited as a major figure until the feminist movement of the 1970s and 1980s—and even then, she appeared only once in *Essence*, the popular black woman's magazine. It almost goes without saying that Paule's literary exclusion was the result of the "vast literary whiteness" of the publishing industry, but the important literary debates over black culture and literature during the 1960s and 1970s were carried on in black spaces where black women writers were subject to hostility, sexism, and indifference.[14] Strikingly, except for Nikki Giovanni's dismissive review of *Chosen Place*, Paule's name is not mentioned in the entire ten-year run of the highly influential *Black World*, "the central archive" of the Black Arts Movement in the 1970s.[15] When black male critics did notice black women writers, it was often to question the legitimacy of their standing in black traditions.[16] In his 1986 *New York Times* article on black women writers, literary critic Mel Watkins pronounced their banishment self-inflicted: "Those black women writers who have chosen black men as a target have set themselves outside a tradition that is nearly as old as black American literature itself."[17]

Paule most certainly did not feel banished or marginal in the literary salons she cultivated on the Upper West Side of Manhattan. In the period between the publication of "Shaping the World of My Art" in 1973 and the appearance, ten years later, of *Praisesong for the Widow,* Paule was traveling at warp speed. She confined her travel back and forth to Haiti to holidays and the summer because she had to be in New York for Evan's school year. That schedule allowed her to be active in the New York literary and social scene and, after her time at Yale, to maintain an adjunct teaching position at Columbia University. Howard University professor Eleanor Traylor remembers meeting Paule at Mikell's, a rhythm-and-blues and jazz club at 97th and Columbus Avenue on the Upper West Side, another site for literary and cultural meetings that drew this crowd, especially after Baldwin's brother David became the bartender. While Evan was attending the Riverdale Country School in the Bronx and living at home, he remembers his mother participating wholeheartedly in political events, even though she jealously guarded her private time for writing.[18] She held a meet-and-greet at the apartment to fundraise for the 1968 presidential campaign of fellow West Indian Brooklynite Shirley Chisholm. When Evan transferred in 1978 to Wilbraham and Monson Academy, a boarding school in Massachusetts, both mother and son were delighted with their newfound independence.

In her memoir *My Soul Looks Back,* culinary historian and author Jessica B. Harris designated the black cultural world of New York in the 1970s as a *belle époque,* similar to Paris in the 1920s or the existentialist 1950s, or London in the 1960s.[19] Harris placed James Baldwin at the center of a circle that included writers Maya Angelou, Trinidadian American Rosa Guy, Louise Meriwether, culinary writer Vertamae Grosvenor—and Paule Marshall. Harris named Paule's apartment at 407 Central Park West party central: "If it was chez Paule, it was party time."[20] The apartment, with its long entrance hall, the kitchen and the living room at one end, bedrooms at the other, its high ceilings and windows overlooking Central Park, was often filled with Paule's guests and friends. The nucleus of the group was Maya, Rosa, Louise, and Paule, all born in the 1920s and all dedicated to writing. But Paule's salon included many other artists and intellectuals: singer Abbey Lincoln and her husband drummer Max Roach; bassist Ron Carter; saxophonist Archie Shepp; radical anthropologist Connie Sutton and her husband Sam; visual artist Ernie Crichlow; actors Ossie Davis and Ruby Dee—any of them might appear at a party chez Paule. The only reference to Nourry during this period in Paule's active social and professional life is as a member of that party scene at her house; Paule reported to Evan she had caught Rosa at one party making a pass at her husband. Harris proclaimed Maya and "Jimmy" Baldwin as the force behind this New York black literary and cultural moment. Unable to penetrate Paule's reserve, Harris decided that Paule was simply unknowable, "a cipher."[21] However, on the Upper West Side of New York City in the 1970s, from her desk, her kitchen, and her living room at 407, Paule Marshall was a force that energized black literary culture.

Paule was also a generous mentor and friend. She had a special relationship with Nourry's niece Chantal, who recalls, "She was always there for me. She was a mentor. When I wanted to pursue higher education, she advised me. She was the first visitor when I had my first child and brought me the Dr. Spock book and told me this was to be my Bible of childrearing."[22] When Chantal moved to New York, she got to see what Paule's life was like in the city. "She had so many friends and used to have nice social gatherings at her place. Sometimes she would invite me to accompany her to an event. Whenever she was in town, we would go out to either a restaurant or to a Broadway show. My husband and I attended most of her book signings."[23] Paule invited Chantal to an award ceremony hosted by Governor Mario Cuomo at the Metropolitan Museum, where both Paule and Leontyne Price received the New York State Governor's Award, and where she was captured in a photo with the former U.S. secretary of state Condoleezza Rice. At the after-party at the home of one of Paule's friends, it became clear to Chantal that Paule would have never traded her life in New York for Haiti; Paule asked Chantal once in confidence, referring to this whirlwind of New York cultural activities, "Can you imagine me giving up all these things?"[24]

In February 1977, a black women's cultural group organized by June Jordan and Alice Walker met at Jordan's apartment on 8th Avenue in Brooklyn to eat gumbo, drink champagne, and talk about their work as writers, activists, and feminists and to support and advocate for black women writers and artists. The group, which eventually included Vertamae Grosvenor, Alice Walker, Lori Sharpe, Toni Morrison, June Jordan, Dr. Sananda Ananda-Maynard, Ntozake Shange, Audreen Ballard, and Paule Marshall, called themselves the Sisterhood.[25] When cultural scholar Courtney Thorsson did the archival work to uncover the story of the Sisterhood, she concluded that this was the group that defined the 1980s as the decade of greatest visibility for black women writers in the United States. Paule became a stalwart member, an involvement that may have begun with an invitation from Toni Morrison, then an editor at Random House, to read Toni Cade Bambara's short story collection *Gorilla, My Love* and presumably to help promote it. Although Paule never refers to the Sisterhood in her notes or interviews, she was an active member. The women traveled throughout New York to meet in one another's homes in the East Village, the West End, Harlem, 8th Avenue and Park Slope in Brooklyn, the East 60s in Manhattan, the Wellesley Club in the Biltmore Hotel, and at least once at Paule's apartment at 407 Central Park West.

Paule put this new interest in black women in political perspective: "The climate improved sharply due to Black cultural revolution and militancy," she wrote in her impressionistic unpublished notes. "Publishers began to take us seriously. Bookstores and libraries had whole sections devoted to . . . More black editors—Marie Brown at Doubleday who brought out *Blk. Eyed Susans, The Black Woman.* Must never forget that it was the students facing the police dogs in the south, beatings, jailings that made the publishing industry of America respond. Made possible 2nd Renaissance of the 60s and 70s." The iconic photograph of the Sisterhood shows eight of the women gathered around a picture of Bessie Smith.[26] Literary scholar Hortense Spillers wrote what could be the caption of that photograph: "The community of black women writing in the United States can now be regarded as a vivid new fact of national life."[27]

Paule wasn't present for that historic photograph of the Sisterhood because at the time it was taken in New York she was on the global stage. The metaphorical return to the motherland that Paule proposed in "Shaping the World of My Art" became an actual physical return in January 1977 when she traveled to Nigeria as part of the official U.S. delegation to the Second World Black and African Festival of Arts and Culture in Lagos, a month-long festival of the arts, unofficially called FESTAC '77. Paule, Evan, and her friend Ernie Crichlow, the visual artist and fellow Brooklynite, flew into Lagos on the jam-packed State Department–chartered plane with a contingent that included Louise Meriwether, Rosa Guy, Randy Weston, Joan Sandler, head of the U.S. delegation, and Sandler's daughter Kathe.

FESTAC, attended by half a million spectators, was "a mecca for more than seventeen thousand black artists, who came from the Caribbean, Australia, South America, Canada, Europe, and the United States, as well as throughout Africa."[28] As Nigeria was "the richest black-ruled nation on the continent," mainly as the result of the oil boom, the government went all out for the festival, building a multimillion-dollar National Theatre, reconstructing the sixty-thousand-seat National Stadium, and creating a fifteen-thousand-unit housing complex outside Lagos called FESTAC Village.[29] Although new expressways were meant to relieve the legendary traffic jams in Lagos, the horrendous traffic into the city from the festival village was a major obstacle for the group; they were also unprepared for the housing problems—water not running regularly, inadequate food, and some unfinished units in the village. The public was outraged with the government for the extravagance of the festival, the money spent on visitors instead of local people, the shoddy work on the new buildings, and the investments in bribes. Paule and Evan left the village and moved to the Palace Hotel. According to Paule, the local folks complained bitterly about the millions of *naira* (the Nigerian dollar) being spent to surpass the black arts festival that had been held in Dakar, Senegal, a decade earlier.

For Paule, it was "the second major plum of an all-expense-paid overseas cultural conference" after her trip with Langston Hughes to Europe. Several people took their children, and the political and emotional significance was so strong that many, in tears, kissed the ground when they landed on African soil.[30] Evan, then seventeen, remembers the excitement of seeing uniformed black soldiers patrolling the streets and black faces on the money. He met famous black artists such as American jazz pianist Randy Weston and Nigerian band leader and composer Fela Kuti, and he made a number of trips to the bathroom where the brothers were smoking so he could get a hit. One night their host took them to the Afrika Shrine, a club in Lagos, to hear some music. There was great excitement when word got around that Fela, who was not expected to perform, had showed up.[31]

Ebony covered the opening parade, which was modeled on the Olympics' opening ceremonies, each national delegation running a lap around the track in celebratory welcome. Paule was taken with the African women performers at the opening ceremony, describing in detail the Egyptian delegation, the "Sahara-brown" beauties, she called them, who were riding in the opening parade seated high on the backs of white Arabian show horses. They were "as sumptuously costumed as their mounts in great billowing Scheherazade trousers, tunics, and sheer flowing scarves. Their arms and ears bejeweled. The glint of jewels as well in their elaborately dressed hair. Kohl rimmed their eyes, adding to their drama. Each rider was a Cleopatra look-alike holding aloft an outsized red, white and black Egyptian flag."[32]

In contrast to such elaborately outfitted and choreographed African delegations, the U.S. contingent, to Paule's embarrassment, came totally unprepared. With no special clothing or costumes, no souvenir flags bearing the image of President Gerald Ford, and no organized performances, they rolled onto the stadium grounds and simply improvised. One group started with Black Power salutes, while another sang versions of a "jazzed-up, belligerent-sounding version of the old 'Amen' gospel hymn," competing with yet another U.S. group trying to drown them out with whatever verses they could remember of the Negro National Anthem. Paule described the U.S. spectacle: "Unprepared. Unrehearsed, Improvised. Disorganized."[33]

Despite their impromptu performance, when the ragtag U.S. contingent appeared, the entire African audience in the stadium rose "in a single body to roar its welcome in nonstop applause"—

an outsized welcome, Paule speculated, to acknowledge the Americans as representatives of the wealthiest and most powerful nation in the world.[34] But Paule also interpreted this extravagant display of pride and joy as masking their "guilt and sorrow" for the part that Africans had played in having once reduced these *returning children* "to mere articles of trade, commodities, merchandise, goods, cargo, *chattel cargo!* to be bought and sold and whipped and worked for free!"[35] As her character Silla Boyce says in *Brown Girl, Brownstones*, "Look how those whelps in Africa sold us for next skin to nothing."[36] When Paule spotted a tearful ancient-looking African woman sitting next to her, she silently forgave her, imagining that the woman might be weeping over her own collusion in the buying and selling. Many years before Saidiya Hartman and many other scholars turned to these questions, Paule was examining and questioning those myths of kinship.[37]

Over the next four weeks, Paule's African colleagues at FESTAC followed the Americans, whom they recognized as resembling their own relatives, seemingly "desperate to make amends for the past," Paule thought. They argued over whether Paule was Ashanti or Bemba, checking out cheekbones, foreheads, eyes, heads, lips, nostrils, and jawlines, and she was claimed and reclaimed, embraced and singled out, until resistance was futile: "To be claimed by so many! To possess a face that was generic apparently to the entire continent below the Sahara!"[38] Paule was now encountering a personal, intimate diasporan history and discovering that some ties could not be easily discarded.

Paule gave a reading at the colloquium in the National Theatre in Lagos for the seven hundred writers, artists, and scholars, though much of the festival attention was on the musicians and dancers and other performers such as Stevie Wonder who so delighted Evan. Plans for an annual festival fizzled out because most nations didn't have the funds to continue it.

Paule's teenaged son accompanied her to Africa; her husband did not. The marriage with Nourry had been fraying as the 1970s wore on. Evan was aware by the end of the decade that things might be unraveling as both he and the girls began to sense the tension between Nourry and Paule. Then in 1979, when Evan was about twenty, the "other woman" appeared on what would be one of Paule's final visits to Haiti. Usually, Nourry would collect his daughters at their home in Port-au-Prince and join Evan and Paule at the relatively inexpensive Plaza Hotel. On this trip, however, Nourry arranged for Evan and Paule to meet him at the elegant and expensive Hôtel Oloffson, where he was apparently already staying. Evan was surprised because they had never stayed at such an expensive hotel, going there only for dinner or drinks. "When we got to the hotel in Port-au-Prince, he was already booked," Evan recalls, and "I could sense the tension, which was about a white woman both she [Paule] and Nourry knew, who was also staying at the hotel. Maybe my mother had discovered their affair. I remember vividly that she was angry and upset about something."[39] When the woman joined them at the dinner table, Paule said to Nourry in French: "What is that woman doing here?" As a flustered Nourry tried to explain, Evan knew that Paule would not hold back, and he expected there would be a heated exchange later.

CHAPTER 8

A Journey Backward to Find Her Own Tribe

PAULE STAYED ON IN HAITI as Evan returned to Hampton University for the spring semester. The rift with Nourry seemed to be healed. She wrote to Evan in January 1980 that the setting in Haiti was not "conducive to a peaceful meditation," that her meditation sessions in "Haiti haven't been very satisfactory," four dogs barking "without letup day and night—especially night." She was able to convince Nourry to get rid of only one of them. Later, in the same letter, she writes that her fifteen minutes of daily meditation seemed to be working because "Nourry and I are getting along beautifully. My being more relaxed has made our relationship more harmonious and easy going. Praises to Allah." Her writing, however, was not going so well because she was experiencing "some tension and anxiety I'm not aware of." The signs that their ten year marriage was coming to an end are woven throughout the letter. At fifty, Paule was about to separate from Nourry, from Haiti, and from the two stepdaughters she had come to love. She did not return to Haiti after 1980. She went back to New York to finish writing *Praisesong for the Widow*, "the novel I had fled to Kenya to escape from and also the one that had helped me to recover from the unfortunate second marriage."

In a 1979 interview in *Essence,* Paule told Alexis De Veaux that there were changes in her life that would show up in her next novel, some of them witnessed only by Evan.[1] Back in New York after the 1977 FESTAC trip and another one to Kenya and Uganda, she had gained weight and was so determined to lose it that she cleaned out the refrigerator and filled it up with tofu and low-calorie drinks, leaving Evan to forage for himself. She considered getting a face lift but apparently settled for a contraption she kept in the bathroom cabinet that allowed her to exercise her face and prevent drooping jowls. She had taken to riding her bike around Central Park for exercise and relaxation. She had joined the Sisterhood of black women artists and writers and began studying transcendental meditation taught by Sisterhood member NaNa Maynard, hoping it would help her to be less judgmental and less severe—with herself as well as with others. Whenever she talked about the new novel, she would claim that the idea for the widow in *Praisesong,* a "middle-aged, middle-class black woman, [who] has made it," appeared mysteriously. Later, she admitted, "Perhaps she had something to do, I thought, with the fact that middle age had descended on me with a vengeance at the time."[2]

Paule was about to launch her third novel, *Praisesong for the Widow,* during the most exciting twenty-year period in the history of black women's writing. Toni Morrison published her first three novels in the 1970s and appeared on the cover of *Newsweek* magazine. Alice Walker became an editor at *Ms.* magazine and would win a Pulitzer Prize in 1984 for *The Color Purple.* Ntozake Shange's choreopoem "for colored girls who have considered suicide / when the rainbow is enuf" played to capacity crowds in cities across the country from New York to San Francisco and on Broadway. Andrea Lee and Jamaica Kincaid became staff writers at *The New Yorker.* Many black women fiction writers published for the first time in the 1970s and 1980s: Octavia Butler, Gloria Naylor, Toni Cade Bambara, Jamaica Kincaid, Fran Ross, and Sherley Anne Williams. Hortense Spillers declared this explosion of writing by black women "a vivid new fact of American life."[3] Literary scholar Deborah McDowell called it "an epochal moment in U.S. publishing and intellectual life."[4] Citing Paule as one of the figures behind this new epoch, Cheryl Wall reintroduced the 1959 *Brown Girl, Brownstones* as "the novel that most black feminist critics consider to be the beginning of contemporary African American women's writings."[5]

Spurred into action by this new interest in black women writers, Paule began negotiating the sale of *Brown Girl, Brownstones* to the new Feminist Press, then headed by noted feminist scholar Florence Howe. *Brown Girl* became a windfall for the press, selling sixty thousand copies by 1991. Paule would eventually end up in a battle with the press over the rights to *Brown Girl, Brownstones,* which she had unwisely signed away in perpetuity, but Howe had no intention of relinquishing her best-selling title: "We republished *Brown Girl, Brownstones* in 1982, when no one was aware of its importance, and we have marketed it to a whole generation of readers who are using it in thousands of classrooms across the country."[6] Paule understood, though she came to resent, the compromise: "The press resurrected the novel, and it has done exceedingly well," and, since it kept the doors of the Feminist Press open, "it has been a beautiful trade-off."[7]

Howe also suggested, wisely, that Paule should republish some of her earlier stories in a collection called *Reena and Other Stories,* which the press published in 1983. Paule shaped *Reena* into a feminist anthology, selecting the stories that centered on women and composing new autobiographical and critical headnotes to focus on women. These two publications, along with *Praisesong* and her 1980s articles on black women in the *New York Times,* produced the breakthrough Paule had long struggled for. By the 1980s, when she contracted with Atheneum to publish

Daughters, she received a $100,000 advance, more than three times any previous advances (and about $325,000 in today's dollars—a major book deal by any standard).

In another interview, she suggested both personal and political incentives for the novel: "How do I, as a woman and a writer, a black woman and a black writer, live in a society that daily undercuts my sense of self."[8] Paule began planning a spiritual journey for the main character of *Praisesong*, the middle-class, middle-aged widow Avey Johnson. She plucks Avey off of a luxurious ocean voyage, sends her to the Caribbean island of Carriacou in Grenada, then back to the Gullah Islands in South Carolina, and finally home to White Plains, New York. In her 1973 essay "Shaping the World of My Art," Paule had described the triangular route she planned for her novels, one aspect of which was a "return to the motherland," a physical return that she meant as a metaphor for the psychological and spiritual return back over history, "which I am convinced Black people in this part of the world must undertake if we are to have a sense of our total experience and to mold for ourselves a more truthful identity."[9] Although Avey does not travel to Africa, Paule meant *Praisesong* to record a journey on the transatlantic trade route, undertaken in search of a truer self and maybe provide the answer to both Avey and Paule's middle-age panic.

Paule had long resisted the pressure to write a novel set exclusively in the States, even as her friends and colleagues warned her that setting her fiction in the Caribbean "somehow goes against me. That it makes me less 'folks,' less African American," out of sync with the black cultural nationalism of the 1970s.[10] She compromised, setting *Praisesong* in Brooklyn; White Plains, New York; Tatem, South Carolina; Grenada; and Carriacou, a combination that allowed her to deal with the intersecting histories of the United States and the Caribbean. She made the main characters

Avey and Jerome Johnson African Americans and lined *Praisesong* with references to cultural texts by African American figures, such as Robert Hayden, Langston Hughes, James Weldon Johnson, Nina Simone, Mamie Smith, James Baldwin, Amiri Baraka, Ma Rainey, and Lester Young. Scholar Cheryl Wall noted that the novel reads like "a song in praise of African American literature."[11] With this change in setting, *Praisesong* would be her first novel to reach a wide black American audience and became her most popular novel for many reasons, not least because of its timing and because it was celebrated as a successful conversion narrative.

Praisesong begins with the widow Avey Johnson traveling with her two women friends on their annual luxury Caribbean cruise aboard *The Bianca Pride*. Avey becomes disturbed both physically and spiritually by the extravagance of the cruise—from the high-end shopping on board, the chandeliers, tapestries, gilt-framed mirrors in the Versailles dining room, the layers of sweet peaches in syrup and whipped cream in the peach parfait à la Versailles, by all the "whiteness" that surrounds her: the ship, whose name translates as "White Pride," "is a 'glacial presence' set against the mauve, rose, and pale yellow sky over the warm Caribbean sea."[12]

The cruise reminds Avey of the excesses in her life: "the wall-to-wall carpeted house in North White Plains, the overflowing closets, the patrician car (a Lincoln), too many mink stoles, the investments, the annual cruises to the Caribbean," a search for material wealth that led Avey and her late husband Jerome (Jay) Johnson to abandon the African American customs and rituals that had been passed down to them and once defined them—the blues, gospel music, dance, greens and cornbread, "those small rites . . . that joined them to the vast unknown lineage that had made their being possible" and that "had both protected them and put them in possession of a kind of power." As she confronts the materialism of her life, Avey is also seized by troubling memories of her husband and their bitter struggles to escape poverty in pursuit of the American dream of success. They had lived in an African American community, a rundown neighborhood marked by "ruin and defeat" while Jay became consumed with his accounting business so that they could afford a life in White Plains.[13] Avey remembers their desperate climb up the economic ladder, and the ways their marriage became a site of anger and accusation because of that striving. Pregnant with their third child, Avey attempts to force a miscarriage and accuses Jay of having affairs with the white women at his job.

This picture of Avey and Jay's failed marriage and their disconnection from communal ties sets up the second half of the novel, which dramatizes Avey's transformation and healing through a ritual journey that begins with a series of powerful dreams of her childhood visits to her great aunt Cuney in Tatem, South Carolina, and culminates in an almost mystical pilgrimage to the island of Carriacou in Grenada.[14] When Avey finds herself walking on the beach in Grenada in a state of psychic shock, she meets an elderly Grenadian man named Lebert Josephs who has "special powers of seeing and knowing."[15] He persuades Avey to accompany him on the annual excursion of the out-islanders to their native island of Carriacou, where she undergoes a series of experiences. In Paule's words, that journey enables Avey to "recapture that sense of self, that sense of history, which then permits her to move to another level in her life. To stage a private revolution and win it. And it's that capacity for change that I was trying to deal with in that novel."[16] In many interviews Paule would promote Avey's *Praisesong* journey as a spiritual and psychic victory, claiming that Avey is able to recover her " 'true-true name,' her rightful self. And with that she's once again centered, rooted and thus personally [and politically] empowered."[17] Paule's words in her interviews and the ones in her novel are often at odds.

Avey's healing takes place at the Nation Dance in Carriacou, where the dancers move in a counterclockwise circle identical to the Ring Shout she learned in South Carolina with Aunt Cuney. After Avey is given a ritual bathing, and a massage by his daughter Rosalie, Lebert then leads Avey to a small, unsteady schooner to join the out-islanders on Carriacou. In an ancient dirt yard, Avey is induced to join the Big Drum dance. As she watches the dancers form a ring and salute their "Nation"—their African ancestors—Banda, Moko, Temne, Cromanti, Chamba—she begins to move with the others, as though unconsciously responding to a past memory with Aunt Cuney, perhaps a collective African memory, and suddenly she feels "the myriad of shiny, silken, brightly colored threads . . . streaming out of everyone there to enter her, making her part of what seemed a far-reaching wide-ranging confraternity."[18]

But Paule's elegiac descriptions of Avey's Carriacou experience undercut any sense of Avey achieving an uncomplicated "wholeness" as a result of this excursion. Avey arrives in Carriacou to a place of impoverishment. The ceremony takes place in darkness in a large dirt yard by the side of a dilapidated house lit by two gas lamps. There is a table with drinks and a few bottles of rum, and nearby young boys are playing makeshift drums made from small rum kegs. As the frail elderly dancers step forward for the ceremony of the Big Drum and the Beg Pardon, Avey sees that "all that was left were a few names of what they called nations which they could no longer even pronounce properly, the fragments of a dozen or so songs, the shadowy forms of long-ago dances and rum kegs for drums. The bare bones. The burnt-out ends."[19] The elderly dancers evoke a powerful lamentation that Avey recognizes as the sound of "separation and loss."[20] What Avey reclaims is the recognition of the fragmentary nature of African traditions in the Americas, and a reckoning with the embers of the "burnt-out ends" that still remain. Paule gives Avey's Carriacou excursion another kind of power, not an uncomplicated "victory" but a sign of how people keep alive the "longings," "feelings," and "memories" that over the years "had proven more durable and trustworthy than the history of trauma and pain out of which they had come."[21]

Paule was not pleased with the early reviews of *Praisesong*. When it was published in 1983, mainstream white reviewers were mystified by Avey's diasporan trek to Carriacou and impatient with what they considered the novel's didacticism. In the *New York Times*, Christopher Lehmann-Haupt, who had slammed *Chosen Place* for being too political, wrote a caustic review that reduced the novel to "a cautionary tale about the consequences of cultural alienation": "Don't get caught up in the white man's world," "Don't lose touch with music and dancing, or the rituals of the Baptist Church that are the closest thing to African culture that most American blacks have."[22] In the British *Times Literary Supplement*, Mary Kathleen Benet's review, "The White Death," suggests that Avey's search for meaning by connecting with her racial past is another kind of "white" status symbol. Is this search for roots, Benet queries, a "modern, acceptable equivalent of the straightened hair and white ways she is renouncing"?[23] In the *Village Voice*, Carol Ascher viewed Avey's return-to-roots journey as another kind of middle-class privilege, a sign that Avey can join "that white male-created middle-class." Yes, Ascher wrote, you can go back to retrieve your roots if "your children are grown, and you have a job, property, money in the bank."[24] In *Freedomways*, Marian K. Borenstein, an educator and community activist in

New York, recognized that Paule was less familiar with African American families than with Caribbean ones, and chastised her for criticizing African Americans for striving for material comfort: "Are we to assume, then, had they stayed poor, barely able to make ends meet, they would have retained their blackness at full strength? Does being a middle-class achiever necessarily make one soulless, a diluted Black?"[25] Anne Tyler ended her review in the *New York Times* pronouncing, skeptically, that she would stand aside and allow black readers to be the ultimate judges of *Praisesong*: "Will black Americans, reading of Avey Johnson's rebellion against her homogenization, sympathize with it? Will they willingly accompany her on her journey backward to find her own 'tribe'?"[26]

African Americanist scholars and communities of readers were as divided about the meaning of *Praisesong* as Paule was. Some answered Tyler's challenge by reclaiming *Praisesong* as the model text of black diasporic literature. The terms that commentators often used to characterize *Praisesong*, such as a journey toward "wholeness," indicated the slippery way the novel could be read as if Avey had somehow achieved a transformed existence with certainty and confidence.[27] In *Toward Wholeness in Paule Marshall's Fiction*, Joyce Pettis sees all of Marshall's fiction as part of a journey toward "wholeness," which, Pettis argues, is achieved in *Praisesong*.[28]

But Paule had cautioned readers with the narrative clues she had so carefully inserted not to conclude that Avey had somehow reached a state of transcendence, or that this was a finished or easy process. In the page and a half at the end of the novel devoted to Avey's future plans, Avey wonders if her experience in Carriacou was "a mirage" rather than an actual place, "*something conjured up* perhaps to satisfy a longing and need."[29] The final epigraph in part 4 from Susan Sontag—"Ultimately the only response is to hold the event in mind; to remember it"— is a directive from Paule that *Praisesong* was to be a memorial, a probing for the meaning of a diasporic identity that had to be created out of the fragments of history and memory.[30] Scholar Courtney Thorsson carefully parsed the word *conjured* and reaffirmed Paule's intention that Avey's achievement of a diasporic homeland be viewed as "a shared archive" of "longings and the feelings," not a transcendent self.[31] Marshall scholar Cheryl Wall also resisted the "wholeness" narrative: "African Americans will never be able to recuperate the past completely, cultural knowledge will always remain fragmentary."[32]

It's also telling that most critics and readers bypassed the cautionary epigraph in the final section of the novel that focuses attention on an aging woman: "*Oh, Bars of my . . . body, open, open!*" from Randall Jarrell's poem "Woman at the Washington Zoo."[33] The speaker in the poem, a middle-aged woman like Avey and Paule, is at the zoo watching the animals in their cages and experiencing a kind of spiritual and psychological crisis. The woman is a clerk in a government office in Washington, DC, dressed in a dull navy blue outfit, prim and proper like Avey. She feels desperate and entrapped, sees herself in the eyes of the animals—"these beings trapped / As I am trapped"—and proclaims her desire to escape the aging body and the bars of convention she has made for herself. Her desire to be changed like the wild beasts, pecked and torn in pieces, is savage. She screams for the vultures to tear into her flesh: "You know what I was / You see what I am: change me, change me!" The poem turns our attention to the personal traumas in Avey's life—widowhood, loss, abandonment, aging—that represent the kind of spiritual crises that might not be cured by a trip to Carriacou.

None of these scholarly or critical pronouncements would deter Paule's readers from loving and appreciating *Praisesong*. She received many fan letters from black men who considered Jay Johnson a positive image because "he chose not to abandon his family, but stayed, gritted his teeth, worked hard and succeeded," though at great cost to himself.[34] Paule would have been heartened by several personal letters from other writers that prefaced the eventual embrace of *Praisesong* by black scholars and readers. She received the Before Columbus Foundation American Book Award from the foundation founded by her friend Ishmael Reed, not known for embracing black women writers. Alice Walker wrote from San Francisco that *Praisesong* was "wise, very moving, and beautiful," adding a personal note that *Praisesong* had helped her with her relationship with her then boyfriend Robert: "It helped me understand much of our life together on a deeper and feeling level."[35] John O. Killens was almost ecstatic in his praise for the novel's portrayal of "some beautiful black-man-woman love scenes almost unheard of in modern American literature, all praises due to God, or Allah, and Paule Marshall." Writing his first "fan letter to another novelist," Killens predicted that "Black men will be eternally grateful to you."[36] He also praised Paule's focus on a middle-aged woman protagonist as "a gift heretofore unprecedented."[37]

Praisesong for the Widow achieved a kind of iconic status in 2024, appearing in the novel *Great Expectations* by Vinson Cunningham, a young black *New Yorker* writer who encountered the novel in a black women's literature course taught by a black woman professor. Cunningham was so amused by what he considered the novel's obvious symbolism and the professor's incompetence that *Praisesong* (as well as the course and the professor) was easy fodder for his biting critique. He labeled Paule's metaphors of black middle-class corruption—Avey's pearls threatening to strangle her and her excessive luggage—"creaky explanatory crutches." The novel seemed so ridiculous to Cunningham that he recast the scene of Avey taking the boat trip to Carriacou as the basis of a joke that begins, "A nigger walks onto a boat . . ."[38] The fact that Paule's novel was now instantly recognizable, and belittled, even without being named, is perhaps another milestone in Paule's writerly life.

Having finished the novel that had helped her to recover from "the unfortunate second marriage," Paule wrote her friend John Killens, "I am off to China," and thanked him for his review of *Praisesong*. She had already begun to work on her next book, and the trip provided a badly needed respite before she could settle down to the desk again. In June 1983, she joined twelve American women writers leaving San Francisco as part of the U.S.–China Peoples Friendship Association tour for American women writers to meet prominent Chinese women writers. Paule agreed to serve as the delegation leader for the tour, for which she would get an all-expenses-paid trip, a "Bajan 'free-ness,' " as she called it. On the twenty-one-day tour to Beijing, Nanjing, Suzhou, Shanghai, Guilin, and Guangzhou, American women were to meet and converse with their Chinese counterparts, while also seeing and experiencing as much as possible of China—"the colossus of a country."

Four of the women on the China tour were women of color—Indian American Canadian novelist Bharati Mukherjee; Alice Walker, who had just won the Pulitzer Prize for her novel *The Color Purple;* poet and activist Nellie Wong; and Paule. The other eight writers—novelist Lisa Alther; poet Tess Gallagher; novelist and journalist Blanche McCrary Boyd; professor Susan Kirschner; journalist Kathryn Kellogg; poet Kathryn Kilgore; fiction writer Tillie Olsen; and novelist Valerie Miner—were white. Paule considered the women "an amiable group that both tolerated and respected each other's personality differences."

Paule kept notes of the trip in a slender four-by-eight-inch inch dark green leather-bound journal that she bought in Beijing.

I discovered it in 2018 among the papers in the Richmond storage facility, the twenty-seven-page diary diary, one of only one of only two written documents where Paule comes close to "letting it all hang out," as she promised John Keene. This diary is the only record we have of Paule's panic, anxiety, and muteness in the face of her public performances or of her reactions to deeply humiliating racist insults, and the only one that hints at her bisexuality. The diary opens with Paule chastising herself for failing to take journal writing more seriously: "Here I am with the trip more than half over only now beginning to put down a few impressions. I'll try to backtrack, even as I move forward so that China, like Kenya, Uganda, and all the other places I've visited won't become a thing of the past—the clouded past—the day after I leave here."

Most of the notes in the journal are perfunctory lists of Paule's duties as the tour leader, but they also create a picture of the busy, varied daily activities that engaged her, some pleasant, some tedious, some distasteful: keeping track of the schedules for dinners, performances, meals, programs, sightseeing, mountain climbing, boat rides, purchasing tickets, announcing when to put the luggage out for the next day, organizing ferry schedules, changing money, checking passports, and arranging shopping trips. At times it was overwhelming. Other activities, like looking for gifts for a few special people, were pleasurable. She was looking for raw silk shirts for Evan and David, Evan's childhood friend and Paule's godson; gifts for writer Louise Meriwether and Paule's best friend Connie Sutton. There were two reminders to look for a silk blouse for Lucienne Numa, a physician and, according to Paule's son Evan, Paule's lover for a brief time in the early 1980s. She blesses Lucienne for prescribing Lomotil, which saved her from a bad bout of diarrhea.

Valerie Miner praised Paule as an ideal leader: very responsible, gracious, and friendly to all the writers. "She hung out with all of us, went shopping with us (we joked that it became the 'Feminist Shopping Tour of China') and she worked hard."[39] Whatever the tensions and difficulties, she met with all the writers in the evenings, even after exhausting days. She recommended that Valerie try her end-of-the-day ritual of putting her feet up on three pillows and lying on the bed for ten minutes to rev up her energy level. Valerie remembers Paule being very patient with Tillie Olsen, but Paule recorded her annoyance in the journal. When they encountered older peasant women clinging to each other's hands as they moved along, hobbling through one palace after another on their shrunken feet, Paule noted that "Tillie, the oldest member of our group, who could sometimes be sentimental, even gushing in her sincere 'love' of the masses, rushed over to embrace one of the women with bound feet, and the old woman fled her." Paule was embarrassed and angry.

Paule's visual imagination is striking, especially her descriptions of the Chinese landscape that are as vivid as her images of the Caribbean. The group had been warned to stay away from Guilin in the summer because of the rainy weather—hot, humid, and wet. For Paule, the rain was part of Guilin's breathtaking beauty:

> The rain was a nuisance but also very beautiful, creating a low cloud cover of mist which transformed Guilin into the fairytale landscape of Chinese paintings. We climbed to the top of Brocade Hill in a light misting rain, saw the town below like some insubstantial dream with an overloaded ferry boat crossing the Li River and in the mist, from the height, none of it seemed real. Nellie [Wong] said she felt part of a landscape painting; I, on the other hand, felt cloddishly real, substantial, heavy, defined, in contrast to a world that could only, it seemed, be of the imagination.

In contrast to the painterly stillness of the Guilin entry, Paule's description of the Chinese women is all movement and energy:

> People here, pedestrians, take the most daredevil chances with their lives crossing the streets, riding their bicycles. One woman, holding her baby, stood calmly in the middle of the road amid the careening traffic and stepped calmly back an inch or two as our taxi-van came bounding toward her. One young woman in a dress riding a man's bike dismounted and remounted with astonishing grace and went pumping off. In Guilin, a mother opened her umbrella as the rains came down yet again, arranged it over her baby in its seat on the bar of the bike, remounted and went cycling off, one hand steering, the other holding aloft the umbrella over baby.

Some aspects of the trip were more troubling than the rain. In the evening after the Guilin outing, "after an unappetizing dinner," Paule went off on her own for a solitary walk along a road that stretched past orderly rice fields and encountered three teenage boys:

> Three boys laughed anxiously at the sight of me. . . . Three barefoot teenage peasant boys. As I was about to raise my hand to wave to them . . . they came to an abrupt stand-still, then went dashing across the rice paddy. I wanted to tell them—barefoot as they were—that I was one with them—a Third World person, one of the have-nots, never mind, I probably made them think of a dragon. . . . I started laughing—one of those laughs to keep from crying, and raised my face to the sky and called upon Lucy—Lucy Australuis [*Australopithecus afarensis*]. The first mother of us all. Clearly, they had never seen a black person before.[40]

Some years later, writing about this incident in the unpublished travelogue she called *Travelin' Light* triggered an extended riff on the racial incidents she experienced throughout her life. She called up all the times "others had fled the sight of my face—a face the dense undiluted brown of the hot cocoa Adriana prepared for us on winter mornings." The incident sends her back to her young life in New York as she catalogues her experiences of racial assault: at Bushwick High, when her best friend refused to walk with her at graduation; the man in the Manhattan coffee shop who called out "nigger"; and years later in Los Angeles, when a motorist in a passing car called out the n-word at her as she walked out of her hotel: "The word shutting down my brain to the extent where I couldn't call to my aid the repertoire of cuss words, bringing on a paralysis that rendered me speechless." These encounters summoned another voice: "Nina, Nina Simone, her voice suddenly in my head, ministering to me, helping me recover before I reached the hotel: 'I wish I could know what it means to be free.' "

Paule's experience of being shunned by the Chinese teenagers slotted into a pattern of racial shunning and shaming that she traced back to her teenage years. The boys in China had at least seen her "most acutely"; while back in the States, "there's this odd business of white people not seeing me at all. Upon my approach, a sixth-sense delete button eliminated me/deletes me from in front of them—before their brain can register my presence, a switch deletes me from their radar screen." Paule rarely depicted scenes of racial bigotry in her fiction. Her unpublished notes are the evidence of how deeply she was impacted by these slights and attacks and how deeply closeted she kept them.[41]

Alice Walker also recounted racial incidents on the China trip in her essay "A Thousand Words: A Writer's Picture of China," though she did not interpret them as personal attacks, and her first

Paule and Alice Walker (right) in China in 1983, arm in arm, standing outside a Chinese temple.

reaction was to seek community with Paule. When one of their hosts decided to show off her knowledge of black Americans by regaling them with "Old Black Joe," a song she learned when she was studying English in the United States in the 1950s, Alice was called on to smooth over the situation and explain "the reactionary nature of the song."[42] Appalled and saddened that such ignorance still existed, Alice wrote that the incident made her want to move closer to Paule and "put my arms around her, and I want her to hug me back. Here we are, two black women (thank the Universe we *are* two!), once again facing a racial ignorance that depresses and appalls."[43] Alice also reported that she met two young African students studying medicine in China, who told her that they faced social ostracism in China and believed "the Chinese people do not like black people and some call us black devils."[44]

In their small-group interactions, their Chinese tour guides were, to the Americans, surprisingly curious about homosexuality. During an all-day boat ride on the Li River, Paule listened in on an animated conversation among the writers and their two young interpreters He Bi and Lu Tie, "asking all the questions regarding lesbians and homosexuality." The answers, Paule wrote in her journal, were supplied by Lisa and Blanche, whom she called "the declared gays." Paule thought the young Chinese women were snooping. "He Bi can't seem to hear enough." And writer Valerie Miner, one of the self-declared gays, thought that the Chinese guides were spies, appearing "quite horrified and titillated, acting as though they'd never heard of [homosexuality]."[45] Blanche Boyd ("the boldest in our group") quipped with sarcastic humor, "Maybe I could help them out, take them out of their misery, satisfy their curiosity." To the group, Paule seemed reserved, unwilling to join in the discussions of sexuality, but her journal suggests that she was listening quite intently. At fifty-six, the second oldest in the group after Tillie, who was seventy-one, she may not have felt as open as the younger women, especially those who were freer to express their queer sexuality.[46]

Like Miner and most of the group, Paule was convinced that their meetings were carefully monitored and controlled: "Despite our efforts we never were able to meet those writers who were considered 'dissidents.' Always people from the travel service to keep a watch on us. Repression clearly felt." In the sessions with Chinese writers and poets reading their work, Paule recalled that "so many of the poems that were read in our presence were about nature, flowers, etc. The self excluded. Any subject matter of a political nature that might displease the gov't was carefully excluded." The left-leaning Americans had come with the names of specific writers they hoped to meet, writers who were critical of the government or had spoken out against the Communist Party, but "all such requests were politely but firmly turned aside."

The high point of the trip for Paule was meeting Ding Ling, China's foremost feminist writer. At the time, Ding Ling, the pen name for Jiang Wei, was seventy-nine. She died three years later in 1986. By the time she met with Paule's group, Ding Ling had come back into favor with the Communist Party and was living in a six-room apartment in Beijing usually reserved for top officials. Her political beliefs had sustained her through jailings and the execution of her husband. She was, Paule wrote, "a feminist long before the term had even been coined." Even after her conflicts with the Communists, Ding Ling held firm to her belief that "the one billion people of China must unite into one under the leadership of the Communist Party." Valerie remembered that when they met Ding Ling, "she asked us to stand and sing a song she had learned when she was in the United States. The song was 'We Shall Overcome.' " Thinking about the earlier song, Valerie thought, "It was a very lovely moment."[47]

Paule put together a folder of stories and articles by and about Ding Ling when she returned, with notes for teaching her work. She underlined what she admired about the stories: Ding Ling's struggle to be a feminist, her critique of male behavior, her involvement in the underground resistance against the Japanese, her refusal to accept the party line that all literature must conform to socialist realism, her appreciation for women who were freethinkers and accepted free love (in her notes Paule wrote, "shacked up"), and she applauded Ding Ling's choice to marry a man thirteen years younger. Paule believed that Ding Ling's commitment to Marxism gave her "a strength that comes from working for a larger cause—this gives her the strength to reject marriage." As is clear from her notes, Paule was drawn to Ding Ling for her counterculture views and because, like Paule, she was a model of the writer, her life and writing inseparable.

In all of the formal meetings on this trip, Paule appeared poised and self-controlled. Tess Gallagher remembered her as very reserved, "not really saying very intimate or revealing things."[48] Only in her journal did Paule record the internal distress she experienced about her public presentations, now intensified by her role as tour leader. She was obligated to make the official opening greetings and parting remarks, and, according to her companions, she did so with apparent grace and ease, but in the notes she wrote after retiring to her bedroom, she admits being flustered and dissatisfied with "my reticent, ill-prepared statement." The persistent feelings she recorded in the journal were panic and anxiety. After working one night on a toast, she wrote, "It went well; [although] usual panic and stage fright up to the last moment—so tired of the old syndrome." Another time she expressed nervousness about attending a meeting, "since there might be some criticism of my leadership—which I don't need. I just wanted a free trip to China. Perhaps it would have been better if I had paid my way or not come at all." When someone complained about how a meeting turned out, Paule wrote, "I should have said and done more . . . but I still feel so unsure about talking exempt [extemporaneously] and I didn't have either the time or energy to write out another speech. It's a great burden this public holding forth—& I keep promising myself I won't do it unless it's either talking about my own development as a writer or reading from my work. Yet, an invitation comes along, I somehow think I can manage it, and I find myself trapped again, and feeling *panicky and inadequate*—how weary I am of those two emotions."

In another moment of intense self-reflection in the journal, something else erupted, as though this silent poking at deep insecurities and suppressed feelings prompted an uncensored revelation. As the group was waiting for the bus on their last day in China, Paule and the other women were caught in a damp, steamy rain along with the Saturday crowds after a "disappointing shopping trip," where she was unable to find a blouse for Lucienne. Paule noted that "people [stared at me] as if I am some sort of oddity." She described her discomfort in sensual detail: the staring people, the steamy, sauna-like tropical heat, the constant rain, and the crowded, noisy department store filled with sleazy, ill-made goods. She chatted with Lisa Alther, one of the self-declared gays, most well known for her novel *Kinflicks*. Tucked in between the weather, the crowds, and the failed shopping trip, Paule recorded her feelings of attraction for Lisa: "Waited outside chatting with Leza [*sic*] about New York and Central Park, my feelings, as guilty . . . as they make me feel, must be respected. I sense curiosity, friendliness and what could perhaps be described as a mixture of guilt & pity on her part. Might be wrong. Attraction? It's unclear."

This forty-nine-word, five-sentence excerpt, a mosaic of complicated feelings—desire tinged with guilt and shame, the need to honor her feelings, an expectation of rejection, curiosity, and the fear of risk—is the only written record of Paule's same-gender attraction. But even here in the diary, where she has the freedom to say whatever she wants, we still see the habit of obliqueness, the slant way of introducing then sidelining deep feelings. Whose "attraction"—hers or Lisa's? Why does she project feelings of "guilt and pity" onto Lisa? She has just been searching for the blouses Lucienne wants ("size large, no darts, no silk, white linen,

Guangzhou—shopping, last day. A disaster. Crowded stores filled with staring people and cheap merchandise. And the heat—the steamy, sauna-like tropical heat, and the rain that comes and goes constantly. One fans to no avail. Searched for the blouses Lucienne wants; didn't find them. Will look in Hong Kong. The trade fair across from the hotel was filled with sleazy, ill-made goods; the dept store, the biggest in town, was worse: crowded, noisy, people staring as if I am some sort of oddity. Every-where damp & steamy, Sat. crowds. Bus didn't come. Waited outside chatting with [illegible] about

In this excerpt from her 1983 China journal, Paule describes a failed shopping trip amid the heat, crowds, and discomfort of Hong Kong.

embroidered"), but didn't find them. "Will look in Hong Kong." Is Lucienne the reason for guilt over her attraction to Lisa? Or is she still burdened by the cult of respectability and her need for "discretion"?

The revelation of Paule's sexual attraction is particularly stunning because publicly she often privileged black heterosexual unity as the bedrock of black communities and impugned homosexuality. Her 1985 article in *Essence,* "Ties That Bind," called for restoring the black family—always and only presented as the union of black men and women—in order "to rescue our community from what has been called its 'tangle of pathology.' "[49] She

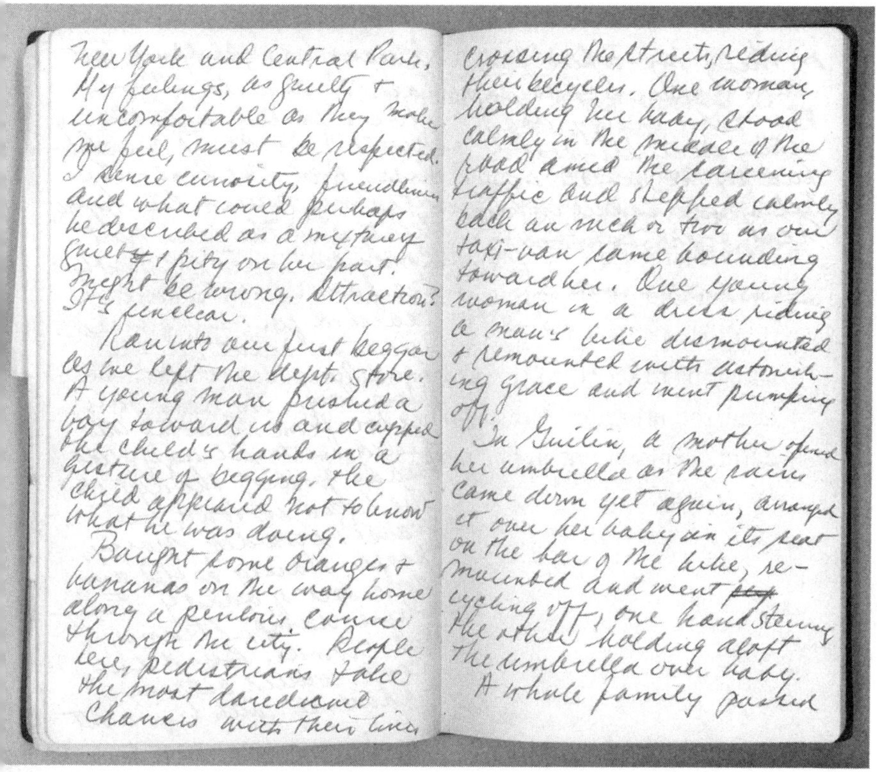

was so perturbed by William Styron's portrayal of Nat Turner as a homosexual in *The Confessions of Nat Turner* that she told the *New York Times* in 1984 she was unable to finish reading it: "I got as far as the scene of Nat and his friend Will tumbling amorously in the grass and called it quits."[50] Is it possible Paule had forgotten that fifteen years earlier, in 1969, in *The Chosen Place, the Timeless People*, she had crafted a beautifully rendered erotic scene of two men "tumbling amorously" in the Caribbean waters of Horseshoe Pool? Or was she still looking over her shoulder and feeling the presence of the black nationalists, who loathed Styron's book? She did not contribute to the collective published response by ten black men, *William Styron's Nat Turner: Ten Black Writers Respond,* but one of the contributors, Vincent Harding, lamented her absence, writing that Paule Marshall as an artist of folk retentions and diasporic connection would have added immeasurably to this conversation.[51] Paule's public distancing from same-sex desire is perplexing, considering that the most vivid, affective, and erotically charged passages and scenes of sexual desire in Paule's work are almost always queer. If she never publicly divulged anything about her own queer sexual desires, the China journal allows us to see that she was working through the voices in her head, rerouting desire through her art, clearing the way for more daring explorations in her next two novels, *Daughters* and *The Fisher King.*[52]

CHAPTER 9

I'm Taking More Risks

PAULE WAS EXPERIENCING a new sense of freedom in the 1980s. Her two marriages—the first that interfered with her writing and the "unfortunate second marriage"—were behind her. She was free of *Praisesong*, which had required trips to Kenya and China to "escape." Evan had graduated from Hampton University and was on his way to a very successful career as a yacht designer and no longer needed large sums for tuition. She traveled with Lucienne to France, where they stayed at a place near James Baldwin's magnificent Saint-Paul-de-Vence estate. Although she was no longer living on the edge financially, she was searching for a permanent teaching position and relief from the stress of Manhattan.

She signed on for two more "itinerant" positions, one at the University of Massachusetts–Boston and the other at the University of California–Berkeley. In Boston she commuted to and from New York or stayed in Roxbury at the home of her friend Elma Lewis, fellow Bajan and MacArthur winner, and founder of the Elma Lewis School of Fine Arts in Boston. Paule's friend the poet Martha Collins, then the director of creative writing at U Mass, sat in on Paule's interview with the dean and observed a surprising side of Paule: "She seemed to me quite formal, I might

Lucienne Numa (left) and Paule, on a shopping and sunbathing vacation in France in the 1980s, stayed at a luxurious hotel near James Baldwin's estate.

even say *proper,* in that old-fashioned sense of the term, sitting up straight, being very polite, quietly naming a quite high salary figure. I remember appreciating the terms she set in this interview. She was proper and polite but self-assured in her valuation of her worth."[1] This image of the "proper" Paule was performance, mask, and disguise, her preferred way of self-presentation; meanwhile she created women characters who were shuffling off propriety and flouting gender and sexual norms.

It was fitting that, in the spring semester of 1984, Paule, now fifty six, began the next stage of her freedom tour in California. She was so elated about the prospect of a sojourn in northern California at the University of California in Berkeley that she turned down Martha's proposal that she would be an ideal candidate for the prestigious Bunting Fellowship at Radcliffe. The Berkeley appointment was spearheaded by her friend Barbara

Christian, the first black woman to be tenured and promoted to full professor at Berkeley. Christian's groundbreaking 1980 critical study, *Black Women Novelists: The Development of a Tradition,* was one of the first books of black feminist criticism, and its extensive section on Paule's work helped to establish Paule's growing reputation among black studies scholars.

Berkeley was the springboard for a number of important changes in Paule's life and writing. This quintessential New Yorker who had never learned to drive decided to buy her first car, a burgundy Volkswagen Beetle, and became competent enough (barely) to drive across the country with a friend. She found a house to sublet that she loved for its views and for its library: "This wonderful little house on a hill overlooking Marin County, San Francisco, Angel Island, Alcatraz, Golden Gate, and the Pacific beyond. I felt I owned all. I'd get up in the morning, go out on my deck, where it would all be waiting to take my breath away." She confessed that this beauty was all she needed to cure herself of the "arrogance" that there was nothing beyond the Hudson River worth seeing.

She was equally impressed with the library in the house, whose owner, a woman's studies professor, was a Virginia Woolf scholar. "Everywhere I turned in the study I encountered the lady from Bloomsbury—shelves of books about her—biographies, essays, critical studies, and a large framed photograph of VW above my desk of her smoking a cigarette in a long black holder, which she was holding at this defiant angle. And then there were those heavy-lidded Virginia Woolf eyes looking down at me all the time. It was rather spooky. Who's afraid of Virginia Woolf? Well, I was, after a time."

By the time of the Second National Conference on Women in the Arts at the University of Wisconsin in 1985, Paule was so comfortable with Woolf's presence that she changed the title of her mother-poets talk to "A Black Woman Writer Thinks Back through Her Mothers," paraphrasing Woolf's famous dictum, "We think back through our mothers if we are women."[2] She also credited Woolf with setting the requirements for a woman to be able to write: a room of one's own, £500 a year, and literary foremothers, "those women who wrote in the face of the most unimaginable odds."[3] In 1989, when Paule was awarded the John Dos Passos Prize, she introduced Virginia Woolf as one of her literary foremothers, a sign of her deviation from the prescriptions of black cultural nationalism. Alexis De Veaux recounts in her biography of poet Audre Lorde that when Lorde and Michelle Cliff, two well-known black feminists, were engaged in a heated discussion about an essay Cliff planned to write about Woolf, Lorde told her flat out that writing about Woolf, a white, upper-class British woman, was "a betrayal of black people."[4] It may have been Berkeley's history of radical activism, or the liberatory spirit of the black activists on that campus, or Woolf's exquisite probing of women's need for "concealment and suppression," or Paule's own "uniquely independent intellect" behind her decision—she would continue to summon the spirit of Virginia Woolf for the rest of her writing life.

Paule received a warm reception in California. Both she and Alice Walker, who had recently won a Pulitzer Prize for *The Color Purple* and was building a house in the hills north of San Francisco, were celebrated in California's black cultural circles. Paule was the guest of honor at a lively party at the home of Dona and Frank Irvin, parents of American historian Nell Irvin Painter, and an invited guest speaker all over the state, including at the famed Eso Won Bookstore in San Francisco. In a casual snapshot at the reception after Paule's talk at Berkeley, she and Alice seem relaxed and comfortable among the writers and academics who knew and admired their work.

At a reception after her reading at the University of California, Berkeley, in 1984, Paule and her friends gathered in a circle on the floor for this photo op. *Left to right:* Mary Helen Washington, Paule Marshall, June Jordan, Barbara Christian, Alice Walker, and Susan Griffin.

With the success of *Praisesong,* Paule received a $100,000 advance from her publisher Atheneum and began her fourth novel, *Daughters,* which she announced would be a departure from her other work: "I'm taking more risks and it's a 'freer' book," more intensely personal and, she admitted, autobiographical: It's "a kind of *roman à clef* that has to do with my relationship with my father."[5] She dedicated *Daughters* to Samuel Burke and her brother Frank, not in admiration or gratitude but as a declaration that she was finally able to "[free] myself of Sam B" and of that "particular domination and dependency."

Whether or not she ever achieved such freedom, *Daughters* enabled Paule to be unusually forthright about how her relationship with her "handsome, charismatic father," had affected many of her adult relationships with men.[6] She described *Daughters* as a form of therapy: "Always looking for this father in the men that I became involved with, and always preparing myself for the end of that relationship. This novel is about the subtle deferring to men that was so much a part of my childhood and the childhood of many women."[7] Paule meant for the novel to be a lesson to young women, as well as to herself, to guard against the subtle experiences "of seduction, of dependency, and of domination" they might feel in relationships with men, including their fathers.[8] "How long it took me to move away from that and to recover, to insist upon autonomy," she reflected.[9] Yet she was perhaps not as free as she thought: when she appeared on the CBS *Today Show* in 1992, shortly after the novel's publication, she did not report the relationship as problematic; she recalled her absent father only as "the light of my life."[10]

Daughters also allowed Paule to disclose for the first time, in a 1991 interview with Daryl Dance, a date rape and an abortion, "a back-alley, coat hanger experience." In her handwritten notes, she added that "*Daughters* enabled me to deal with the one & only abortion in my life. I thought I felt only relief at the time—I was consc. of feeling only relief—but at another deeper level I continued to grieve, to feel guilt." Writing *Daughters* permitted her "to exorcise at last the painful memory of those two assaults. To face the fact that I never got over relinquishing that life, I gave [my daughter] a name—Kendall—and I continued to look for her in the daughter that some other woman bore—but who was really my daughter. I looked without knowing I was looking for years. Until just recently I found her. Kendall. She doesn't know that's her name, but it is. She doesn't realize she's my daughter, but that's all right." Paule never expanded on these disclosures, although they may be a key to the relationship between father and daughter in the novel—and in her life. Dance later confessed that Paule's revelations about the rape and abortion were so "clinical, analytical, and impersonal" that "I simply remained the calm, unflappable interviewer" and did not question her any further.[11]

The idea for *Daughters* came to Paule at an Alvin Ailey dance performance at City Center Theater on West 55th Street when she saw in the program the epigraph to one of the dances: *Little girl of all the daughters / You ain't no more slave / You's a woman now.* As always, Paule wanted to make a statement about political forms of bondage, so that the struggle of a woman to overcome dependency and domination could encompass "the larger struggle of the Third World to free itself of the domination of the West and America."[12] But this epigraph is a gendered mandate that specifically defines girlhood as a site of enslavement and freedom as achieving an emancipated womanhood.

Paule created a catalogue of black women in *Daughters,* giving each a stage for her emancipation from the emotional and psychological domination of men. The celestial names of the four main women characters—Ursa, Astral, Estelle, and Celestine—position them as a part of the constellation that circulates around and is in bondage to the polestar, Primus Mackenzie, a charismatic politician slated to become prime minister of Triunion. Astral Ford is Primus's mistress and manager of his resort; Celestine Bellegarde is his longtime devoted servant with whom he has been sexually intimate; Estelle, "the wife he went and find in America," becomes her husband's political partner trying to stop him from signing onto an American resort scheme that will cut off access to the beach and fishing rights for the native people.[13] Two other American women—Ursa's closest friend, Vincereta (Viney) Daniels, and Mae Ryland, a grassroots organizer in Midland, an inner city of New Jersey—engage in rebellions that tag them as descendants of Triunion's legendary rebel heroine Congo Jane.

Paule used a strategy in *Daughters* that she called "double exposure," allowing the novel to toggle back and forth from the

United States to the Caribbean: chapters 1 and 3 are set in New York (mostly Manhattan) and New Jersey; chapters 2 and 4 are set in the fictional Caribbean country of Triunion. Eighteen hundred miles from New York City, Triunion was a composite of Haiti, the Dominican Republic, and several English-speaking countries—to represent French, Spanish, and English colonial rule—and, like most Caribbean nations, had attained only a tenuous political independence. Of all the reviewers of *Daughters,* Jane Smiley was the one who understood the "profundity and grandeur" of the novel's political vision. Set in the 1980s, it exposed, Smiley wrote, the callousness and cynical greed of the Reagan administration's assault on blacks of privilege and the black poor, both at home and in the Caribbean.[14]

"Double exposure" also refers to Paule's own dual cultural heritage as African American and Caribbean. The main character Ursa is African American through her Connecticut-born mother Estelle and Caribbean through her father Primus Mackenzie, a hybrid status that allows her to move back and forth from the United States to the islands, contrasting scenes of first world privilege and power with third world poverty and dependence, and showing African American daughters acting in collaboration with their Caribbean sisters. The novel indicts the new "charismatic" black leaders of both countries, Primus in Triunion, and Sandy Lawson, the young black mayor in Midland, New Jersey, for ditching their progressive politics as they become seduced by luxury and power.[15] Primus is seduced by an invitation from "the Carnegie people" pressuring him to think "free enterprise" rather than "any socialist nonsense."[16] He abandons his ideas for small farm cooperatives, new housing and hospitals, a cannery or sisal plants—and instead signs onto secret plans to take over public lands and build a conference center, casino, private airfield, and golf course—a playground for the Fortune 500.

Mirroring Primus's role, Sandy Lawson is the hand-picked candidate of the banks and the chamber of commerce in the United States.[17] Like Triunion's shantytowns, Midland City is a place of "abandoned factories and warehouses and defunct train lines, weed-choked vacant lots, junkyards, crumbling buildings and decay."[18] Lawson is estranged from the grassroots community worker Mae Ryland for approving the new expressway that will enable people in the suburbs to get to their downtown jobs and cut through Mae's ward, the poorest one, " 'just like we ain't even here.' " Paule's image of Sandy's capitulation to white control is a striking picture of the unmarked presence of white power. From her car, Ursa looks up and observes Sandy walking down the steep, wide steps of the towering, new, glass-enclosed city hall building, shouldered by two white men, both talking to him as he turns his head from one to the other, "back and forth like someone at a tennis match," all three laughing, Lawson, the black puppet, controlled by an anonymous force in a silent film directed by men "whose white faces and dark suits look almost interchangeable."[19]

If the black masculine subject is imprisoned in his own country, Paule meant for her women to be liberated. Those rebellions begin with Estelle, who raises her daughter Ursa to be free of the strictures of gender, race, and class. In opposition to Primus, Estelle dresses Ursa in overalls, combs her hair into an Afro that the conservative servant Celestine disdains as a "Black Power" hairdo, and invites the poor "doormouth" neighborhood children to play with Ursa to counteract her sense of privilege. Estelle teaches Ursa about the rebel hero Congo Jane, the one-breasted Amazon figure who led a slave rebellion, sends her daughter to the United States to attend a liberal college, and is proud that her daughter does not choose "baby-making as her life's work."[20] Estelle is Paule's ideal mother.

Ursa's friend Viney foments a rebellion that allowed Paule to gesture toward representing a lesbian relationship. Viney confronts her lover Willis Jenkins when she discovers his relationship with the man in the apartment one floor below. She then sells her apartment in Manhattan, buys and rehabs a run-down brownstone in Brooklyn, gets pregnant by artificial insemination—"the closest you can get to an immaculate conception"—and bears a son she names Robeson in honor of the most famous black leftist man in U.S. history. *Daughters* includes an invisible lesbian network. When Robeson is unlawfully arrested, Viney tells Ursa that she has called their old college friend Sharon, a child psychologist who lives with her lover Margaret, to intercede. In this intimate and queerly constructed family, Ursa maintains her own room in Viney's house, her "safe harbor," and together they parent Robeson and an "adopted" daughter DeeDee, an impoverished neighborhood child. When Ursa and Viney travel together to Triunion, two women there, Astral and Malvern, speculate that Viney and Ursa may be "wickers," a slang Caribbean term for lesbians: "She [Ursa] only came down that last time with this woman, this tall something in a pair of sunglasses that took up half her face. For all you know, they might be two good wickers you see them there. The wick of the lamp might be all they care about. The only thing to satisfy them. They might not have any uses for a man."[21] The older woman Malvern surprises Astral by affirming same-sex intimacy as "modern" and blessing the relationship between Ursa and Viney as "God-made": "Is the modern times. Everybody doing as they feel to and saying to hell with whoever don't like it. And who's to say, maybe those women God made so have the right idea. At least they don't wake up one morning and find themselves saddled with a head of children draining every ounce of their strength and their life gone. That's one thing you can say for them."[22]

The British cover of the 2004 Serpent Tail's edition of *Daughters* suggests that even the novel's vague gesture toward lesbianism did not go undetected. The two women on the cover, representing Ursa and Viney, are seated close together, one behind the other. The first woman, wearing trousers with suspenders and a T-shirt, gazes apprehensively into the distance, while the slim woman in a flowered dress standing behind her, her arm thrown over the first woman's shoulder and casually resting on her breast, stares, with a sultry and knowing gaze, directly into the camera. The title, handwritten in cursive above the two women, extends the mystery Paule intended—are they sisters or friends or lovers?

The cover of the 2004 Serpent Tail edition of *Daughters* features two women representing the fictional Ursa and Viney.

Ursa's renunciation of her role as the daughter of privilege begins with an abortion in an elegant West 58th Street clinic. In opposition to her father's ambitions for her, she not only refuses motherhood, she also leaves her corporate job and her Park West Village apartment, sells her furniture and car, cancels her health club membership, and washes out the relaxer in her hair. She takes a job with a nonprofit to do a study of the mayoral race in small, mostly black and poor Midland City. Battle-ready, Ursa flies to Triunion, where she and her mother Estelle conspire to defeat Primus in the upcoming election. The two women deliver the secret resort plans to Primus's opponent, the revolutionary Justin Beaufils (his name meaning "good son"), whose egalitarian marriage to a woman agronomist parallels that of the nineteenth-century Triunion rebels Congo Jane and Will Cudjoe. Through the intervention of his wife and his daughter, Primus is defeated at the polls and never becomes prime minister.[23]

Paule's promise that *Daughters* would be a roman à clef that would unlock secrets about her relationship to her father Sam Burke was unfulfilled. Paule left that mystery intact, but the hint of sexuality between father and daughter, recalled in Ursa's childhood memories of swimming in the pool at her father's resort is unmistakable. In one scene, Primus stands over Ursa at the side of the pool, his head and body "eclipsing the sun." Annoyed with him, the child pulls the water "like a blanket over her head," dives to the bottom of the pool, and sits there "to impress, tease, and frighten him a little."[24] The second pool scene occurs as Ursa is standing next to her father's mistress Astral—again, her father's head is described as blocking the sun. In the third pool scene, Ursa's thoughts of Primus become confused with the trip up to West 58th Street for an abortion.[25] In the fourth pool scene, Ursa remembers the annoyance and anger she felt when Primus's body blocked her from seeing "the trees or even a patch of sky."[26] These are images of sexual dominance: the child pulling the blanket over her head, trying to hide underground, the man's large body overhead blocking access to the outer world, the child's feelings of complicity in his erotic play. At the end of the novel when she finally encounters Primus's mistress Astral, Ursa maintains that she loved her father as much as Astral did, adding cryptically, "and in the same way perhaps as this woman."[27]

Paule created a similar eroticism between father and daughter in *Brown Girl, Brownstones.* When Deighton beats his daughter Selina, she is "aware only of his body against hers, his muscles moving smoothly under his skin as he flailed her, and his heaving chest crushed against hers. She had been fused with him; not only had he breathed for her but his heart had beaten for the both."[28] We know that in *Daughters* Primus exerts a kind of control over Ursa that disrupts her romance with her lover Lowell, but *Daughters* never shows Ursa directly confronting her father.[29] She finally admits to herself that her relationship with her father interfered with her relationship with the man in her life, and she joins her mother to engineer Primus's political defeat, putting his opponent, the young radical Justin Beaufils, in office. Overthrowing her father politically thus becomes a substitute for a direct confrontation about his sexual domination. Ursa's emancipation from her father's seductions remains in the margins, overwritten by the story of his election defeat. Paule never gives us the key that would unlock the mystery of Ursa's eroticized relationship with Primus or hers with Sam Burke.

When interviewer Daryl Dance asked Paule if *Daughters* could be considered a "feminist statement," Paule was at great pains to elude the term *feminist:* "Whatever feminist note is struck in the novel is not meant to obscure what I hope will be seen as a major theme in *Daughters:* the need for black men and women to come together in wholeness and unity."[30] That disavowal undercut the struggle of Paule's fictional women to free themselves from patriarchal structures—"Little girl of all the daughters, / you ain't no more slave"—but it also deflected attention from the serious trauma they experienced as women. Paule's statements implied that communal bonds are based primarily on heterosexual unions and that women's fight against male domination and struggles for equality might hinder or endanger those bonds. Quite the contrary: affective communities in *Daughters* are not dissolved because the women emancipate themselves; their struggles against the corruptions of patriarchy are what begin to heal the community.[31]

The reviews of *Daughters* rolled out one after another in all the major mainstream venues—all deeming the novel "a triumph." Reviewers called it "flawless in its sense of place and character," "remarkable in its understanding of human nature," Paule's "most ambitious, mature, and sharply political" novel. Uniformly glowing, these were the first reviews that put Paule's fiction in the context of her entire body of work, showing that she had achieved enormous technical maturity.[32] They marvel at the intricate structure of the novel in its layering of past and present.[33] They comment on the skill with which she orchestrates multiple women characters, showing them gaining personal and political independence. All the reviewers noted the honesty with which Paule interrogated the ambivalence of the black middle class as people of privilege living "at the increasingly compromised center of political power."[34] How, Paule asks in *Daughters,* does this upwardly mobile generation make itself useful to those who are still struggling? The *New York Times* named *Daughters* "a brave book," "a triumph in every way," and included it in the list of the "notable books of 1991."[35] None commented on the lesbian theme.

Paule would need one more book to free herself from Sam B., and she did so in her next and final novel, *The Fisher King,* through the main character Hattie Carmichael, a foster child, whose mother Dawn Carmichael is confined to a state mental hospital. Hattie, the "city child," drifts from one foster home to another, eventually becoming a writer, performer, and one part of a sexual triangle she initiates. Hattie's father remains unnamed, fictionally nonexistent. Hattie is known only as the daughter of Dawn, the freest character Paule would ever create.

Paule's move to Richmond, Virginia, in 1984 was another step on her freedom tour. She turned out three of her books during her years in Richmond: *Daughters, The Fisher King,* and her memoir *Triangular Road.* Aside from brief sojourns in Manhattan, she lived there for the rest of her life. Paule's friends were openly skeptical about her move. At a conference in Trinidad, her sophisticated friend Cliff Lashley, a professor at the University of the West Indies, a man with "a merciless tongue that could do untold damage," was scandalized that she was not only living in a backwater like Virginia but actually buying a condo there. "Oh," he said, scathingly, "I see, darling. You've gone into semi-retirement." Her financial advisor Aaron Smith was also baffled that this "star" of the literary world had landed in a place like Richmond: "It seemed too small for her."[36] Another colleague, Mill Harris, Paule's wealth manager, could not understand why she would leave her lovely Manhattan apartment and cosmopolitan New York for the center of the Confederacy.

Publicly, Paule said she went to Richmond because she needed a job that was more stable than recurring visiting positions. The opening occurred when Paule's friend Daryl Dance, writer and scholar of folklore and Caribbean culture at Virginia Commonwealth University (VCU), nominated her for the Visiting Commonwealth Professor series. Initiated in the wake of black student demands for more black faculty, the series was part of a statewide equal opportunity program to attract "distinguished scholars" to Virginia public colleges and universities. Others recruited for the series were writers Nikki Giovanni, Maryse Condé, Joanne Gabbin, and the musician Ellis Marsalis, Jr., Paule was offered an untenured two-year visiting position—another in a long list of such contracts—in the creative writing program at VCU. She agreed to a one-semester schedule, teaching two writing classes in the fall, on leave in the spring, at a salary of $25,000 with a $10,000 allocation for travel, secretarial support, and other related expenses.[37]

Founded in 1968, the year Martin Luther King was assassinated, VCU was trying to establish its identity as an urban research university while at the same time grappling with the Vietnam War protests and rebellions and racial issues specific to Richmond, a southern city with a history of massive resistance to integration. In their history of VCU, John T. Kneebone and Eugene Trani, who became president of the university in 1990, looked back at VCU's racial history and noted that it "lagged . . . badly . . . in hiring black faculty and administrators." Even as late as 1979, then VCU president Edmund Ackell, who was worried about the effects of urbanization—meaning blacks and nonconforming hippies—warned that if "conservative Richmond" people see students wearing jeans or with long hair, or see " 'a black and white [student] walking together,' they could get 'the wrong impressions about the institution.' "[38] Black students expressed their dissatisfaction with the racial climate and attitudes like Ackell's in the campus newspaper: "It's time to address the seemingly racist administration here at VCU and to inform them that their mission to eliminate, destroy, discriminate and deprive the blacks on campus, is indeed impossible despite the deceit, lies and fallible master plan."[39]

The Visiting Commonwealth Professor series and Paule's appointment were signs of change. Her office on the third floor of the Hibbs Building facing the James Branch Cabell Library was centrally located on campus, although Paule spent very little time there except for classes and appointments and occasionally meeting Daryl for tea in the Hibbs lounge. She was a writer and not much interested in the minutiae of academic life or politics. Richard Fine, the associate chair during Paule's tenure, remembered her as a colleague who always did her teaching and other work in the department effectively and without complaint, but one who set boundaries with students and with the administration: "I'm also from the North (in my case, Boston), so I understood and appreciated Paule's frankness and her directness in setting those limits, which was always done graciously but firmly."[40]

As usual, she scouted out the kind of apartment that suited her, a spacious condo on the second floor of a lovely old-style southern building, where she hosted gatherings with her students and friends. Apartment #6 at 503 South Davis sported a large front balcony overlooking Byrd Park and Fountain Lake, renowned for its perpetual fountain that changed colors at night. Paule was, of course, tuned into the backstory of William Byrd Park, named for a notorious owner and abuser of enslaved people. At first, the Confederate statues lining Monument Avenue and the occasional performances of actors dressed in Scarlett O'Hara hoop skirts or Confederate uniforms were a constant reminder that Richmond was a part of the antebellum South, but Paule looked to Richmond as a place "to decelerate." She valued the peacefulness and quiet at her condo facing the lake, where she could focus and do her work. "My dear," she told her friend Norrece T. Jones, a historian and colleague at VCU, "I look at this as buying part of the park."[41]

In the summer of 1992, when Paule was sixty-three, the telephone call came that changed her life and career. Paule had just hung up from talking with a friend in Paris and was working on an article for the *New York Times* when the phone rang at precisely 2:32 p.m. There was a pleasant voice at the other end, Sara Lawrence-Lightfoot, a professor at Harvard, who had recently been elected chair of the MacArthur Board. Lightfoot was calling to inform Paule that the foundation had just concluded its annual meeting to select the year's recipients, and that the winners had been declared. Lightfoot suggested that "if I wasn't sitting down, I might want to do so because as of two o'clock that afternoon I had become a MacArthur Fellow for life." Paule described her reaction as "dumbstruck silence," especially after Lightfoot informed her that she would receive a rather tidy sum well into the six figures, a large grant because of her age. "I was never so glad of my sixty odd years." As a fellow, Paule would be provided with one of the most comprehensive health insurance plans in the country, paid for by the foundation. She barely heard Lightfoot's concluding words: "Let me be the first to congratulate you, Ms. Marshall." When Paule finally managed to reach Evan in London with the news, he first tried to be restrained, telling her, "Now, Ma, take it easy. I always knew it would happen." Then he started whooping and Paule couldn't get him to stop. "You could hear him across the heavens via satellite," Paule recalled.

Once Paule received the MacArthur award, the university predictably latched onto it for publicity and fund-raising purposes. Professor Fine recognized that Paule understood the game and was willing to play along with it, agreeing to interviews and a few events or meetings with potential donors, but declining all offers to socialize privately with wealthy donors, gracious but firm in deflecting any attempts to exploit her winning of the MacArthur. On one occasion, at a lunch in the President's House that included Fine, the university president Eugene Trani, and Paule, a potential donor invited her to a cocktail party at their house, and she declined graciously, saying that she was a hermit at the moment and needed all her time for the book she was working on. Fine sympathized with her situation: "As an aging white male, I can now only imagine how many different obstacles she needed to negotiate in those situations, especially thirty years ago and in the South." But Paule was comfortable in her own skin and, according to Fine, she tried to meet people where they were without compromising her core beliefs. "I really admired the way that she dealt with the demands VCU placed on her time—deftly and with great tact and integrity."[42]

A year later, in 1993, Paule was nominated for and won VCU's Distinguished Scholar/Artist Award. Glowing letters from the top scholars in the field of African American literature—Houston Baker, Paula Giddings, Trudier Harris, and Henry Louis Gates, Jr.—came in support of Paule. President Trani wrote of the university's pride in an illustrious faculty member: "It was a great honor to have Dr. Paule Marshall as a member of the faculty of Virginia Commonwealth University for 10 years, 1984–1994, and she was a greatly valued member of our university community for two years before she joined the faculty as Writer in Residence. It was a personal honor for me, as President of Virginia Commonwealth University, to bestow upon Dr. Marshall the Distinguished Scholarship Award in 1994, at VCU's Commencement Ceremony."[43] In her support letter, Berkeley professor Barbara Christian, one of the earliest Paule Marshall scholars, agreed with Trani that VCU should consider itself the honoree: "She is one of our great New World writers. Your granting of your Distinguished Arts and Scholar Award [to Paule Marshall] will lend honor to your University."

Paule made few public comments about VCU. One compared it to Iowa, Berkeley, Yale, and Columbia as "far less prestigious," a sign perhaps of her resentment of her treatment at VCU or her dislike of teaching—or her elitism.[44] She felt that it was only after winning the MacArthur Fellowship in 1992 that her VCU colleagues became noticeably friendlier: "People on the faculty who had been very snooty," she told a friend, "would now exclaim 'Our wonderful Paule Marshall.' "[45] Alvin Schexnider, the associate dean for academic affairs, provided a black administrator's view: "We knew she was a catch; there was no one else on the faculty of her caliber, and she was probably the highest paid faculty in the department. She was also very private, a warm spirit, collegial, and, for a person of her stature, accessible and approachable. She represented her craft and herself as a strong black woman well. Frankly, I thought she walked on water."[46] Here's that duality again—the warm spirit, apparently accessible, but so apart from everyone that she seemed as remote and unreachable as a goddess.

If Paule set limits on the time she spent in department work or academic politics, she was very much involved with her students in the writing program. One of Paule's former MA students at VCU, Bert Ashe, now a professor at the University of Richmond and the author of a memoir, *Twisted: My Dreadlock Chronicles,* remembers that in Paule's writing workshops she was the no-nonsense, tough truth-teller. They discussed two stories at the once-a-week session, with the author instructed not to talk but to listen to a conversation about his or her story, including both compliments and criticism, and let the story speak for itself. Unlike some creative writing teachers, Paule was the authority in the room; she refused to allow the "always-talkers" to dominate and encouraged the silent ones to join in. To Bert, "she was a fascinating combination of being thoughtful and engaging while also pointedly leading the discussion so that everyone in the room could apply the commentary to their own compositional efforts."[47] Once she related an anecdote about her relationship to Langston Hughes, about the years when she was the apprentice and Hughes was the mentor and teacher, urging her to write more. To Bert, that moment felt "magical"—"to have a *legend* at the front of the table, referring to another *legend*."[48]

Erica Vital-Lazare, now a published writer and professor at the College of Southern Nevada, headed to VCU when she discovered that Paule was doing a reading on campus. After the reading she stood at the end of the line, too much in awe to approach the famous author. Paule waved her up, signed her book, asked if she wrote, and said, "Send me something." Erica sent a few short stories and a novel, and Paule secured a place in the graduate school program and a teaching fellowship for her so that she did not have to pay tuition for graduate studies. "I had that kind of support, but was she tough on me? Her notes were tough, but she gave you room to find your way." In the "salons" she held in her office and at her home, mostly for the black students, Erica recalls, "We sat at her feet. We had tea. When I got married in a little park, she was there. She came over the bridge to Hampton to have barbecue with my mother and me on the Fourth of July, and when I had my first child, she stopped in Las Vegas on her way to California to bring a gift. Whatever I do it's because of the spirit of that woman calling me over and asking me if I were a writer."[49]

Students in her undergraduate classes knew that Paule was a "big deal" outside of VCU and were somewhat intimidated. Mary Lou Hall, now an associate professor at VCU, remembered that undergraduates thought she was "snooty and rigid." Then, at some point in the semester, she invited her undergraduate creative writing class to her apartment, and Hall discovered that "it was fun to see her warm up and treat us differently. That night humanized her for me."[50]

In informal meetings with students such as the Richmond Black Writers Group, who met at each other's homes, the power dynamic was different—Paule was one of the community. She often hosted her end-of-the-year get-togethers on the Saturday or Sunday after commencement at her apartment overlooking the park. In 1991, when Bert's wife Valerie was "tumblin' big" with their first child, Bert recalled Paule seeing them off at the door as he joked about the absurdity of the OB-GYN predicting the exact due date of the birth. When Val turned to say goodbye, Paule suddenly extended her hands, and "with a light in her eyes, placed one hand on each side of Val's belly, threw back her head, and offered a loud and exultant 'Ahhhhhhhhhh—LIFE!!!' " They all laughed, and baby Jordan, born on the exactly assigned due date, delighted Paule: " 'Yup. She's arrived on time. Ready to take care of business!' " Bert felt that Paule was absolutely the best role model a graduate student could ask for: "She had a wonderful way of threading the needle between serious, fiction-seminar engagement and relaxed and pleasant hostess."[51] Bert, Erica, and Mary Lou were among the students she included in her intimate circles. As always, your view of Paule Marshall depended on where you were standing.

Paule's social self was on full display in Richmond. She joined Habitat for Humanity, doing hands-on work helping to build houses. A serious walker and health advocate, she was in walking distance of all the boutiques, cafés, and stores in the artsy area of Cary Street. She loved shopping at Ellwood Thompson's organic market on N. Thompson Street, where she bought the ingredients she needed for her rigorous regime of healthy eating. She dined at many of the restaurants on Cary Street, including the CanCan Brasserie for dinner. She saw *Who's Afraid of Virginia Woolf* at the Firehouse Theater. Slowing down from the hectic pace of Manhattan allowed her to "unburden myself of a lot of negative programming and work on my inner being," and she saw herself becoming a happier, more relaxed, and younger person even as "I became a Gray Panther."[52]

Paule was invited everywhere in black Richmond, a rich and satisfying social life made possible largely because of Professor Daryl Dance, who had contacts in the cultural, political, social, and academic circles of Richmond. Their friendship began when Daryl nominated her for the Commonwealth Professorship at VCU and lasted for the rest of Paule's life. That friendship is documented in Daryl's memoir *Remembering Paule: A Photo Memoir of Her Richmond Years,* in which Daryl assembled the photographs and announcements and invitations of Paule's Richmond years. Paule and Daryl went to movies, restaurants, lectures, and university events, sometimes reading their work together, often with Daryl driving the reluctant driver Paule. They traveled together to the African Americans in Europe Conference at the Université de Paris III. With Paule's entrée to black expatriate literary circles in Paris, she took Daryl to visit Richard Wright's Paris home and other African American expatriate hangouts. Paule sent postcards to Daryl whenever she was traveling and brought back a lovely Haitian folk painting for her. They were together at Howard University in 1995 when Howard established the Sterling A. Brown Chair, which included a memorable after-party with Toni Morrison and Toni Cade Bambara in Washington, DC, at Howard professor Eleanor Traylor's house, followed by brunch the next morning at James Baldwin's mother's house in DC.[53] When Daryl traveled to Barbados, Paule put her in touch with the widow of the first Barbadian prime minister. In 2007, they traveled together to Baltimore to celebrate the thirtieth anniversary of the founding of the literary journal *Callaloo.* Daryl invited Paule to celebrate with her family at many holidays and considered Paule a part of her family.

Daryl's memoir shows Paule's life intersecting seamlessly with both African American and Caribbean communities in

Richmond. Along with events sponsored by the Association of Jamaicans in Richmond and an annual Christmas party sponsored by Trinidadians, Daryl's memoir pictures Paule at several African American venues: the Elam Baptist Church, occasional parties at the home of Wendy and Randy Johnson, the African Americans in Europe International Conference, Women's Day at the Koinonia Independent Methodist Church, VCU's African American Alumni Council Black History Month Reception, the African and African American Writers and Their Communities conference at the University of Richmond, and the Wintergreen Women Writers' Collective. Black literary and cultural groups in Richmond, those who read and appreciated Paule's work, and African American and Caribbean people reached out to her, and for nearly thirty years embraced her warmly in their circles.

Throughout the photo memoir, Daryl tried to understand the dynamics of what was a close yet perplexing thirty-year relationship. Despite her own social and professional status—she had written a supporting letter for Paule's MacArthur award and helped to get her the position at VCU—Daryl thought of herself as a kind of disciple to Paule, much as Paule was to Langston Hughes, and she struggled to find the terms to describe their friendship, vacillating between *close friends, congenial friends, not chums, not soul sisters, not confidants, not intimates.* They traveled together, but Paule never shared any family secrets. Daryl settled on a consoling explanation: Paule was "a dedicated writer married to her craft."[54]

Norrece Jones, a professor of history at VCU, shared Paule's love of art and music and became another close friend. He would later be on call when she began to show signs of dementia. He was Paule's companion on visits to the Virginia Museum of Fine Arts and at the museum's jazz performances. He helped to celebrate her birthday at the Crossroads, a club in Richmond, with music, dancing, and a live band, and was pleasantly surprised that Paule was comfortable in such a casual, down-home setting. When Paule secured an invitation for Toni Morrison to do a reading at VCU, Norrece agreed, at Paule's request, to host the after-party at his apartment. Paule's anxiety over party preparations precipitated an encounter that revealed something about her prickliness to what she considered slights. During the gathering, probably due to her own anxiety, Paule began giving orders that Norrece felt were somewhat presumptuous and he became offended. She was miffed and chose to distance herself from him after the party. When they finally agreed to talk about the incident, Paule took Norrece's hand and warmly offered her apology: "It was just a peacock feather," she confessed, a metaphor for her rare diva performance.[55]

In contrast to the ease of Paule's friendship with Norrece and Daryl, it took years for Toni Cooper, a white divorced mother and Paule's neighbor across the hall at the South Davis condo, to break through the walls Paule erected. Toni became one of Paule's running buddies and eventually a close friend. They shared an interest in the arts and attended events at the Virginia Museum of Fine Arts and went to movies together. Toni enjoyed Paule for her sense of humor, her intellectual interests, and as an available partner for movies, museums, dinner, social events, and long walks, but what moved them beyond neighbors was Toni's association (as a volunteer) with the Elegba Folklore Society and the Friends of African and African American Art at the Museum.

Toni, who thought of Paule as "a grand lady," seemed sure that race never played a part in their relationship, even though Paule's sharp comments belie that blithe assumption. The fact that two of Toni's boyfriends were black produced this reaction from Paule: "Why the attraction to black men?" she wanted to know. Once when they were discussing another racial issue, Paule reminded Toni, "You always wake up with your white self," chiding her for not recognizing her white privilege. Toni could not recall her response to any of this "race talk," but she did remember that when they were at the Richmond Museum and encountered a group of Links, an exclusive social club for prominent and professional black women, Paule told Toni she understood why the Links was a blacks-only organization: "Whites excluded them and now they are not interested in integration."[56]

In 1987 Paule was invited to the inaugural retreat of the Wintergreen Women Writers' Collective. Founded by James Madison University professor Joanne Gabbin to welcome poet Nikki Giovanni as Distinguished University Professor at Virginia Tech, the retreat was meant to be a buffer against the kind of chilly reception that Gabbin had experienced at James Madison. One of the Wintergreen women, Carmen Gillespie, called it "a balm for the brutality of the dangerous spaces women writers occupy."[57] Daryl drove Paule to the retreat, being held a little over an hour from Richmond in the Blue Ridge Mountains. The original ten participants were Joanne Gabbin, Nikki Giovanni, Trudier Harris, Mary T. Harper, Sandra Y. Govan, Opal Moore, Daryl Dance, Paule, and two graduate students, Carmen Gillespie and Catherine Rogers. Originally intended only for scholars in Virginia, those who were just over the border in North Carolina clamored to be invited. People floated in and out, but the regulars—Daryl, Opal, Sandy, Trudier, and Joanne—usually attended every year. Over thirty-seven years, sixty-five women came to Wintergreen.

Although Paule attended only once, she was considered a founding member, a Wintergreen Woman, and a model member for participating in all of the activities. She was in wonderful physical shape, even though, at fifty-eight, she was one of the oldest members. Arriving for Wintergreen's traditional morning walk in a chic brown velvet jogging suit, she led the walk from the

Peddler's Edge House up to the Summit at the height of the resort, beating everyone up the hill. Joanne confessed that "even though she was twenty years older than I was, I was huffin' and puffin' up that hill."[58] Trudier Harris also remembered how Paule outwalked almost everyone: "I thought I was a fast walker—and I am—but Paule challenged me. I was shocked that that skinny little woman could walk as fast as I did. She told me that when she went walking in Barbados, little kids would point to her and shout, 'Soldat! Soldat!' "[59] Along with her Wintergreen colleagues, Paule read her work, and when the filming of a video was cut short when a bear came wandering across the porch, "Paule was running and screaming with the rest of us." An expert swimmer, Paule joined the women in the pool, her hair always expertly coiffed. Joanne and a few others suspected she was wearing a wig, but she wore a bathing cap over it and never let anyone see her without it, never uttering a word about the alopecia she developed in her thirties. To Joanne, Paule was "one of the sweetest spirits that ever came to the Wintergreen collective."[60] With the keen sense of a poet, Opal Moore observed that "Paule was always gracious, serious—and circumspect."[61] Although Paule enjoyed the experience at Wintergreen, she never returned.

Joanne asked Paule to contribute to the 2009 collection of essays by each of the Wintergreen writers about a defining moment in her life. Entitled *Shaping Memories: Reflections of African American Women Writers,* these are deeply personal essays about growing up black and female, about racism in the universities, about family, physical disability, friendships, their love of writing, their commitment to work, and their experiences at Wintergreen. Joanne described the final text as a vision of the souls of black women.[62]

Paule's contribution to the Wintergreen collection was an excerpt from the 1973 essay "Shaping the World of My Art," a recycled essay that returns to the mother-poets who influenced her writing as she was growing up in the Bajan Brooklyn community. It features the thirty-year-old Paule Marshall writing about the ten-year-old Pauline Burke, forgoing the opportunity to say something about the seventy-something Paule Marshall. Joanne was disappointed, but she accepted this older piece because she didn't want to leave Paule out of a communal endeavor. "She was very kind to me," Joanne remembered. "We cared about each other. She was also a very private person. She never said to me, 'Joanne, you must come and visit me.' I never asked her about her ex-husbands, which is unusual for me. With my girlfriends, I usually know about that the second time we meet." Paule was a presence, a supporter, "a sweet spirit," but still private, elusive, maintaining, as always, a lock on the door to her interior world.[63]

Like many in her life, Paule's son Evan remembers this guarded person, outwardly gregarious but private, someone who was never lost without company. "She didn't need flattery or a shoulder to cry on, and, somewhat like me, she quite easily retreated and felt more comfortable in her solitude, thinking about her work. To her friends, Paule was always a bit distant and reserved, hard to figure out, perhaps a bit superior, not into emotional drama, never giving the full intensity of her life."[64]

Against this portrait of a remote, distant Paule, there are many others of her as sociable, generous, kind, and thoughtful. David Sutton, Evan's friend from childhood and the son of Paule's close Manhattan friend, NYU anthropologist Connie Sutton, had a singular view of her. Connie and Paule became mothers around the same time and became godmothers to each other's sons, so when David attended Walden School on Central Park West, he would often walk the few blocks after school to 407 where he would stay with Paule until someone picked him up, or he'd spend the night. He loved Paule's cooking—stir-fry chicken and cold Asian noodle salad—and especially her strange health food dishes, such as a pudding dessert made with blended tofu and peanut butter served over fresh apple sauce. Many evenings after Evan went off to boarding school, it was just David and Paule, times when she read aloud poems like Yeats's "Sailing to Byzantium" and gave him tips on how to read Irish poetry and James Joyce. For his college graduation, Paule gave him a monographed suitcase, urging him on to future travels, and when he was working on his book on food and memory, she gave him a set of madeleine cookies in reference to Proust's famous encounter.[65] She bought his daughter James McBride's *The Color of Water* and Edwidge Danticat's *Breath, Eyes, Memory,* two of her favorites. The warmth of David's feelings for Paule are clear in his memory of the firm but gentle person he called his "other mother," an artist who sometimes had to retreat but someone David always felt "was *there,* not somewhere else" as some artists can be.[66]

CHAPTER 10

The New Generation

IN 1994, NEW YORK UNIVERSITY offered Paule the distinguished Helen Gould Sheppard Professorship in Literature and Culture, a position she would hold until she retired in 2008. Sheppard, whose wealth was inherited from a notorious nineteenth-century robber baron father, was a philanthropist and contributor to NYU as well as a devout Christian fundamentalist, vice president of the segregationist Daughters of the American Revolution, and such an ardent anti-Communist activist that she feared the "Reds" might come after her. Paule did not decline the professorship, even if the donor's name might have been offensive. She did, however, resist NYU's offer of one of the ordinary faculty apartments. Designed by modern architects I. M. Pei and James Ingo Freed, they were, in Paule's savvy view of New York real estate, too plain, "with nothing to arrest the eye," she told writer Edwidge Danticat.[1]

Paule was determined to hold out for one of the older prewar apartments owned by NYU, with high ceilings, large rooms, floor-to-ceiling bookshelves, and fireplace. After some negotiations with NYU, she finally got one of the coveted apartments at 37 Washington Square overlooking the park and a tiny portion of the Hudson River. When Danticat, who would eventually join her in NYU's creative writing department, asked how she had nabbed her fabulous apartment, Paule said that when the dean asked her what kind of apartment she would like, she "looked around his lavish office and said, 'Something like this will do.' "[2]

Paule had an enviable teaching schedule at NYU. She taught her courses in the fall and headed back to Richmond after the Christmas break to devote the spring and summer to writing. She and famed novelist E. L. Doctorow were the two permanent professors in the Creative Writing Program, located at 18 University Place until 2007, when entrepreneur Lillian Vernon donated the Creative Writing Building at 58 W. 10th Street in Greenwich Village. Doctorow's fame meant that he commanded the big office on the second floor. Paule netted a lovely corner walk-up office on the third floor. Paule particularly admired Doctorow's novel *World's Fair,* which she called a "beautifully done book about growing up Jewish in the Bronx"—and Doctorow saw to it that Paule and Evan had front-row tickets to the Broadway hit *Ragtime,* based on his 1975 novel.[3]

Galway Kinnell, the leading poet in the program, was passionate about attracting working people, so classes were taught at night so that people who worked during the day could attend. Poet Sharon Olds pointed out that the creative writing faculty also valued diversity. She remembered one semester in which the program attracted students from all seven continents, so there was daunting competition for admission—maybe twenty places for seven hundred or more applicants. Olds, who now occupies Paule's office on the third floor of the 10th Street Building, had been in awe when she met Paule: "I remember her as a person with a subtle vivacity. She had a willingness and eagerness to meet the day, a willingness to participate—a favorite quality of mine. People loved her classes. I was astonished at what she had accomplished. When I think of her, I sit up a little straighter."[4]

Paule taught both the Writing Workshop in Fiction and The Craft of Short Fiction class, and students remembered her, as they did at VCU, as the undisputed authority in the room. You can almost hear that authority in her teaching notes. She defined the writing workshop as a place to learn the "nuts and bolts. Technique. To increase your skill and confidence in handling and manipulating the elements of fiction." She insisted that her students read widely, and in her craft class on the short story, she introduced them to a variety of writers, including Ernest Hemingway, Flannery O'Connor, Franz Kafka, Yukio Mishima, Ursula Le Guin, John Cheever, Louise Erdrich, and Bobbie Ann Mason. She defended her inclusion of John Barth's postmodern short story collection, *Lost in the Funhouse,* saying, "I thought I'd give you a taste of the avant-garde, so you can't accuse me of being a hidebound conservative—I encourage students to take chances, to be wild and way out." She also warned students about the limitations of writing courses: "What I can't teach: the gift. Habit of art. Someone on whom no experience is lost. Possibilities. Hidden meaning. Good eye. Vision."

Poet and memoirist Shamar Hill took both the craft class and the workshop in 2002 and welcomed Paule's toughness: "It might be hard to hear it, but it forced you to grow. Some professors were very gentle, would only tell you what was working. She was not unnecessarily tough. She wanted us to have the drive to make the work better. She wanted us to have a sense of wonder. She was the first black female writing teacher I ever had, and I am sure she was the only black woman teaching in the writing program. She had a fierceness, but she also laughed a lot."[5]

The students like Hill who saw Paule outside of class saw a completely different side of her. Hill remembered that in private meetings, "she was much gentler, trying to support you in a different way." At the end of the semester, she invited students to her apartment and afterward she took them to an Italian restaurant, the North Square. In contrast to the view of Paule as an intensely private person, Hill saw her as the life of the party. "She was a ball of energy. I had no idea how old she was, but she had the energy of someone much younger than she was. There was a kind of humor and wisdom she brought to the seriousness about the work—a lot like being black. I really did adore her."[6]

Among her students was John Keene, later a MacArthur winner himself and the author of *Annotations,* an experimental autobiography about growing up in St. Louis; *Counternarratives,* an exhilarating collection of postmodernist historical fiction; and *Punk,* a National Book Award–winning volume of poetry. Keene, who first encountered Paule in 1995, used the word *proper* to describe her, adding, "She was an incisive reader and editor, but also generous and warm in her own way." He submitted a story for the workshop, "My Son, My Heart, My Life," about a queer preteen struggling with his sexual identity and was unsure how Paule would receive it. She "took it in stride," Keene wrote, and with her excellent editing, he was able to get it published while still in graduate school.[7] Keene acknowledged Paule's influence on his fiction and lamented the absence of critical attention to her work. He felt both a conscious and unconscious relationship with his former professor's work, explaining that his experimental and autobiographical first novel *Annotations* "might be an African American queer man's post-modern rejoinder to *Brown Girl, Brownstones.*" His collection of stories, *Counternarratives,* is in conversation with *Soul Clap Hands and Sing,* a collection that Keene says "dazzled me" with "a daring that really has not been accounted for in our critical literature."[8] Paule's story "Brazil" in *Soul Clap Hands,* which focuses on a black comic-minstrel entertainer, finds its counterpart in Keene's story "Cold," a fictional account of the suicide of Bob Cole, a minstrel performer in the United States at the turn of the twentieth century. This literary kinship between Paule and Keene—both historians of complex and heterogeneous blackness—highlights Paule's imprint, mostly unacknowledged, on modern and postmodern black literary history.[9]

Paule put her imprint on twenty-first-century U.S. cultural history in another unlikely direction. Ben Rhodes, twenty-two and fresh out of college, enrolled in her writing workshop in the fall of 2000 with plans for a writing career. Paule encouraged Ben to move from the constraints of the short story to a novel in order to experiment with the lives of the other characters, not just his own. The values she preached as a creative writer were the ones she lived by—inclusivity, trying to inhabit the worlds and perspectives of different people, particularly those who had been marginalized or shut out, which was especially important for those students who came from fairly privileged backgrounds like Ben's. She felt the novel was a better form than the short story for that kind of expansiveness. In Ben's later political life—he spent eight years as President Barack Obama's speechwriter and deputy national security advisor—that novel helped him see into the lives of others. (It also came back to haunt him when the right wing discovered he had an unfinished novel in his drawer called "Oasis of Love.")[10]

Ben was so impressed by the modesty of such an important American writer that he began to do some research on her: "Who was this person I was taking this workshop with?"[11] Along with other students in the workshop, he looked for and read *Brown Girl, Brownstones* and discovered the very interesting and fairly radical life Paule had lived. Seeing her in an Afro as a young woman in contrast to the somewhat soft-spoken, kind woman at NYU was an eye-opener. He discovered that she had more credentials in radical politics than a lot of other people at NYU who were more outspoken. She never talked about how important she was, never reminded the students of her extraordinary career, nor did she express any bitterness about not being given the credit or recognition she deserved. She conveyed to Rhodes a sense of someone who was comfortable in her own skin, at peace with herself and with the career she had in spite of the fact that she should have been more celebrated. Ben's evaluation of his experience in Paule's class, in the light of his later closeness to President Obama, would have stunned and delighted Paule:

> She had that aura about her, that kind of lived experience that lent her credibility, but she didn't have to advertise it. The fact her work ended up having this life so that people kept discovering it, returning to it over and over, is a kind of testament to her because she was doing this kind of work before it was trendy. I am not trying to overstate this, but there's something interesting about the fact that my post-university journey started in Paule Marshall's workshop and then I began working for the first black president, helping him to tell stories that were accessible to people—empathy, economy of writing, effective storytelling—all of that is relevant to political communication. I'm proud to be a very tiny part of Paule Marshall's legacy in the world.[12]

When Paule was planning to go on tour after the publication of *The Fisher King* in 2000, she asked Shay Youngblood, author of *Black Girl in Paris,* to teach her writing class at NYU. When Shay began sharing some of her ideas for the class, thinking she should tell the students more about the business of publishing, how to negotiate a contract, and the skills they would need for publication, Paule nodded, then very clearly discouraged that idea. "Disabuse them of the notion of instantaneous fame—top of the *NYT*'s best seller list. Toughen them up so they can stay the course. They need to be able to write, to concentrate on craft. Not everyone has the commitment to writing or the skills. Even if they have the gift, that's not enough: they need discipline, doggedness, cussedness, luck."[13] Shay learned later that she was right.

Paule's recognition of Shay's ability was a turning point: "This is how she helped people like me who did not have a lot of academic or writing models. She set me up in a leadership position, offering me the opportunity to see what I could do. I was deeply affected by the confidence she showed in me." Shay had first met Paule in the pages of *Brown Girl, Brownstones* but never dreamed she would meet her in person. "I was giving a talk on my book *Big Mama Stories* at the National Council of Teachers of English (NCTE) in Atlanta, my first big talk, called 'Educating the Imagination,' and Paule was in the audience. This giant of a person came up and introduced herself and congratulated me on the talk and on my book. Later, when I moved to New York, she invited me to read in the prestigious New Generations series at NYU along with Patricia Powell and Dennis Williams."[14]

Shay understood Paule's personal life was out of bounds, but not her art: "She dressed rather conservatively, kind of like a West Indian librarian but one with a rich inner life. I couldn't imagine her 'cuttin' loose,' though she 'cut loose' in her writing. She might not have known the names of my best friends, but she chose some of us to uplift. She welcomed some of us to the world of writers. It was a kind of an anointing."[15]

Paule also used her position at NYU to shape the field of diaspora studies. Working with Doctorow, photographer Deborah Willis, and cultural critics Clyde Taylor and Manthia Diawara, Paule initiated the Paule Marshall & the New Generation series at NYU to give young writers a platform for their work. For over ten years, the NYU series showcased a diversity of black writers from Africa, the Caribbean, and the United States. Often the newer writers were paired with more well-known ones. The series took place in several elegant New York venues: the Greenberg Lounge of Vanderbilt Hall, 40 Washington Square South; MacDougal & West 4th Streets; or D'Agostino Hall on West 3rd Street. Paule filled those rooms, provided the introductions, and sold their books. This "New Generation," as Paule called her young novelists, included, among others, Colson Whitehead, Danzy Senna, Dennis Williams, Ajumah Kamal, Patricia Powell, Glenville Lovell, AJ Verdelle, Edwidge Danticat, Moses Isegawa, David Anthony Durham, Tayari Jones, Christine Lincoln, Uzodinma Iweala, Mohammed Naseehu Ali, Usem Akpan, Florence Ladd, James McBride, Kwadwo Agymah Kamau, Z Z Packer, Thomas Glave, and Nalo Hopkinson. In December 2006, to celebrate the tenth anniversary of the series, Paule presented three emerging African writers—Uzodinma Iweala, Mohammed Naseehu Ali, and Uwem Akpan —very deliberately using the New Generation series to expand the canon of black writers beyond the United States.

Mel Tapley, the arts and entertainment editor at the *New York Amsterdam News,* covered the first New Generation program at NYU's Greenberg Lounge on a Friday evening in 1995. Tapley knew Paule well enough to lament her twelve-year absence from New York: "She's back and revealing some very promising celebrants of her craft." Tapley was so enthusiastic about her return, he sprinkled mixed metaphors throughout the article, envisioning the event's participants as a wedding party, throwing beautiful, colorful flower petals in front of the bride, clearly inappropriate for the feminist and progressive artists, but also displaying a deep enthusiasm for the writers and respect for Paule. When Paule read portions of *Daughters,* her latest book, Tapley continued to sprinkle metaphors: "It was like releasing butterflies, pretty, winged petals of all colors, into the air."[16] The writers who followed Paule were as excited as Tapley. Edwidge Danticat read from her novel *Krik? Krak!* and was singled out for special attention because she had been nominated for the National Book Award. Shrewd about public recognition, Paule told Danticat that a nomination was just as good as winning the award. Shay Youngblood remembered that she sold fifty books that night. "[Paule] took us out afterwards to an Italian restaurant and was so gracious and warm, making everyone feel comfortable."[17]

At the end of the fall semester, around 1995, Paule headed back to Richmond to work on *The Fisher King*. In her notes, Paule wrote that the theme of *Fisher King* was inspired by three writers: Olaudah Equiano, Ralph Ellison, and James Baldwin, but she signaled her new interest in formal experimentation by naming two visual artists as inspiration, the African American sculptor Martin Puryear and the German impressionist Gabriele Münter. She wanted this new novel to imitate their economy of style, a paring-down that she called "putting a restraining order on myself." Like Puryear's piece *Untitled*, a large black wire mesh form in the shape of a human head, and Münter's Expressionist painting *Girl With Doll*, she wanted *Fisher King* to be enigmatic and mysterious, impressionistic and spare. She also claimed that the novel's inconclusive ending and its spare modernist style came out of a desire to simplify her life. When she went to Richmond, she was in the process of what she called "discarding." She couldn't explain to friends that she had been slowly fashioning a life to complement a bare-boned existence: "Spaces to live in that would be spare, understated, yet with one or two accents." A little over 200 pages, *Fisher King* (in contrast to the 472-page *Chosen Place*) is a short, compact novel that Paule hoped would "involve the reader more, having the reader use his (her) own imaginative skills," like the avant-garde work of Puryear and Münter.

She might very well have cited (but did not) her writer's workshop, her students' work, and her syllabi as instrumental in her turn toward experimentation. She had expanded her syllabus to accommodate her students' interest in modern and postmodern aesthetics. The time she spent helping John Keene to refine and publish his story "My Son, My Heart, My Life" may have allowed her to imagine the queer sexual triangle at the heart of *Fisher King*. When she encouraged her students to be "wild and way out," she must have been giving herself the same advice. In this last novel, she created a woman character, Hattie Carmichael, who was different from any other woman in her fiction: a "City-Child," a foster child, ethnicity unknown, father unknown, schizophrenic mother confined to a psychiatric institution, eventually an expat living in a shabby area of Paris and working in the Club Violette as wardrobe mistress to *danseuses exotiques*. Like the European flaneur, Hattie freely claims her right to explore, declaring, "I've been a walker in the city from way back."[18] Hattie embodied the spirit of modernity for Paule.

But when Paule spoke publicly about *The Fisher King,* she presented it as a somewhat conventional story about a male jazz musician, inspired by the memory of her cousin Sonny, a baritone saxophonist, whose large formal photograph sat on the upright piano in her home in Brooklyn throughout her childhood. Paule said she wanted to pay homage to those rebellious young men and women she knew like Sonny, who braved family and community disapproval to become dedicated jazz musicians. Sonny was the dissident, the artist, who defied his West Indian community, where success was measured in the number of doctors, lawyers, and teachers the community could count, and music was tolerated only if it was establishment music—classical, European. Paule would admit in her unpublished notes that *she,* like her cousin, was also a dissident artist and that book writing was as much disdained by the community as jazz—"Strictly verboten!" Even a brief synopsis of the novel shows that Hattie is the central character. But in her public statements, Paule deflected attention from Hattie and once described her as an appendage to the jazz musician Sonny-Rhett: "I gave him a mother, a wife, and an 'other woman.'"[19] To make it even more difficult to identify Hattie's importance, Paule allowed the promotional material for the novel to feature two males—Sonny-Rhett as a jazz pianist and his grandson Sonny as the mythical Fisher King, the hope for healing the conflict between families. The cover illustration of the novel, most certainly approved by Paule, is a Romare Bearden collage, *Jammin' at the Savoy,* featuring an all-male jazz band.

Given these gendered miscues, Paule's commentary begs to be read with a critical and skeptical eye, and *The Fisher King* with greater attention to Hattie. The novel begins in the 1940s in the Bedford-Stuyvesant neighborhood of New York, where three teenagers—Cherisse Jones, African American; Sonny-Rhett Payne, West Indian; and Hattie Carmichael, ancestry uncertain—are drawn together by their love of black music. As a teenager Hattie works in a music store, where she meets Sonny-Rhett, a promising jazz pianist. She starts an all-girl singing group, the Maconettes, in order to give a starring role to Cherisse, who becomes her first lover. Sonny-Rhett eventually falls in love with and marries the beautiful (and bi-sexual) Cherisse, despite the ethnic rivalry between their families, and the couple move to Paris, where he begins his meteoric jazz career.

The couple urge Hattie to join them, and eventually she becomes Sonny-Rhett's business manager and his lover as well as Cherisse's. Hattie envisions their triangle with herself as the base, the foundation, all living together in an apartment in Paris large enough for three, "like the connected sides of the triangles she used to draw in geometry." She thinks to herself, "It might be the way—the only way—to have them both."[20] Cherisse is so comfortable with this three-way sexual relationship that she whispers the French word *partager* to Hattie, reminding her that "it's the verb 'to share.' "[21] Hattie encourages Cherisse and Sonny-Rhett to have a child, JoJo, whom she raises after Cherisse dies from cancer and Sonny-Rhett dies in a suspicious accident in a Paris subway station. JoJo gives birth to Sonny. The father, a Cameroonian man, is discovered "sans papiers," arrested, and deported. JoJo disappears after giving the baby Sonny to Hattie, whom she calls derisively "the *goine*," the lesbian. After Sonny-Rhett's death, Hattie returns to their old Brooklyn neighborhood, invited there by Edgar Payne, Sonny-Rhett's brother, for a memorial concert in his honor and to reconnect Sonny with his Caribbean and African American families represented by the two matriarchs—African American Florence McCullum-Jones and the Caribbean-born Ulene Payne—and to try to reconcile the ethnic tensions between them.

This entire complicated family saga is filtered through the script Hattie writes for the memorial concert. It is important to note that the moment Edgar signs Hattie to a contract to write the script, we have the novel's first iteration of the central role of the writer. Hattie will write and perform the story of the life and work of Sonny-Rhett at the Putnam Royal, a former men's club, weaving together the story of the trio's love affair, Sonny-Rhett's career and his music, and the history of jazz in the United States and in Europe. Paule provides all the stage directions in this section of *Fisher King*, so that Hattie's pivotal role is unmistakable.

Once Hattie steps to the lectern to narrate the concert, she is both the author and the star who has "the audience deposited at her feet." She dons a dramatic costume for her performance, designed to turn all eyes to her: "the loose-fitting, wide-sleeved tunic and long matching skirt. . . . Instead of cotton or wool, they were made of layers of sheer airy georgette or silk. Black, of course, but with a dusting of beadwork at the neckline that flashed silver each time she moved."[22] As the stage lights dim over the band, "a single bright cone of light came to focus on her as she opened the folder containing her notes."[23] In between sets, Hattie sits in "a chair with a high carved back and the seat and armrests padded and cushioned in maroon velvet, *a diva's chair*," while the band plays Sonny-Rhett's celebrated hits that trace the arc of his career: "Sonny-Rhett Plays Sonny," "The Crossing," "Europhoria," "In the Upper Room," "P'tite JoJo," and "Continental Free-fall."[24] At the same time that she is paying homage to the black artistry of Sonny-Rhett,[25] Hattie, the true fisher king, is preserving a black diasporic cultural history and rewriting the story of the uber-masculine world of jazz culture and history.

Contrary to critic Harold Bloom's uninformed dismissal of Paule as a writer who "attempts few formal innovations," *The Fisher King* is full of them.[26] First, there is the sheer boldness of appropriating the cultural script of jazz history that had been for decades the provenance of men. The triangulated relationship in *The Fisher King* between Hattie, Cherisse, and Sonny-Rhett, initiated by Hattie, is the only example of a harmonious marriage in Paule's entire oeuvre and the closest Paule came to representing a family that allows autonomy and freedom and a genuinely collaborative artistic community—another bold experiment. Cherisse is in her element in the haute couture culture of boutiques and fashion salons in a city that seems to have been created with her in mind as she frequents the cafés and salons with the wives and mistresses of other musicians, while Hattie and Sonny-Rhett collaborate in his musical career. Hattie revises the definition of family: "There're all kinds of family and blood's got nothing to do with it!"[27]

The representation of a black sexual love triangle as "normative and happy" is also a significant departure from, maybe even an apologia for, her negative portrayal of the lesbian relationship in *The Chosen Place, the Timeless People.*[28] It is also consistent with Paule's account of her own bisexual life: not as transgression but simply as a form of self-expression. The teenaged Evan asked his mother in the 1970s about her relationship with Lucienne, and he remembered her nonchalant but direct response: "I love women and I love men."[29] Paule may have chosen the name Hattie Carmichael to highlight her experiments in *Fisher King*; the name may allude to the entertainer Hattie McDaniels, another struggling black woman artist, and maybe to Mary Carmichael, the imagined writer in Virginia Woolf's feminist classic, *A Room of One's Own,* who introduces a concealed lesbian story with the famous line, "Chloe liked Olivia."[30]

In her unpublished notes for *The Fisher King,* Paule wrote about her connections to the jazz community: "It was nothing for example to walk down the street back then and run into the young Max Roach, already a world-class drummer, standing talking with friends. The brilliant Charlie Parker and Bud Powell played our local clubs. So did other giants of jazz such as Lester Young (Prez) who used to say 'Ding-dong' instead of hello when you greeted him. At eighteen I had a massive crush on Kenny Dorham, a trumpeter out of Texas. I was always front row center whenever Kenny played B'klyn." She was introduced to live jazz in Brooklyn in the 1940s through clubs like the Putnam Royal, begun in 1946 for men of color "to promote social welfare and community spirit in Bedford-Stuyvesant."[31] Paule claimed it as "our local jazz club." She herself sang in a local singing group like the one in *The Fisher King.* The club boasted twenty-two hundred members, a dining room, reading room, card room, meeting rooms, and a cocktail lounge. Jazz greats such as Max Roach, Cecil Payne, Duke Jordan, Bud

Powell, and Wynton Kelley played there, sometimes at the Sunday matinees, allowing them to play gigs in Manhattan later in the evenings. When Paule and Kenneth moved to 407 Central Park West in the 1960s, bebop vocalist Babs Gonzales lived downstairs, and Max Roach and his then wife Abbey Lincoln lived one block north. Roach and Lincoln attended her parties along with bassist Ron Carter and his wife, who lived in an apartment in the tonier West End in the 1970s.

Paule often cited the influence of women jazz artists, including Abbey Lincoln, who appeared with her and Alice Childress and Sarah E. Wright on the 1966 panel "The Negro Woman and American Literature" at the New School. Lincoln claimed that she herself was part of the tradition of female singing pioneers such as Bessie Smith and Billie Holiday, who set the pace for the "creative singer of contemporary African-American music." Their influence, she asserted, had been felt throughout the world "in the concert halls, on the vaudeville stage, on Broadway, in the intimate night club, and by way of the prosperous recording companies, who have much for which to thank her."[32]

Paule certainly had her friend James Baldwin and his famous jazz story on her mind when she was thinking about *The Fisher King*.[33] Like John Coltrane's rendition of "My Favorite Things" from the musical *The Sound of Music*, the echoes of Baldwin's 1957 story "Sonny's Blues" in *The Fisher King* are unmistakable. "Sonny" is the name of the main jazz figure in both stories, but in place of Baldwin's masculinized community of brothers, uncles, fathers, sons, and male musicians, Sonny-Rhett is immersed in a female community, mentored and nurtured by his mother, his wife Cherisse, and his friend, business partner, and lover Hattie. Sonny-Rhett's brother Edgar, who abandoned him as the brother does in Baldwin's story, begins to understand his brother only after listening to his music. In "Sonny's Blues," the

A casual snapshot of Paule and James Baldwin, 1970s.

two brothers reconcile, whereas in *The Fisher King,* Hattie does not let Edgar forget that she was there for Sonny-Rhett when he wasn't. Brotherly reconciliation is not so easy as it is with Baldwin. Paule was disrupting masculinist jazz traditions with a narrating female voice, a female nurturing community, and a female familial culture.

In another re-(vision) of Baldwin, who imagined jazz as a battleground for the black soul, whose freedom can only come from enduring suffering and loss, Hattie imagined Sonny-Rhett's music as thrilling and dangerous, and expanded it beyond the boundaries of race. In an extended metaphor of an amusement park ride, Hattie narrates Sonny-Rhett's music as charting an unfamiliar terrain that took the young riders on

> a joyous, terrifying roller coaster of a ride, turning them all into twelve- and thirteen-year-olds from around the block again, strapped into the Cyclone and the Hurricane at Coney Island . . . repeatedly soaring skyward in the rattling steeplechase cars, close to the sun, high above the Atlantic nearby and with what they liked to think was a bird's eye view of Prospect Park in the far distance and beyond that, their world of Bed-Stuy, or Central Brooklyn . . . then seconds later, the cars plunging down again taking them headlong toward what could only be an atomic ground zero, all of them screaming in terror while loving every second of it, their stomachs left somewhere high above them in the air.[34]

Such a vivid and precise description suggests that Paule had been a frequent visitor to the Coney Island amusement park when she was young. This image of wild, unrestrained pleasure on the Cyclone coaster maps jazz-as-pleasure onto the city-as-pleasure, even as it evokes death in the image of Icarus flying too close to the sun and the ground-level menace of the atomic bomb: the modern world of pleasure, excitement, and terror.

Darryl Pinckney wrote in the *New York Review of Books* in 1983 that Paule Marshall's fictional women never lose. "No matter the odds," Pinckney asserts, "the women with enough nerve can win even when the deck is stacked and the other players hostile."[35] But to understand Paule's larger vision is to recognize that none of her women is able to entirely escape the power of patriarchy. Hattie knows she cannot win the fight for custody of Sonny against the affluent and well-connected Edgar. Her family, Cherisse, JoJo, and Sonny-Rhett, the musician-artist-lover who inspired her artistry, are all dead. As if to confirm her inability to see a future for herself as an artist, Hattie anticipates her death, even though she is only in her late fifties. She announces that she has already bought and paid for her plot in the Cimetière de Montmartre in Paris, an eerie premonition that seems to imply the end of Hattie's quest. Or, perhaps, since the Cimetière de Montmartre is where some of France's most celebrated artists are laid to rest, including Dumas fils and originally Zola before he was moved to the Pantheon, she was claiming herself as a writer and artist, even in death.

Women critics and scholars were much more attentive to the price women pay for entering "the wild zone," spaces where experimental women dare to challenge a dominant male culture. Such daring in women's fiction often leaves them alone, exhausted, and alienated from communal bonds; that wild zone is hard and not always successful, but always undertaken.[36] Hattie, especially, exemplifies the price paid by women who challenge the limitations of their lives. Hattie is left without family, separated from Sonny and from Sonny-Rhett, whose music inspired her writing. We might think about Paule at this point in her own life. When *The Fisher King* was published in 2000, she was seventy and twice divorced. Her son was living on his own in London and crafting a successful career as a yacht designer. Both her brother Frank and her beloved sister Anita were dead, and she may have sensed that *The Fisher King* was her final novel. She was, understandably, exasperated with readers who were perplexed about the "unhappy" ending, which leaves Hattie bereft and apparently powerless. "Well, the book is not about happiness, for god's sake," she asserted, "it's about the way we are as humans."[37] Perhaps she meant it's the way we are as women artists.

CHAPTER 11

Portrait of the Artist

When John Keene was in Paule's writing workshop at NYU in the 1990s, she told him that when she wrote her memoir, she would "let it all hang out." When she published *Triangular Road* in 2009, Keene was surprised: "It struck me as *offering only oblique views* into what I imagined has been a fascinating life, though as always, the writing sparkled."[1] Contrary to what she told Keene, she did not intend to write about her social life, her marriages, motherhood, her teaching career, her many friendships—or her inner life. What might better be called Paule's anti-memoir says more about her resistance to self-disclosure than it does about her fascinating life. At eighty, at the apex of her career and with a lifetime of writing to reflect on, Paule wanted to be remembered for what she wrote, for her creative imagination, for her discipline and dedication to writing. *Triangular Road* was a tightly controlled portrait of an artist attempting to shape and guard her artistic legacy.

In April 2006, when Harvard University professor Henry Louis Gates, Jr., invited her to give a series of three lectures in the Alain Leroy Locke series at Harvard, she began planning the public version of her memoir. She delivered these lectures on three consecutive days at the Barker Center on Quincy Street in Cambridge, warmly received by a respectful and attentive audience composed mostly of scholars. In the videotape of the lectures, Paule is dressed conservatively (visible only from the waist up): one night in a light gray tailored suit jacket; the next in a warm orange cardigan sweater; and finally in a pale green V-neck linen top, each outfit accented with a simple one-strand cowrie shell necklace. Her tone is formal, and she is poised and in charge as she reads from her script.

One way to encounter a more complex, contradictory, and contrarian Paule Marshall than the one she constructed for the Harvard audience is by reading in—or more precisely from—the unpublished and unscripted parts of her autobiographical writing: the video recording of the Q&A following her lectures, when Paule was without the safety net of a prepared script; the deletions she made in her 2008 published memoir *Triangular Road;* and the uncensored or, more precisely, self-censored autobiographical notes called *Travelin' Light*, which were left on the desktop of her iBook G4 computer when she passed away in 2019.

At the first of the three Harvard lectures, Paule cautioned the audience that her presentations would be in the form of memoir, narrative, and reminiscence rather than academic treatise or formal lecture: "*I'm a fiction writer*, after all."[2] True to her word, Paule presented a highly artful narrative. The Cast: Paule Marshall, artist; her father and mother, Sam and Adriana; Langston Hughes. The Setting: New York, Paris, Copenhagen, Richmond, Barbados, Grenada, Carriacou, and Nigeria. Elements of the Plot: choosing writing above everything else, tracing her writerly heritage back to Barbados, documenting her literary status in Grenada, her parents as catalysts for her writing, forgiving her parents as permission to write, immersing herself in the history of the slave trade, traveling, reconciling her Caribbean and African American identities, shunning personal revelation. These are elements and themes she had worked over intensively in her fiction and in interviews, so there was nothing surprising or new here—it would never be easy for this very private, reserved woman to "let it all hang out."

In the first of the three lectures, "Homage to Mr. Hughes," there is a subtext: how Paule became a writer. She begins with the invitation she received in 1965 to travel with Langston Hughes on a State Department tour to Paris, London, and Copenhagen. Running alongside this tribute to Hughes, her longtime friend and mentor and the man she deemed the "towering figure of 20th century African American literature," is the story of her artistic apprenticeship. As a teenager, she reminds us, she discovered Hughes's two autobiographies, *The Big Sea* and *I Wonder as I Wander*, and was inspired to become a writer and a "travelin' woman," like her mentor.[3] Hughes attended her first book party in 1959, "a literary icon come to celebrate me." "Mr. Hughes" was a constant in her literary life, sending postcards to congratulate her on each novel or award she won, as well as hounding her about what he considered her low productivity and the obscurity she might be courting by not publishing faster. Throughout the lecture, Paule referred to herself as "a mere fledgling of a writer" and "this little provincial from Brooklyn," although she had already published a well-received novel and a volume of short stories, produced an award-winning television show on CBS, won a Guggenheim, and worked internationally as a professional journalist for *Our World* in the Caribbean and South America. She was one step beyond her mentor, who always carried a satchel of his books to sell. The "fledgling writer" had brought along copies of *Brown Girl, Brownstones* and was on the lookout for a European publisher.[4] We can see in this opening lecture Paule artfully crafting, in the margins of the "homage" to Hughes, the narrative of "a writer's life."

In the Q&A after the first lecture, the audience (not visible on the video), not surprisingly, wanted to know more about Hughes: "Was Paule planning a biography of Hughes?" "No," she insisted; her lecture was meant to present a more complex view of the man and to address the fact that he was "brave enough to commit to being a writer." The word *brave* triggered some anxiety for Paule. Her dossier had surfaced in her State Department interview, and she knew that Hughes had cooperated with but also challenged Senator Joseph McCarthy in 1953 during the Senate investigations of his Communist past. Paule defended Hughes's willingness to sacrifice everything for his work: "He didn't want anything that was going to prevent him from being able to write and to carry on with his work and to move about the world. He had seen what this country had done to Robeson—took away his chance to function as an artist. Langston was committed to his art, and I needed that because I was getting objections from any number of quarters, including my family."[5] In Paule's subtle shift to first person—"I needed that"—she transferred Hughes's determination to save himself from the blacklist to her decision to write in defiance of her family, her in-laws, her husbands, and motherhood. For Paule, the obstacles were just as great, and "the writer's life" required the same kind of total commitment.

The next question came from Professor Gates, who asked if she had an opinion about the claim of Hughes's biographer Arnold Rampersad that Langston was asexual. "No," Paule replied, then, reconsidering, "Well, not really. [*pause*] I just know some of the bars he took me to, some of them were gay bars and he was gone all night and he was not taking me with him." She and the audience began to laugh. "But I was respectful enough not to ask questions, not even to ask myself." Gates pursued the issue: "Did it ever *even* occur to you?" She threw up her hands in mock incredulity: "Langston would never answer those things about his life.

There were things about his life that were private." Then she fumbled about looking for something on the lectern and produced a postcard Langston had sent her in June 1965 from Tunisia, and waved it back and forth: "I mean—this whole thing in Tunisia—these lovely boys on the card. But you respected. You don't intrude. You don't ask questions." But did Paule intrude? Her speculation to the audience about Langston's nights out at gay bars and the apparently spontaneous production of the Tunisian postcard implied his homosexuality. Her exposure of Hughes's private life deftly deflected the mutuality of their sexual nonconformity and once again exposed her reticence about her own autobiography.

A more freewheeling Paule might have pointed out the affinities between herself and Hughes, and perhaps made reference to the subtle but pervasive representations of homoerotic desire in her characters, whose sexual rebellions were often an expressway to empowerment. Think of Selina and Suggie rising from the bed and walking together to the door of Suggie's room, where "a wide bar of light from the hall made a path for them and the rich colors of their laughter painted the darkness."[6] Or the novel *Daughters,* which suggests an alternative lesbian family.[7] Or her final novel *The Fisher King,* which treats the three-way sexual relationship between Sonny-Rhett, Cherisse, and Hattie as a new way to be a family and to be in an artistic community. Alongside the Tunisian postcard, she might have shone a light on her enormous imaginative and empathetic powers by pointing out the orgasmic swimming scene between two men, Vere and Allen, in *The Chosen Place, the Timeless People,* as they ride the Caribbean waves of Horseshoe Pool together. Paule was forthright about using her fiction to deal "with aspects of my own personal history," in order to work out issues that were painful for her, including her marriages, conflicts with her mother and father, a date rape and a back-alley abortion, and sibling rivalry.[8] She is, however, silent about queer and sexually nonconforming relationships in her own life, letting her fiction unveil what Paule conceals, just as Langston Hughes did in his poetry.

In the second section of the memoir, "I've Known Seas: The Caribbean Sea," Paule becomes a documentarian, standing behind the camera, filming the "fascinating" life of the artist that Keene had hoped for. It's 1957, she is twenty-eight years old, traveling to Barbados with an advance contract from Random House for her first book, and marching orders from her editor Hiram Haydn to revise her six-hundred-page manuscript. The Caribbean is something like a writers' retreat, where she could stretch her modest advance and focus on her work, a reprieve from day-to-day concerns. The camera pans over Barbados, at 166 square miles the closest point in the Caribbean to West Africa, the origin of the chattel slave trade and also the source of the geography, politics, and culture of her fictional characters, the spiritual center of her work. It's the birthplace of her parents, and staying there, she thought, might help her to better understand them. Since she and her husband led fairly independent lives, she could, she thought, spend the better part of a year there; "Marriage would pose no problem."[9] Later, she would record in her unpublished memoir a friend's skeptical reaction to her leaving her husband for such a long time: " 'I know I'd never go away for nobody's year leaving my husband alone.' A friend spoke the truth."

As the second lecture continues, we see the writer in Barbados treating herself to a weekly "sea-bath" after a day's work, spending time at the museum and historical society researching her family, and joining a small group of friends who were part of the pro-independence movement slowly getting underway on the island. These activists, mostly men, had returned from study in England as young barristers, doctors, economists, and other professionals, eager to seize power in their homeland and envious of the changes in places like Ghana.[10] Paule is listening for the voices that will live in her fiction: " 'Look at Ghana, man! I hear it gon soon be independent! So why not us? What the bloody hell wrong with us, nuh! Is we sweat and blood build the place.' "[11]

The fascinating writer's life now moves on to the next Caribbean writer's retreat, a sojourn in Grenada, where, at age thirty-three, she began work on her second novel *The Chosen Place, the Timeless People.* Here she portrays herself as a fully vetted writer, a celebrity from the States, in search of a new landscape for her epic novel. When Odessa Gittens, a transplanted Bajan, saw a brief biography of Paule in the "Visitors to the Island" column in the newspaper describing Paule as "an American writer of Barbadian parentage," she descended on Paule, arranging for a housekeeper, a cook, and a nanny for three-year-old Evan ("the book-party baby") so that Paule could "settle in" and everything would run smoothly.[12] In the opening scene of her Grenadian period, Paule is in a bright, airy, freshly painted study, her Virginia Woolf room, filling her desk with writing supplies, setting up her new Royal typewriter, and arranging the steno pads full of new historical material. Here she does not have to negotiate racism or the condescension of white editors and publishers, or the drudgery of domesticity. In the afternoon, when she is exhausted from writing, she takes a soothing "sea-bath" in the coral waters of the island. Even the writer's block she suffered for weeks in Grenada confirms her status as writer.

What is most notable is that Paule was showing how her writing emerged from her deep engagement with places, people, and politics, especially in the Caribbean. When her writer's block made it impossible to write, she took off and followed a group of islanders to a political rally on one of the makeshift buses, observing the women hawkers selling their snacks to the drivers and passengers. She passes the sugarcane fields, tin-roofed houses, and beautiful limestone hills. Above all, she is taken with the stoic power of the women "headers," who cut cane and carry bundles on their heads in the hot sun, reminding her of rebellious slave women such as Nanny Griggs. She takes a side trip on a local schooner to the tiny island of Carriacou and joins in the Big Drum/Nation ceremony performed by the few old folks left who still remember Africa in song and dance. Nothing is lost on the writer—the political rally becomes background for *The Chosen Place;* the Carriacou trip will become the basis of her next novel, *Praisesong for the Widow.*

Paule ends the third lecture (and the written memoir) in Africa, completing the "triangular road" at the Pan-African festival of the arts in Nigeria, FESTAC '77, a continent- and diaspora-wide celebration of black artistic achievement and the end of colonialism. At forty-eight, she is a world-renowned writer. She does not write about the children in the streets or the food or about the city of Lagos, but about four weeks of "meeting, conversing and interacting with *fellow artists* in a spirit of confraternity."[13] She recalls the history of the slave trade and is forthright about the role of Africans in the commerce that reduced their descendants to chattel cargo. Although none of her books is set in Africa, she remembers her writer friends, two of the "best and brightest" of the continent, Nigerian writer and activist Wole Soyinka, and Kenyan writer Ngũgĩ wa Thiong'o, both imprisoned at times and exiled for opposing the misrule and corruption of their governments. This is far from what Paule imagined as a symbolic completion of the diasporan "triangular road." On African soil, Paule was firmly grounded in the material and political realities of Africa.

The smooth ending for the Africa segment Paule had scripted was disrupted by the next questioner, a woman who had recently heard Ngũgĩ speak at Harvard about the importance of African writers using their indigenous language rather than the language of the colonial power. She asked if Paule had ever "yearned, in terms of finding a home and a place, to have access to an African language." Paule responded with a clear "No" and then began to elaborate, "What I yearn for is an acceptance of all the forces and cultures that have gone into making me, to live as this complicated person, to bring a reconciliation of those different currents within myself and to live as this complicated person in whatever space I'm in." In her answer, Africa became a discursive figure, a symbol, a haunting, not a homeland. The woman persisted with a question about Shakespeare's character Caliban in *The Tempest*, a figure that scholars of postcolonialism claim uses mimicry as a form of resistance to colonial power: "So, [you have] no Caliban complex about using the Master's language to destroy the Master's house?" It was kind of a trick question and a veiled critique, assuming a knowledge of postcolonial theory and referencing black feminist theorist Audre Lorde. Paule was quick with a deliberate play on words that evaded the question but also silenced the questioner: "No, just master it."[14] Then Paule and the audience have a hearty laugh in response to her clever retort.

A final questioner at the Q&A after the third lecture, whose parents were from Barbados, asked Paule if she ever felt any tension between being both Caribbean and American. Paule replied that she did not feel any "marked tension" over her dual identity. She described the ease of her life in the diverse world of her childhood, Bajan at home, part of an African American community in the neighborhood, and an A-plus American in school, sitting next to Jewish and Irish kids. But then she resurrected the painful story of her experience at Dartmouth when a young African American student questioned why Paule, accompanied by Toni Cade Bambara, had been invited to an African American event.

Paule was so "charged up and angry" at the question of her non-belonging that Bambara had to intervene and explain that Paule was a writer of the entire diaspora. Paule called the young Dartmouth student "a poor misguided soul," adding caustically that she had heard that the student was on her way to do graduate work at the University of Chicago: "Pity the university." Paule turned to the Harvard questioner and admonished her: "Just don't take on that kind of talk."

Despite her protestations, Paule was not entirely at peace with her dual identity. Her anger—even years later—over the assumption that she didn't belong at an African American event and her response to the questioner were signs of her own inner tensions. Maybe, after thirty years of preaching, performing, modeling, and representing black unity, being named an outsider was particularly galling. Had Paule turned to her fiction for her answer, she might have shown that her sense of doubleness had been fertile ground for her as a writer. She had always consciously positioned her fictional characters—African American, Caribbean American, Caribbean, and African Caribbean—side by side on the page, in conversation, in collective action, in intimate relationships: Selina and Miss Thompson, Estelle and Ursa, Ursa and Viney, Avey and Lebert, Reena and Paulie. In *Brown Girl, Brownstones*, for example, a racist incident leads the young Selina to understand that her power is in being joined to a community of color and she understands that "she was one with Miss Thompson [the African American hairdresser], . . . one with the whores, the flashy men, and the blues on Fulton Street, and she was one with the mother and the Bajan woman who had lived each day what she had come to know."[15] Paule might have told the questioner about the vision of black unity embodied in the boy Sonny in her novel *The Fisher King*, who is African (through his Cameroonian father) and Caribbean and African American (through his mother

My Work in the Canon

Categories Place of work in Am Lit

12

Saadawi-"Woman at Point Zero." Lamentable state of women...

Only just started reading memoirs. "Defending the Spirit." and "The Debt." If not reparations at least a memorial on the Mall. The Hours - Mike Cunningham

HOW DO YOU SEE YOURSELF IN RELATION TO OTHER WRITERS? Categories

1) I see my work as part of the literature that defines this country. As part of the American canon. There are those who might say otherwise, but that's their problem.

2) I also see my work as part of a long tradition of African-American Letters that began with that first novel, "Clotel" by William Wells Brown in 1867, two years after the Civil War. (Object also to Renaissance. Max Rodriguez in QBR Black Book Review) Continuity of ~~writing~~ blk writing

3) Also see myself as a writer of the Diaspora--in that my work links the AfAm experience with the Caribbean and by inference to Africa. (Africa is always present in my work, in images, ceremonies, direct references). Praisesong speaks to commonality; our experiences & culture

emphasize the connections

(1) I've been questioned as to my "category"--in what category should my work be placed: W.I? [Caribbean] AFAM? [Am? fish or fowl] I was about to say as usual "You can put me where[ver] you want to. I'll fit." when Bambara answered the question for me. A writer of the Diaspora. A great complement. I come by this wider view of our literature naturally.

4) In relation to the young writers on the scene today, I

What do you consider yourself?

When Paule was asked to comment on how she saw herself in relation to other writers, she produced this document, "My Work in the Canon," in which she describes her work as part of the American canon and part of a long tradition of African American letters, calling herself a writer of the Diaspora.

and grandparents). Sonny's African American great-grandmother claims him as a sign of the future: "You got some of all of us in you, dontcha? What you gonna do with all that Colored from all over creation you got in you? Better be somethin' good."[16] Paule might have reminded the audience that her character Sonny reaffirmed the theme of her 1964 black nationalist speech—that black is not just a color but a way of enlarging the struggle and the resistance.

Dementia and death occurred before Paule was able to carry out her plans to finalize a manuscript called *Travelin' Light: People and Places*, which she intended to send to Beacon Press for the series Bluestreak: Celebrating Black Women Writers. *Travelin' Light* is an unevenly organized potpourri of memories and memorials, and a written account of Paule's most personal revelations. She compiled the notes for *Travelin' Light* on her iBookG4 computer, which I found buried at the bottom of a packing box in the storage facility in Richmond, Virginia, its existence made known when I discovered a small black-and-white photo showing her working at her desk, the computer in the background. It is a precious document. Without it, a part of Paule's intensely felt intimate life would have been lost.

Since no password was needed, there was easy access to the files, which she kept on the desktop in folders that included tributes to other writers; various lecture invitations (her "standard" fee after the MacArthur was $4,000 plus expenses); photographs of her two beloved grandchildren, Nina Prudence Marshall, born in 2005, and James Julius Marshall, born in 2006; reminders to herself (now that she had begun forgetting things) of how to use the phone and the dates her caregiver was to come.

Travelin' Light is divided into five sections that often overlap and include brief, unfinished tributes, called "Homages," to

Langston Hughes, Ralph Ellison, James Baldwin, Richard Wright, Paul Robeson, Malcolm X, and Gwendolyn Brooks; Paule's travels to China, Africa, and Haiti; the story of her mother and father's migration to the United States; memories of what she called "the thieves" of her early years; and a partial account of her marriage to Nourry Menard. These two sections of *Travelin' Light*—"A Life" (five pages) and "*en passant*—Haiti,"(forty-one pages)—are the closest Paule would ever come to revealing what she called "those different currents" in the complicated person Paule Marshall.

Paule's tributes to the five male writers in Homage I and II were composed with a calculated goal in mind—to aim her camera at the women who always seemed to be in the margins of literary canons and famous men's stories. Thus, the homage to Langston Hughes became a story about Paule's apprenticeship to Hughes. In the homage to James Baldwin, Paule recounts a story of helping to save Baldwin from being scammed by two people who had invited Baldwin to their penthouse. She described the couple as a man "hiding his sexuality behind a 'paper marriage' to a 'paper wife,' from some impoverished Latin American country sitting there unable to say even a few words in English." She thought Baldwin was simply "delighted at being in the spotlight, the cigarette, the bug-eyes, the Harlem urchin's face." The host and his "paper wife" were apparently trying to extort money from Baldwin, and, in the absence of his sister Gloria, "who served as keeper of the purse," the money would have been gone in no time. Paule hints that she and some of Baldwin's friends rescued him from these "hungry bees round the honey pot," and saved his money. She planned to devote a section to Baldwin's influence on the style and content of her writing: Baldwin "reacquainted me with the inclusive politics of my childhood. The larger world of people of color."

The very brief notes for the homage to Malcolm X suggest that Paule had not yet formulated her thoughts and ideas about Malcolm's meaning in her life. Looking back on his presence when she was giving her 1964 speech at Town Hall, she foregrounds the importance of his support of her writing career: "his face smiling up at me, approvingly." She also recalls Malcolm asking her if she thought he too could get a Guggenheim, and Paule assured him that he could.

The setting of the homage to Ralph Ellison is a party at the home of an (unnamed) white poet, where the sociable Fanny Ellison, quite the opposite of her husband, is the figure that caught Paule's attention. Setting aside Ellison's habitual coldness toward her at formal events, Paule recalled his essays on art, culture, and literature in *Shadow and Act,* especially "Hidden Name and Complex Fate," her bible of literary craft. At the party, Ellison remained hidden "behind his impenetrable glass wall," while Fanny, at one point in the gathering, remarked from across the room so that all could hear, "Ralph! Oh, he's a bastard!" Paule interpreted the outburst not as an insult but as a playfully sardonic comment on Fanny's resignation to a long and difficult marriage. The remark, Paule wrote, was "said with laughter and unquestionable love/wonderfully resigned love [that] humanized [her husband] in the most wonderful way." This was Paule's homage to Fanny.

In the homage to Richard Wright, Paule inserted stage directions to signal her intentions: "Concentrate on Julia Wright." The setting for Wright's tribute is an event in February 1992 in Paris, honoring Wright by installing a marble plaque with gold lettering on the door of his apartment at No. 14 rue Monsieur-le-Prince inscribed: *Hommes de lettres. Noir Americain. Habite cet immeuble de 1948–1959*. Paule was in Paris for the conference "African

Americans and Europe," which assembled an entourage of Richard Wright writers and scholars (among them Robert Bone of Columbia University; Michel Fabre, Wright's biographer; sculptor and writer Barbara Chase-Riboud; Gerald Frazier of the *New York Times;* representatives of the Congressional Black Caucus; members of the Richard Wright Circle at Northeastern University in Boston; and Wright's wife Genevieve and daughter Julia). The group of over one hundred walked from the Institut du Monde Anglophone at the University of Paris to Wright's house at 14 rue Monsieur-le-Prince, singing hymns and giving speeches, ending with "Lift Every Voice and Sing." The speaker, who, in Paule's estimation, "restored Wright to a vivid flesh-and-blood man," was Julia. She had been a shy, tongue-tied child when Wright introduced her to the dignitaries who frequented their home—Chester Himes, James Baldwin, Katherine Dunham, Albert Camus, Jean-Paul Sartre, Ralph Ellison. Of all of these distinguished visitors, Julia remembered Martin Luther King most vividly because her father had insisted she look at the chest wound King sustained when a woman stabbed him in New York. Wright told her that looking was "the price of freedom." Julia was brought to tears as she remembered reading her father's 1945 autobiography *Black Boy* and imagining the hungry little boy growing up in Mississippi drinking gallons of water to mute his hunger pangs. Paule was captivated by the sight of the "near-white" Julia, standing next to her dark brown son named, after another warrior, Malcolm.

In the homage to Gwendolyn Brooks, Paule kept the focus entirely on Brooks, whose 1953 novel *Maud Martha* seemed to preview so much of what Paule wanted to accomplish in her own writing. Brooks was her model for giving women characters "a textured inner life." She admired Brooks for making her women characters dark women, "no cream-colored thing with curly hair." Brooks allowed her women to feel rage and still manage to be sympathetic and tender with the men in their lives. Brooks was also the model for Paule of modernist experimentation, and in her final novel *The Fisher King,* Paule aimed to imitate the "spare, compressed, impressionistic style" of *Maud Martha.* These formal tributes to writers were strategic, very efficiently establishing Paule's place among her peers in the African American canon, but most important, she was doing her own canon-building, citing Brooks and *Maud Martha* as her heritage and legacy.

Paule credited her writing and thinking in the next two sections of *Travelin' Light* "A Life" and "*en passant*—Haiti" to several forms of meditation she had begun practicing in the early 1970s, including transcendental meditation and a Hindu-inspired practice called Kundalini, both of which she expected would produce a sense of inner peace and relief from the tensions in her life. In "A Life," filed on her computer between 1969 and 2004, she began examining—or, more exactly, documenting—the lifelong pain she had endured from her mother, teachers, lovers, husbands, and the way she had always reacted to these insults with a "shameful paralysis," feeling anger so deep "it chokes off my voice." She was intent on fashioning a life that would be "spare and understated," and for that she needed to discard spiritual detritus as well as material excess.

In "A Life," she compiled a list of encounters that "stole my self-worth," a catalogue of "thieves" that went back to high school: Catholic Mary, the study-hour buddy and best friend who refused to walk with her at graduation (here Paule inserted a note to herself to use scenes of suppressed anger from Gwendolyn Brooks's *Maud Martha*); the speech teacher who discouraged her because she had a hissing "s"; the guidance counselor who urged her to go to a commercial high school instead of an academic one; the lovers "who abused your good thing with their incompetence"; her mother, who called her a failure at age thirteen. Added to the list of "thieves" were "former husbands, lovers who sought me out, who were attracted to me because I was a writer, someone with work and a life all her own, yet only to turn around and punish me for it, by attempting to turn me into a scullery maid. Or who expected me to play all the roles without a hitch." She includes her own failings on this list: "The painful list of family members, friends, and lovers I failed, the part of you that's not available to your child." Then, just as she seemed to be feeling the full impact of this catalogue of thievery, Paule turns to metaphor, describing the process of eliminating these thefts in quiet, domestic terms: "Folding them neatly and setting them aside. Rising from the bed, walking from the room, with only the one bag of barest necessities in hand." She writes this as if the anger and pain of these years could be as easily managed as putting away the laundry.

The longest section of *Travelin' Light*, called "*en passant*—Haiti," is the forty-one page, never-before-told story of her second marriage, exposing for the first time, in Paule's own words, the personal cost of her commitment to "the writer's life." "*en passant*—Haiti" begins in 1970 with her first trip to Haiti, where she met Nourry Menard, whom she refers to throughout as MN, reversing Nourry's initials, or SH, for Second Husband, "for discretion's sake." She took this trip to Haiti (following in the footsteps of Frederick Douglass and dancer Katherine Dunham) to rest and recuperate from the seven years it took to write *The Chosen Place, the Timeless People*. She was planning to play the typical tourist until she met Danielle, who encouraged her to throw away her guidebook and see the city through the eyes of a native. Danielle, a guide and traveling companion, took her up to Cap-Haïtien and to a modest guesthouse, where Nourry Menard was the only other guest.

"*En passant*—Haiti" charts the part of her blissful life Paule called "shangri-la," the first few years she spent in Haiti after her marriage to Nourry in 1970. She was immersed, apparently happily, in family life with her husband, her son, Nourry's two daughters, Rosemonde and Nancy, and sometimes more than one barking dog. During the half year she spent in Haiti, Paule oversaw homework lessons, arranged day trips to the movies or swimming pool and, when Nourry was free, planned vacations in their new SUV. Later, as she reflected in "*en passant*" on her Haitian marriage, she noted that black American women who married West Indians or Africans often struggle to adjust to what is sometimes a radically different culture. "I was one of them."

It was a sign of the difficulties ahead, especially after marriage became deeply entwined in the political scene in Haiti. A photograph in a guidebook of the huge, white, domed Palais National, which housed "the aging ailing despot inside," Duvalier *pere*, the notorious "Papa Doc," reminded Paule that "his repressive heel had been firmly on the neck of the country for over a decade." Paule was well aware that the support for Duvalier by the U.S. State Department came in return for his "highly vocal, rabid anticommunism," millions of U.S. dollars lining his pockets or swelling his Swiss bank accounts, while he terrorized his country. She also knew—or thought she knew—that Nourry shared her view of Duvalier.

The rupture of Paule and Nourry's marriage was precipitated by a presidential "visit" from Duvalier's son, President Jean-Claude Duvalier (Baby Doc) in the mid-1970s. President Duvalier sent orders that homes, shops, and public buildings lining his route through town were to be refurbished in preparation for his official visit to Le Cap. It was both a political shock for Haiti and a personal one for Paule and Nourry. While Paule was at home with the children, Duvalier's troops came to the house in an armored vehicle outfitted for battle, "complete with a swivel machine gun, full combat gear, topped by a green beret set at a menacing angle on his head—all of it probably U.S. Army surplus." The soldiers left quickly. It seems that confronting a "black woman with an Afro who stood up as though ready to challenge them, four frightened children and a spoiled stupid dog who gave only a half-hearted bark" was not worth the trouble. In town, Nourry had a worse time. Duvalier's men commandeered their new SUV, bought to travel that summer with the family to the Dominican Republic. The men returned it damaged and covered in mud, humiliating Nourry in front of his workers. Paule sat up with him for most of the night while he raged about the Duvalier government. "They have all ruined the country."

An even bigger shock for Paule was that shortly after the encounter with Duvalier's troops, Nourry appeared for dinner in a "mysterious good mood" and told Paule excitedly that the president had seen his bottling plant and was impressed with its efficiency and size, and now " 'On parle de moi au palais'—there was talk of him at the palace." Nourry tried to quiet Paule's fears about his joining the government, saying it was just talk at this point, but he began to take long and frequent trips to the capital, advised that his presence there might expedite his case. He dismissed Paule's fears about the corruption of the Duvalier regime as the problem of a foreigner who does not understand Haitian politics. He hinted that his role might even "require" him to have a mulatta mistress. Mocking Nourry's voice, Paule scorned his suggestion that "a sensible Haitian First Lady would accept the situation for what it was, a custom. But certainly not a feminist and writer wife from America." Paule responded with the only kreyol curse term she knew, *"Ca-ca rat! Rat shit!"* Paule was enraged, but that one curse was hardly sufficient to address Nourry's insult or his next gesture: "His raised hand forbade any further word from me on the subject." Now, she began to wonder how much of the time he spent in Port-au-Prince was devoted to finding "the kind of high-yaller" mistress that might be required of him. Their quarrels, she wrote, "became uglier than any in *Whose Afraid of Virginia Woolf.*" Finally, she wrote, "there was no living with him." Paule did not indicate how long she stayed with Nourry after his suggestion of a mulatta replacement for her.[17]

Thirty-one pages into the forty-one pages of "*en passant—* Haiti," the word *entrapped* appears as Paule allows her doubts about the marriage to finally surface, especially regarding its effects on her writing. "This dual, back-and-forth life of mine, as fulfilling as it was, despite all the pleasures it brought, was, yes, a kind of trap—a pleasant one, yes, but one that did not allow me to go about my work as I should." She had been prolonging the extensive note-taking for her third novel, *Praisesong for the Widow,* because she knew the hours of concentration the actual writing would entail. For some time, she had been feeling an impending sense of entrapment. Paule then inserts the lines she had been avoiding: "There was little or no time for the writing. Life getting in the way of work. I had started the new novel but was getting little work done on it."

In contrast to her spacious study in Grenada, where she had an entire house to herself, her workplace in Haiti was in a corner of her bedroom with Nourry, where she was often interrupted by the children. Her marriage became "my Haitian misadventure." She intersperses the words *trapped* and *shame* repeatedly: she felt *utterly ashamed of* the desire and need "to escape to a nirvana," *shame* for having had the luxury of writing the entire day, as she did in Grenada; she reports a vague *unreasonable* sense of *entrapment;* she is absurdly envious of her friend Danielle who is leaving for the United States. She feels "*utterly ashamed of myself. And ashamed. Utterly ashamed.* " "Feeling *shamefully* to give full attention to the work. *The writer's life*. Not much to be envied about it" (my emphasis). With apparently no effort to edit, Paule narrates the end of "en passant-Haiti" in stream of consciousness, repeating the words *trap* or *entrapment* and *shame* so many times they seem to be flying out of her head and onto the page.

As self-revealing as these notes may seem to be, much remains mysterious. Paule gives no idea of the sequence of events in the breakup of the marriage. Did she know from the beginning that she would "go her own way—knowing the dangers"? When did she realize that a transatlantic marriage would interfere with her work? Did she begin to feel trapped after Nourry sought an appointment in the Duvalier government or before? Did she desire family life for herself, or was it for Evan, for Nourry? Was Nourry seeing other women during the long periods when Paule was back in New York? Did she have other lovers? Why "shame"? Was it because she put up with these indignities for too long? On the important issue of whether or not Nourry supported her work, Paule is silent. As if seeing a still-frame image of her divided self, she reminds us to look over at her cramped workspace in the corner of the master bedroom.

In the years following her separation from Nourry, Paule went on long trips to Kenya and China; she took a female lover, Lucienne; she published *Praisesong for the Widow*, which, she said, helped me "to recover and move on." From 1983 to 1991, she was working on her fourth novel, *Daughters*. Published in October 1991, *Daughters* was her first novel with multiple women characters, the first to foreground female solidarity, and the one she described in the 1991 interview with Daryl Dance as filled with "large, enraged silences."[18] The word *silence* provoked an unusual willingness to talk about anger: "I have my doubts as to how many of us are actually able to talk about our real feelings with the men in our lives. Many of us still sit out our grievances in silence until we explode and start to yell or take some form of action. Silent sometimes till the point when we finally pick up the gun and just blow him away." Paule suggests, somewhat obliquely, that these silences characterized her own relationships: "I used to find it exceedingly difficult to express what I truly felt with my partners. Perhaps the silence in *Daughters* comes out of that part."[19] She viewed *Daughters* as a kind of therapy that enabled her to break the pattern of deferring to men, to overcome dependency and domination, and to insist upon autonomy.

Paule also wanted the novel to name other forms of bondage that included "the larger struggle of the Third World to free itself of the domination of the West and America."[20] But the epigraph she chose, from an Alvin Ailey dance program—*Little girl of all the daughters / You ain't no more slave / You's a woman now*—is a statement specifically about female emancipation and womanhood; the enraged silences in *Daughters* are female silences: Estelle watching her politician husband being waited on by a poor woman with a crying baby and thinking, but not saying, "Why couldn't he have brought the coffee over himself?"; Estelle seething in bed beside her husband after discovering that he has a mistress; the mistress, Astral, watching silently as Primus rises from the bed and dresses to go home to his wife, and reading months later in the newspaper that he has returned from the States with his wife and their first baby. When interviewer Dance suggested to Paule that the novel is a feminist statement about the women who are able to overcome the male symbolically blocking their view of the sun, Paule hastened to cover her feminist tracks: "Whatever feminist note was struck in the novel is not meant to obscure what I hope will be seen as a major theme in *Daughters:* the need for black men and women to come together in wholeness and unity." Once again we see this gesture of withdrawal from intensely held feelings, a self-imposed censorship, "for discretion's sake."[21]

Many scholars, among them Kevin Quashie, Candace Jenkins, Deborah McDowell, Elizabeth Alexander, Hortense Spillers, Christopher Freeberg, and Darlene Clark Hine, have written about the difficulty of public exposure for black women. Quashie is particularly illuminating in his description of the interior as "expansive, voluptuous, creative; impulsive and dangerous," not a quiet place.[22] The irony of these acts of suppression and withholding is that we learn little about the desires and fears of the person and more about practices of concealment, "the aesthetic[s] of the mask."[23] Even in these private drafts Paule left on her computer, where only she could see them, it was difficult for her, this person with so many "different currents within," to reveal, accept—or even know—her whole self. Despite the self-revelations in "*en passant*—Haiti," it is full of gaps and silences and evasions.

These scholar-critics alert us to the untameable quality of the interior and to the reluctance of black women writers to express that interior self publicly—and even privately. Given the stereotypes and negative images of black women in the larger society, Hine argues that black women crafted a "veil of secrecy" and perfected "the art of dissemblance" to protect their inner lives.[24] Representing the black female interior is an apt description of the *artistic* work Paule Marshall produced for fifty years. In her fictional world, she examined, explored, and/or gave us a heightened awareness of the veils of secrecy and dissemblance experienced by the black women she imagined.

Paule remained a single woman after her second marriage. She ended "*en passant*—Haiti" by quoting the writer Doris Lessing: "I have no talent for marriage." Her "Haitian misadventure," as she called her marriage, confirmed that "lack." The title of this account of her second marriage—"*en passant*—Haiti"— translates as "by the way," as if Haiti were a passing encounter, another oblique gesture that undercuts the intensity of Paule's feelings about her marriage to Nourry. It also accurately describes the marriage as a detour from "the writer's life," which, Paule concluded, is what sustained her: "All those [romantic relationships] I had tried over the years, both at home and in the islands, had come to naught. Yet, curiously, with each 'naught,' with each failure, I somehow always felt given back to myself, back to my flawed and imperfect loner self. And there was an odd sense of rightness in that. Given back to my life's work as well."

CHAPTER 12

In the Presence of the Ancestors

PAULE RESIGNED FROM NYU IN 2008, just as her memoir *Triangular Road* was about to be published. Evan was surprised that she was allowed to leave so abruptly in the middle of the semester, putting the university in what he thought was kind of a lurch. "Oh, no," she told Evan, "they understood, and they agreed." Evan remembers her saying that things were getting challenging, and some of the graduate students had complained to the department that "Mrs. Marshall is not on top of things."[1] He had the sense that his mother was aware that her mental faculties had begun to slip, which was the reason she was retiring, but she still seemed to be mostly herself.

The first real indication that something was wrong was just before Christmas in 2012, as Paule was planning to visit Evan, his wife Femke, and two grandchildren, Nina and James, in London. The thirteen-hour, two-stop flight from Richmond to New York to London had never been too much for such a seasoned traveler, and Paule agreed that she would make the reservations. When Evan called a few days before her trip to confirm the date and asked if everything was all set, she seemed perplexed: "All set for what?" As soon as she realized she'd actually forgotten, she quickly tried to correct her lapse: "I'm just not up for it."

It was clear to Evan that she had forgotten the entire trip, but she insisted that she was "just a bit tired."[2]

A few weeks later, Paule called her friend Norrece and told him she was in New York at a conference and needed to get to the airport. He asked where she was staying but she could not remember the name of the conference nor her location. Norrece pressed her further, asking her if there was some identification on the phone. She said she was at a literature conference, perhaps the MLA (Modern Language Association). He still did not think anything was wrong because she was speaking lucidly enough, but as she became more upset, he became alarmed and asked her to go to the door and give him the room number. Realizing that Paule was in her apartment in Richmond, Norrece spoke to her long enough to calm her down. Not long after that, he went down to Richmond to check on her and he could see that she was not doing well. "When my friend Betty and I visited, we saw the deterioration. Her refrigerator was bare and there were tattered clothes hanging in the bathroom that she obviously had been washing by hand."[3]

On Evan's next trip to Richmond after the missed London trip, he began to make arrangements for this new stage in Paule's life. He scheduled a meeting in Richmond with her financial advisor Mill Harris to talk about her finances. On the way to the bank, Paule suddenly wanted to know, "Where are the children? Why did we leave them at the house?"[4] This was the first inkling that Paule's condition was growing worse. Though they rarely discussed what was happening in her private life, Paule began to talk about how much her memory loss frustrated and angered her. Evan wanted her to try to relax her mind, but he knew that Paule was easily stressed under the best circumstances.

She made gallant attempts to hold onto her sense of independence. Eventually, Evan convinced his mother to see a doctor. Her first visit to the distinguished African American internist Dr. Roderick Haithcock at Bon Secours Medical Group in Richmond confirmed the results of the cognitive test: "mild dementia." Following successive visits, the diagnosis got progressively worse, but Paule would not consider any kind of assisted living, nor would she give up her apartment. Evan insisted on someone coming in to help every day. In order to maintain her independence, Paule agreed. A friend suggested someone, and during her first meeting with Paule, the woman began to express her religious beliefs that "Jesus and God are here with you and they will look out for you." Paule, who had never been religious, said a polite goodbye before telling Evan, "No way is that woman coming here."[5]

Norrece suggested his friend Valerie Robinson, who became Paule's caregiver for the last four years of her life. Paule accepted Valerie but was not happy about anyone coming into her private space. She would repeatedly ask, "What is that woman doing in my apartment?" and would often tell Valerie very firmly to get out, she didn't need help. Nonetheless, Valerie adapted and would take her to Ellwood Thompson's for grocery shopping, Paule's favorite health food store, and quickly learned Paule's preferences—she wanted only healthy food, granola and fruit, and always Perrier.

Paule continued to go out for the walks that she loved but began to get more confused and unable to find her way home. After the police twice had to retrieve her, the doctor told Evan that she would have to go into a residential facility. Evan was finally able to convince her to move into assisted living. Because she was insistent that she wanted to be with other people of color, not in a white suburban facility, Evan found Brookdale, a lovely and well-maintained facility in a wooded area of Richmond, a choice some people questioned because Brookdale also housed people subsidized by the state, but Evan intended to abide by Paule's wishes.

There were times when Evan could see flashes of the old Paule. At Brookdale's restaurant, which was often full, if they had to wait their turn, she would ask, in her most imperious voice, "When is our table going to be ready?" Evan would remind her not to worry, that their names were on the list. When he wheeled her around Brookdale, she would speak to people they passed in phrases that sounded like her former self: "I'm very fine today, how are you?"

Both Paule and Evan knew that early and quite severe cases of Alzheimer's ran in her mother's family.[6] Adriana's sister Marie would come to 407 to cook cuckoo for Paule, a family ritual that Paule continued, making sure that Marie remembered how to prepare it. When Marie was eventually placed in a nursing home with dementia, Paule took care of her financially, visiting her and paying all her expenses. Paule told Evan that another aunt, Branford Catherine, became completely senile at eighty-five years old and would often slip out of the house on the hilly Scotland side of the island and try to walk to the main market in Bridgetown. Branford Catherine once peered at Paule and called her "Adrie," her pet name for Adriana, another disconcerting omen for Paule.[7]

With Evan at her side, Paule died in Richmond on August 12, 2019, at age ninety. Her memorial was planned for the spring of 2020, but had to be canceled because of the national lockdown during the COVID pandemic. Mill Harris said that by the time of her death, Paule was worth over $2 million. He was impressed that Paule, a single working mother for most of her adult life, had been able to amass a financial legacy for her son and two grandchildren: "How is a professor able to save that amount of money?" As everyone in the family knew, Paule was a very frugal person who deliberately lived very simply, who knew how "to cut and contrive" as well as Adriana.[8]

For many years the iconic coming-of-age stories in mid-twentieth-century black literature had been James Baldwin's *Go Tell It on the Mountain* and Richard Wright's *Native Son* and *Black Boy.* Because of the interventions of black feminist scholars, Paule's *Brown Girl, Brownstones* now belongs in and enlarges that space. During the Black Arts Movement of the 1960s, literary figures like Baldwin, Baraka, Hansberry, and Brooks were lionized as black nationalist figures, but Paule's 1964 groundbreaking though unacknowledged black nationalist speech and her 1969 novel *The Chosen Place, the Timeless People* set the standard for understanding those revolutionary aims as part of a worldwide struggle. In the 1970s through the 1990s, other writers took the top awards—the Pulitzers, the National Book Awards, the Nobel Prizes. Still, Paule left a legacy of books that raised the issues of race, gender, and colonial oppression. She garnered awards like the Guggenheim, the National Institutes of Arts Award, and the John Dos Passos Prize for Literature, as well as a MacArthur Fellowship that finally accorded her the recognition that she had not received in the writing community. In her work, she brought the black world together under her diasporan magnifying glass and was, as James Hall called her, "a crucial mediating figure" in the fields of black feminism, black arts, postcolonialism, civil rights, and political philosophy.[9]

Toni Morrison died seven days before Paule. The news of Morrison's death spread quickly on social media and via the national and international press; the news of Paule's death came more slowly. Haitian American writer and former NYU colleague Edwidge Danticat learned of Morrison's death at sunrise and Paule's at sunset, and on August 17, 2019, the *New Yorker* published

Danticat's eulogy for both writers, "The Ancestral Blessings of Toni Morrison and Paule Marshall." Danticat wrote that she had first discovered both writers in the 1984 collection of essays edited by poet Mari Evans, *Black Women Writers: A Critical Evaluation.*[10] Later, when Danticat was a newly published author, both Paule and Toni embraced and encouraged her in very personal ways. Morrison's 1984 essay "Rootedness: The Ancestor as Foundation" had assured Danticat that she was working in the presence of ancestors, the tribe of women writers who gave her permission to write.[11] But it was Paule's essay "The Making of a Writer: From the Poets in the Kitchen," about ordinary homemakers like Danticat's relatives in Haiti who cooked and did housework or toiled in factories and rarely had a pen in their hands except for writing letters to Brooklyn, that made Danticat realize she could be a writer. In the pages of the *New Yorker,* pictured side by side with Morrison, in the testimony of one of that next generation of black women writers she had helped produce, Paule was granted the stature she so richly deserved.[12]

NOTES

Unattributed quotations from Paule that appear in the text come from her personal documents in the author's possession. In the fifty notebooks that comprise her papers, there are handwritten manuscripts of her novels, letters and cards, awards, handwritten notes, copies of her speeches, lectures for her classes, and photographs. In 1983, she kept a diary of her trip to China. On her computer, also in author's possession, she left notes for a memoir she called *Travelin' Light*. She also left on her computer remembrances of Langston Hughes, Malcolm X, Gwendolyn Brooks, James Baldwin, Ralph Ellison, Richard Wright unfinished notes on Paul Robeson.

Introduction

1. Henry Louis Gates and Valerie Smith, eds., *Norton Anthology of African American Literature,* 3rd ed., vol. 2 (New York: Norton, 2014), 957.

2. "Black Women Novelists: New Generation Raises Provocative Issues," *Ebony* 40, no. 1 (November 1984): 64.

3. Jacqueline Trescott, "The Daughter of the Mother Poets: Novelist Paule Marshall Exploring the World of Black Immigrants," *Washington Post,* October 7, 1991, https://www.washingtonpost.com/archive/lifestyle/1991/10/08/the-daughter-of-the-mother-poets/6b73e530-f466–474b-a866-c9f5b7359085/.

4. Alexis De Veaux, "In Celebration of Our Triumph," in *Conversations with Paule Marshall,* eds. James C. Hall and Heather Hathaway (Jackson: University Press of Mississippi, 2010), 45.

5. Sabrine Brock, "Talk as a Form of Action: An Interview with Paule Marshall" (1982), in Hall and Hathaway, *Conversations with Paule Marshall,* 65.

6. Hall and Hathaway, *Conversations with Paule Marshall.*

7. As early as 1980, there were many scholarly and literary studies of Paule Marshall. The first full-length studies of her work are Barbara Christian's *Black*

Women Writers: The Development of a Tradition, 1892–1976 (Westport, CT: Greenwood, 1980), and Dorothy Hamer Denniston, *The Fiction of Paule Marshall: Reconstructions of History, Culture, and Gender* (Knoxville: University of Tennessee Press, 1995).

CHAPTER 1. These Is New York Children

1. Paule Marshall, *Brown Girl, Brownstones* (Chatham, NJ: Chatham Bookseller, 1959), 68.

2. Paule Marshall, *Triangular Road: A Memoir* (New York: Basic Civitas Books, 2009), 76.

3. Marshall, *Brown Girl, Brownstones,* 4; Gwendolyn Brooks, "The Ghost at the Quincy Club," in *Blacks* (Chicago: Third World Press, 1994), 359.

4. Angela Elam, "To Be in the World: An Interview with Paule Marshall," in *Conversations with Paule Marshall,* ed. James C. Hall and Heather Hathaway (Jackson: University Press of Mississippi, 2010), 152.

5. Alexis De Veaux, "In Celebration of Our Triumph," in Hall and Hathaway, *Conversations with Paule Marshall,* 42.

6. Marshall, *Brown Girl, Brownstones,* 73.

7. Paule Marshall, "Black Immigrant Women in *Brown Girl, Brownstones,*" *Case Studies* (special issue: Afro Caribbean; Caribbean Life in New York City: Sociocultural Dimensions) 7, no. 1 (January 1989): 79–85.

8. Marshall, "Black Immigrant Women," 82.

9. Marshall, "Black Immigrant Women," 82.

10. Marshall, *Triangular Road,* 72.

11. Marshall, "Black Immigrant Women," 82.

12. Marshall, *Triangular Road,* 74–75.

13. Marshall, *Triangular Road,* 74–75.

14. Marshall, *Triangular Road,* 76–78.

15. Marshall, *Triangular Road,* 78.

16. Adam Green, *Selling the Race: Culture, Community, and Black Chicago, 1940–1955* (Chicago: University of Chicago Press, 2009), 2.

17. Joyce Pettis, "A MELUS Interview: Paule Marshall," in Hall and Hathaway, 85.

18. Sandi Russell, "Interview with Paule Marshall," in Hall and Hathway, *Conversations with Paule Marshall,* 78.

19. George Lamming, *In the Castle of My Skin* (Ann Arbor: University of Michigan Press, 1991), 37.

20. Russell, "Interview with Paule Marshall," 78.

21. Paule Marshall, "To Da-Duh, in Memoriam," in *Reena and Other Stories* (New York: Feminist Press, 1983), 103.

22. Marshall, "To Da-Duh, in Memoriam," 103, 97.

23. Marshall, "To Da-Duh, in Memoriam," 106.

24. Melody Graulich and Lisa Sisco, "Meditations on Language and the Self: A Conversation with Paule Marshall," in Hall and Hathaway, *Conversations with Paule Marshall,* 145.

25. Russell, "Interview with Paule Marshall," 79; De Veaux, "In Celebration of Our Triumph," 46.

26. Pettis, "A MELUS Interview," 85.

27. Russell, "Interview with Paule Marshall," 82.

28. Russell, "Interview with Paule Marshall," 79.

29. Marshall, *Triangular Road,* 85.

30. Marshall, *Triangular Road,* 91.

31. Marshall, *Triangular Road,* 80.

32. Leonard Norman Primiano, *Vernacular Religion: Collected Essays of Leonard Norman Primiano* (New York: NYU Press, 2022), 199.

33. Marshall, *Triangular Road,* 92.

34. Marshall, *Triangular Road,* 94.

35. Paule Marshall, "Shaping the World of My Art," *New Letters* 40, no. 1 (Autumn 1973): 97–112.

36. Mary Helen Washington, "A Talk with Mary Helen Washington," in Hall and Hathaway, *Conversations with Paule Marshall,* 57.

37. De Veaux, "In Celebration of Our Triumph," 42.

38. De Veaux, "In Celebration of Our Triumph," 42.

39. Washington, "A Talk with Mary Helen Washington," 56

40. Paule Marshall to Mary Helen Washington, May 1990.

41. Paule Marshall, "From the Poets in the Kitchen," *New York Times,* January 9, 1983, section 7, 3, https://www.nytimes.com/1983/01/09/books/from-the-poets-in-the-kitchen.html.

42. Marshall, "From the Poets in the Kitchen," 3.

43. De Veaux, "In Celebration of Our Triumph," 42.

44. Marshall, *Triangular Road,* 90.

45. Jazz 90-Cross Talk interview with Ernest White, 1990.

46. Marshall, *Triangular Road,* 74.

47. Marshall, "From the Poets in the Kitchen," 11.

48. *The Today Show,* interview with Deborah Norville, 1990.

49. Quotations from the Harvard lectures are available on YouTube.

50. Thomas J. Campanella, *Brooklyn: The Once and Future City* (Princeton: Princeton University Press, 2019), 3.

51. Marshall, *Triangular Road,* 85.

52. Marshall, *Triangular Road,* 95.

53. In *The Blue Period: Black Writing in the Early Cold War* (Chicago: University of Chicago Press, 2024), Jesse McCarthy spotted the way *Brown Girl, Brownstones* also connects sexual assertiveness "with specifically African American (as opposed to Barbadian) culture" (138).

CHAPTER 2. A Sort of Extraordinary Kind of Person

1. Linda M. Perkins, "Hunter College and the Education of the African-American Women, 1873–1945," *Hunter College Echo: Commemorative Journal* (1995).

2. Paule Marshall, headnotes, "The Valley Between," in *Reena and Other Stories* (New York: Feminist Press, 1983), 15.

3. "Gideonse Assails AYD as Communist," *New York Times*, March 26, 1944.

4. "Hunter May Bar AYD, After Board Action," *New York Times*, November 21, 1947, 11.

5. Paule Marshall, *Triangular Road: A Memoir* (New York: Basic Civitas Books, 2009), 7.

6. *Dust off Dreams: The Story of American Youth for Democracy*, box 4, folder 9, American Left Ephemera Collection, 1894–2008, AIS 2007, 11, Archives Service Center, University of Pittsburgh.

7. Mary Helen Washington, *The Other Blacklist: The African American Literary and Cultural Left of the 1950s* (New York: Columbia University Press, 2014), 269.

8. Marshall, *Triangular Road*, 7.

9. Paule Marshall, "Reena," in *Reena and Other Stories*, 71.

10. Marshall, "Reena," 81.

11. Alexis De Veaux, "In Celebration of Our Triumph," in *Conversations with Paule Marshall*, ed. James C. Hall and Heather Hathaway (Jackson: University Press of Mississippi, 2010), 43.

12. *New York Amsterdam News*, September 1931.

13. De Veaux, "In Celebration of Our Triumph," 43; Hiram Haydn, "A Discussion with Dr. Hiram Haydn and Others on *The Chosen Place, the Timeless People*," in Hall and Hathaway, *Conversations with Paule Marshall*, 19.

14. Dorothy Hamer Denniston, *The Fiction of Paule Marshall: Reconstructions of History, Culture, and Gender* (Knoxville: University of Tennessee Press, 1995), 3.

15. Evan Marshall, in discussion with the author, 2022.

16. Evan Marshall, in discussion with the author, 2022.

17. Evan Marshall, in discussion with the author, 2022.

18. Marshall, "The Valley Between," 15.

19. Marshall, *Triangular Road*, 98.

20. Evan Marshall, in discussion with the author, 2022.

21. Paule Marshall, "Brooklyn," in *Reena and Other Stories*, 27.

22. Marshall, "Brooklyn," 27.

23. Marshall, "Brooklyn," 27.

24. In a 1992 interview with Melody Graulich and Lisa Sisco, when asked if she were still angry with Slochower, she told them no, "not at all," adding that his country place was near to some very good friends of hers, and occasionally she would see him there and they would chat. "I've forgiven him because I was able to exorcize that rage through the story." Hall and Hathaway, *Conversations with Paule Marshall*, 146.

25. Gide's novel is central to the story "Brooklyn." Miss Williams is both shocked and troubled by the novel and by her attraction to what Professor

Berman calls "The salutary effects of sin." *Soul Clap Hands and Sing* (New York: Atheneum, 1961), 44.

26. Linda Dittmar, in discussion with the author, Boston, August 2022.

27. Dorothy Hamer Denniston, *The Fiction of Paule Marshall: Reconstructions of History, Culture, and Gender* (Knoxville: University of Tennessee Press, 1995), 3.

28. Paule Marshall, headnotes, "The Valley Between," 15.

29. Marshall, headnotes, "The Valley Between," 15.

30. Marshall, "The Valley Between," 20.

31. Marshall, "The Valley Between," 24.

CHAPTER 3. An Insane Notion

1. James Hall and Heather Hathaway, "The Art and Politics of Paule Marshall: An Interview," in *Conversations with Paule Marshall*, ed. James C. Hall and Heather Hathaway (Jackson: University Press of Mississippi, 2010), 175.

2. Phillip Bonosky, unpublished memoir of the Harlem Writers Workshop, "Odyssey of a Writers Workshop in New York City in the 1950s," in the author's possession. Bonosky worked full-time for many years for the leftist publications *Masses* and *Mainstream* and was the cultural editor and Moscow correspondent for the *Daily Worker*. The black-oriented Harlem Workshop, a branch of the Committee for the Negro in the Arts (CNA), was originally called the CNA Writers Workshop to indicate its relationship to the Left. In his meticulous journal notes from 1950 and 1954, he reveals that he started the workshop at the request of Rosa Guy. He stepped aside as chair in 1954 but remained in the workshop. Julian Mayfield was chosen to replace Bonosky as chair but was forced to stand down and allow Killens to take over because there was dissension in the group about Mayfield, who, it appears, was "having an affair with someone in the group." In later years, when the workshop became known as the Harlem Writers Guild, Bonosky's key role in its founding would be erased.

3. Bonosky, "Odyssey," 10.

4. Phillip Bonosky Journal, March 23, 1969, courtesy of Daniel Rosenberg, email to the author, November 6, 2020.

5. Bonosky Journal, April 8, 1953.

6. Bonosky Journal, March 23, 1969.

7. Bonosky Journal, May 11, 1953.

8. Claudia Jones, "An End to the Neglect of the Problem of the Negro Woman!" *Political Affairs* 28, no. 6 (June): 51–67.

9. I am highly indebted to Phillip Bonosky for the invaluable material he shared with me about Lloyd Brown, Alice Childress, and Julian Mayfield for my 2014 book *The Other Blacklist: African American Literary and Cultural Left in the 1950s*, and for his memories of Paule Marshall for this book.

10. Paul Buhle and David Wagner, *A Very Dangerous Citizen: Abraham Lincoln Polonsky and the Hollywood Left* (Oakland: University of California Press, 2002), 167.

11. Buhle and Wagner, *A Very Dangerous Citizen*, 169.

12. Hall and Hathaway, "The Art and Politics of Paule Marshall," 176.

13. *Our World* began publication in April 1946, a few months after *Ebony*, and because of their similarities as pictoral magazines and their need to appeal to the same readership, Davis viewed *Ebony* as a competitor. *Ebony* could claim a crew of photographers that included the illustrious Gordon Parks, but *Our World* could claim the talented Moneta Sleet, Jr., later a Pulitzer Prize winner, among its staff of photographers. By 1955, however, Sleet had been hired away by John H. Johnson as the photographer for *Ebony* and *Jet*. The clash between *Ebony* and *Our World* became public when Davis disparaged *Ebony* in a *Los Angeles Tribune* interview as "a white man's idea of what Negroes want in a publication" and blamed the problem on the fact that Ben Burns, a white man, was "high on its staff." Burns, the white editor on *Ebony*'s staff, called Davis's statements about him "malicious" and "reverse racism." Burns counters Davis's charge of white influence by insisting that Johnson, a black man, "owns" *Ebony*, though Burns's book documents his powerful influence as editor. *Nitty Gritty: A White Editor in Black Journalism* (Jackson: University Press of Mississippi, 1996), 129–30.

14. Hilmar Ludvig Jensen, "The Rise of an African-American Left: John P. Davis and the National Negro Congress" (PhD diss., Cornell University, 1997). In the 1930s, Davis, a Bates College and Harvard Law School graduate, was on a mission to pressure the Roosevelt administration to include black people equally in the full range of its New Deal programs. He infiltrated congressional hearings on the New Deal projects and presented such a strong, factual case against racial discrimination that he was ultimately able to open the doors of FDR's White House to prominent black leaders. As the founder and main force behind several militant black labor organizations, including the Negro Industrial League (NIL), the Joint Committee on National Recovery (JCNR), and the National Negro Congress (NNC), he was labeled "Bad Boy Administration Critic" for his persistent and outspoken challenges to the Roosevelt administration. According to his biographer, Hilmar Ludvig Jensen, Davis fearlessly traveled to the South during the 1930s to interview black workers about the abominable conditions they endured, advocating so militantly for their cause during the New Deal era that even W.E.B. Du Bois was leery of Davis's radicalism.

15. Jensen, "The Rise of an African-American Left."

16. Jensen, "The Rise of an African-American Left," 137.

17. Sabine Bröck, "Talk as a Form of Action: An Interview with Paule Marshall," in Hall and Hathaway, *Conversations with Paule Marshall*, 59–71.

18. Bröck, "Talk as a Form of Action," 71.

19. Interview with Christopher Cox, *Soho News*, January 19, 1981, 20.

20. Hall and Hathaway, "The Art and Politics of Paule Marshall," 174.

21. I. Augustus Durham, in conversation with the author, April 18, 2023.

22. "Widows over Fifty," *Our World*, September 1955, 22–25.

23. Zita C. Nunes, "The New Negro and the Turn to South America," in *Cannibal Democracy: Race and Representation in the Literature of the Americas* (Minneapolis: University of Minnesota Press, 2008).

24. Paule Marshall, "Carnival in Rio," *Our World*, July 1955, 36–47.

25. Paule Marshall, "Shaping the World of My Art," *New Letters* 40, no. 1 (Autumn 1973).

26. Hall and Hathaway, "The Art and Politics of Paule Marshall," 175.

27. In 2001, when James Hall describes this photo to her, she says she does not remember it. Hall and Hathaway, "The Art and Politics of Paule Marshall," 157.

CHAPTER 4. The Girl Can Write

1. Helen Benedict, "Filling Silences with Strong Voices: Paule Marshall," in *Portraits in Print: A Collection of Profiles and the Stories Behind Them* (New York: Columbia University Press, 1992), 81.

2. Paule Marshall, *Triangular Road: A Memoir* (New York: Basic Civitas Books, 2009), 100.

3. Sally Lodge, "*PW* Interviews Paule Marshall," in *Conversations with Paule Marshall*, ed. James C. Hall and Heather Hathaway (Jackson: University Press of Mississippi, 2010), 74.

4. Lodge, "*PW* Interviews Paule Marshall," 74; Joyce Pettis, "A MELUS Interview: Paule Marshall," in Hall and Hathaway, *Conversations with Paule Marshall*, 93.

5. Marshall, *Triangular Road*, 96.

6. Marshall, *Triangular Road*, 99.

7. Marshall, *Triangular Road*, 100.

8. Marshall, *Triangular Road*, 101.

9. Marshall, *Triangular Road*, 119

10. Marshall, *Triangular Road*, 103

11. Marshall, *Triangular Road*, 3.

12. Daryl Cumber Dance, "An Interview with Paule Marshall," in Hall and Hathaway, *Conversations with Paule Marshall*, 107.

13. Sabine Bröck, "Talk as a Form of Action: An Interview with Paule Marshall," in Hall and Hathaway, *Conversations with Paule Marshall*, 59–71.

14. Paule Marshall, *Brown Girl, Brownstones* (Chatham, NJ: Chatham Bookseller, 1959), 259.

15. Marshall, *Brown Girl, Brownstones*, 256.

16. Melody Graulich and Lisa Sisco, "Meditations on Language and the Self: A Conversation with Paule Marshall," in Hall and Hathaway, *Conversations with Paule Marshall*, 144.

17. Dance, "An Interview with Paule Marshall," 115.

18. W. H. Allen, "A Review of *Brown Girl, Brownstones*," *Times Literary Supplement*, August 19, 1960.

19. John K. Hutchens, "*Brown Girl, Brownstones*: A Review," *New York Herald Tribune*, August 18, 1959, 17.

20. Hutchens, "*Brown Girl, Brownstones:* A Review," 17. See also John K. Hutchens, "Confidential Report on Candidate for Fellowship," Guggenheim Memorial Fellowship Application for Paule Marshall, December 30, 1960, in the author's possession.

21. Ted Poston, "A Minority Report," *New York Post*, August 23, 1959.

22. John S. Lash, "Expostulation and Reply: A Critical Summary of Literature by and about Negroes in 1959," *Phylon* 21, no. 2 (Summer 1960): 11–123.

23. Dorothy Parker, "A Review of *Brown Girl, Brownstones*," *Esquire* 52, no. 5 (November 1959): 26–28.

24. Henrietta Buckmaster, "Search for Status: A Review of *Brown Girl, Brownstones*," *Saturday Review*, August 29, 1959, 14.

25. Carol Field, "Fresh, Fierce and 'First': A Review of *Brown Girl, Brownstones*" *New York Herald Tribune Book Review*, August 16, 1959, 5.

26. Field, "Fresh, Fierce and 'First,' " 5.

27. See Judith E. Smith, "Making the Working-Class Family Ordinary: *A Tree Grows in Brooklyn*," in *Visions of Belonging: Family Stories, Popular Culture, and Postwar Democracy* (New York: Columbia University Press, 2004), 41–74. Judith Smith catalogues the racial biases of novelist Betty Smith, who wrote in 1942 that twenty-five years ago "the population was mostly Germans and Irish with Jews and Italians the next in numbers. Poles were coming into the neighborhood [Williamsburg in Brooklyn] in 1920. But there were no Negroes then." To Smith, the Negro spirituals were "Negroid but they are not American." Smith thought it would be a blessing if Hitler's bombers destroyed the "evil" section where black residents lived in Willliamsburg. Some of these ideas are reflected in her famous novel, all the more reason that comparisons to Paule's inclusive vision in *Brown Girl, Brownstones* are problematic.

28. Nick Aaron Ford, "Search for Identity: A Critical Survey of Significant Belles-Letters by and about Negros Published in 1961," *Phylon* 23 (1962): 128–38.

29. Quoted in Elizabeth Laura Adams and Carla Kaplan, eds., *Dark Symphony and Other Works: African-American Women Writers, 1910–1940* (Boston: G. K. Hall, 1997), 353.

30. Arnold Rampersad, *Ralph Ellison: A Biography* (New York: Vintage, 2008), 261.

31. Marshall, *Brown Girl, Brownstones*, 303. For the ways that *Brown Girl, Brownstones* and Gwendolyn Brooks's *Maud Martha* depict 1950s modernity, see Jesse McCarthy, "Gwendolyn Brooks and Paule Marshall's Elusions," in *The Blue Period: Black Writing in the Early Cold War* (Chicago: University of Chicago Press, 2024), 104–42.

32. Marshall, *Triangular Road*, 3.

33. Rampersad, *Ralph Ellison*, 409.

34. Hilton Als, *The Women* (New York: Farrar, Straus and Giroux, 1996), 26–27.

35. "The Negro Artist and the Racial Mountain," in *The Norton Anthology of African American Literature*, 3rd ed., vol. 1 (New York: Norton, 2014).

36. Graulich and Sisco, "Meditations on Language and the Self," 135.

37. Marshall, *Brown Girl, Brownstones*, 62.

38. Marshall, *Brown Girl, Brownstones*, 206.

39. Marshall, *Brown Girl, Brownstones*, 210.

40. I am grateful to Professor Elizabeth M. DeLoughrey for the interpretation of this scene in the paper she wrote for my graduate class at the University of Maryland, College Park in the 1990s.

41. Lawrence Jackson, *The Indignant Generation: A Narrative History of African American Writers and Critics, 1934–1960* (Princeton: Princeton University Press, 2011), 496.

42. Marshall, *Brown Girl, Brownstones*, 255.

43. Molara Ogundipe-Leslie, "Re-creating Ourselves All over the World: A Conversation with Paule Marshall," in Hall and Hathaway, *Conversations with Paule Marshall*, 35.

44. Marshall, *Brown Girl, Brownstones*, 288.

45. Marshall, *Brown Girl, Brownstones*, 289.

46. Marshall, *Brown Girl, Brownstones*, 293.

47. Paule Marshall, "How the City Shapes Its Writers: Gone to Heaven at the Apollo," *New York Times Magazine*, April 28, 1985, 60.

48. *TV Guide*, May 14, 1960, 34.

49. Bröck, "Talk as a Form of Action," 65.

50. Randi Gill-Sadler disputes the phrase "ahead of its time" as an inadequate explanation for Marshall's neglect, which Gill-Sadler says is due to its archipelagic setting: "Troubling Place, Troubling Time: Paule Marshall, Archipelagic Form and the Black Literary Tradition," American Studies Association, Montreal, November 4, 2021.

51. Bröck, "Talk as a Form of Action," 65.

52. Marshall, Guggenheim application, Paragraphs 2 and 3: "Student and Creative Career," 10, in the author's possession.

CHAPTER 5. Things Is Different to Before

1. Brian J. Hartig, Brownstone Detectives, "House History Report," April 3, 2019. In the report sent to Evan Marshall, this agency included the ad for 407 Central Park West, New York, that was printed in the *New York Times*, September 1902.

2. Evan Marshall, in discussion with the author, 2023.

3. Alexis De Veaux, "In Celebration of Our Triumph," in *Conversations with Paule Marshall*, ed. James C. Hall and Heather Hathaway (Jackson: University Press of Mississippi, 2010), 45.

4. Evan Marshall, in discussion with the author, 2023.

5. Ossie Davis and Ruby Dee, *With Ossie and Ruby: In This Life Together* (New York: It Books, 2000,) 313.

6. Alexis De Veaux, "In Celebration of Our Triumph," in *Conversations with Paule Marshall,* ed. James C. Hall and Heather Hathaway (Jackson: University Press of Mississippi, 2010), 45.

7. Joyce Pettis, "A MELUS Interview: Paule Marshall," in Hall and Hathaway, *Conversations with Paule Marshall,* 88.

8. Molara Ogundipe-Leslie, "Re-creating Ourselves All over the World: A Conversation with Paule Marshall," in Hall and Hathaway, *Conversations with Paule Marshall,* 32.

9. Pettis, "A MELUS Interview," 88–89.

10. Paule uses the epigraph: "An aged man is but a paltry thing/ A tattered coat upon a stick, unless/ Soul clap its hands and Sing," from William Butler Yeats, "Sailing to Byzantium." *Soul Clap Hands and Sing,* ed. Darwin T. Turner (Washington, DC: Howard University Press, 1988). In his Introduction, Turner writes movingly of being "haunted" by the portraits of these aging men.

11. Paule Marshall, *Triangular Road: A Memoir* (New York: Basic Civitas Books, 2009), 100.

12. Paule Marshall, "Barbados," in *Soul Clap Hands and Sing* (New York: Atheneum, 1961), 12–13.

13. Marshall, "British Guiana," in *Soul Clap Hands and Sing,* 71.

14. Marshall, "British Guiana," 74.

15. Paule Marshall, "Brooklyn," in *Soul Clap Hands and Sing,* 27.

16. Marshall, "Brooklyn," 41.

17. Marshall, "Brooklyn," 44, 35, 44 (my emphasis).

18. André Gide, *The Immoralist* (New York: Vintage International, 1996), 171.

19. Marshall, "Brooklyn" 43.

20. Shirley C. Parry, "Shadows of Resistance: Ambivalence toward Community in the Novels of Paule Marshall" (PhD diss., University of Maryland, College Park, 1995).

21. Karl Sealy, "*Soul Clap Hands and Sing*: A Review," *BIM* 9, no. 35 (July–December 1962): 226.

22. Sealy, "*Soul Clap Hands and Sing,*" 227.

23. Sealy, "*Soul Clap Hands and Sing,*" 227.

24. Sealy, "*Soul Clap Hands and Sing,*" 228.

25. Darwin Turner, introduction to *Soul Clap Hands and Sing* (New York: Atheneum, 1961), xi–xlvii.

26. Darwin Turner, introduction to *Soul Clap Hands and Sing* (Washington, DC: Howard University Press, 1988), xlvi–xlvii. In 1976 Paule was invited to participate in Professor Turner's summer institute on research and teaching in black studies at the University of Iowa. Turner was so impressed with her presentations that he began to systematically read and teach her work. Their collaborations motivated him to begin a serious study of her work and changed his opinion of her fiction.

27. Nick Aaron Ford, "Search for Identity: A Critical Survey of Significant Belles-Letters by and about Negroes Published in 1961," *Phylon* 23 (1962): 128–38.

28. Henrietta Buckmaster, *New York Times,* October 1, 1961.

29. *Kirkus Review,* July 1, 1959, 461.

30. Lavelle Porter, "Paule Marshall's 'Brooklyn' and the #MeToo Movement," *Black Perspectives,* July 18, 2018, https://www.aaihs.org/paule-marshalls-brooklyn-and-the-metoo-movement/.

31. James Baldwin postcard in the author's possession.

32. Marshall, *Triangular Road,* 126.

33. James C. Hall and Heather Hathaway, "The Art and Politics of Paule Marshall: An Interview," in Hall and Hathaway, *Conversations with Paule Marshall,* 178.

34. Marshall, *Triangular Road,* 121.

35. Marshall, *Triangular Road,* 127.

36. Marshall, *Triangular Road,* 30.

37. Hiram Haydn, *Words & Faces: An Intimate Chronicle of Book and Magazine Publishing* (New York: Harcourt Brace Jovanovich, 1974), 267–68.

38. Haydn, *Words & Faces,* 267–68.

39. Haydn, *Words & Faces,* 267–68.

40. Marshall, *Triangular Road,* 135.

41. Marshall, *Triangular Road,* 136.

42. Marshall, *Triangular Road,* 140.

43. Marshall, *Triangular Road,* 121–30.

44. Marshall, *Triangular Road,* 141.

45. Marshall, *Triangular Road,* 149.

46. Marshall, *Triangular Road,* 98.

47. Kenneth E. Marshall, "The Fighting Gang in Transition: A Study of the Structure and Functions of the Urban Adolescent Fighting Gang and An Analysis of Functionally Equivalent Deviant Group Modes," Ph.D. Diss. (New York University, 1969). Schomburg Center for Research in Black Culture. In author's possession.

48. Marshall, "Bops and Other Hipsters," Ph.D.Diss., appendix 2.

49. Evan Marshall, in discussion with the author, July 26, 2019.

50. Evan Marshall, in discussion with the author, July 26, 2019.

51. Evan Marshall, in discussion with the author, July 26, 2019.

52. De Veaux, "In Celebration of Our Triumph," 45.

53. De Veaux, "In Celebration of Our Triumph," 45.

54. Paule Marshall, "Reena," in *Reena and Other Stories* (New York: Feminist Press, 1983), 88.

55. Gloria Hull, "To Be a Black Woman in America: A Reading of Paule Marshall's 'Reena,' " *Obsidian* (Winter 1978): 5–15. Hull's perceptive reading of "Reena" elucidates the hidden meanings in this story by examining Marshall's superb use of imagery, symbolism, and figurative language.

56. Evan Marshall, in discussion with the author, July 26, 2019.

57. Evan Marshall, in discussion with the author, July 26, 2019.

CHAPTER 6. Black Is to Seek a New Way

1. Evan Marshall, in discussion with the author, July 26, 2019.

2. Evan Marshall, in discussion with the author, July 26, 2019.

3. Ossie Davis, in "A Verbatim Transcript of: *A Forum: The Black Revolution and the White Backlash,* sponsored by the Association of Artists for Freedom, June 15, 1964, 46.

4. Kevin Kelly Gaines, *American Africans in Ghana* (Chapel Hill: University of North Carolina Press, 2006), 138. In this study, historian Gaines describes the underlying tensions and challenges of "the new Afro-American nationalism" as a radical critique of integration. Black radicals such as Marshall, Mayfield, and Malcolm X "discerned [in the integrationist camp] a campaign to head off the rising militancy of northern urban blacks." They advocated radical alternatives to the civil rights movement, which "fueled an identification with the anticolonialism of the world's darker peoples." The radicals "questioned whether the integration of blacks would transform and democratize the nation or whether blacks would be remade in the image of a stultifying, inequitable, and morally bankrupt American society."

5. Wilbert A. Tatum, "Acknowledgements and Introduction of Moderator," in "A Verbatim Transcript," 2.

6. Charles Silberman, in "A Verbatim Transcript," 14.

7. Silberman, *Crisis in Black and White* (New York: Vintage Books, 1964), 74.

8. Silberman, *Crisis in Black and White,* 74.

9. A major critique of Silberman's study is Matthew C. Stelly, *Crisis OF Black and White: Charles Silberman's "Crisis in Black and White": A 40-Year Retrospective* (Uhuru Sasa Research Institute, University of Rhode Island, February 2006).

10. Lorraine Hansberry, in "A Verbatim Transcript," 37.

11. LeRoi Jones, in "A Verbatim Transcript," 73.

12. Paule Marshall, in "A Verbatim Transcript," 22.

13. Frantz Fanon, in "Shaping the World of My Art," *New Letters* 40, no. 1 (Autumn 1973): 108.

14. Marshall, "A Verbatim Transcript," 18.

15. Marshall, "A Verbatim Transcript," 19.

16. Marshall, "A Verbatim Transcript," 21.

17. Marshall, "A Verbatim Transcript," 22.

18. Marshall, "A Verbatim Transcript," 21.

19. Marshall, "A Verbatim Transcript," 21.

20. Jack Newfield, "Mugging the White Liberal," *Village Voice,* June 25, 1964, 5–7.

21. Nat Hentoff, "The Town Hall 'Mugging,' " *Village Voice,* July 9, 1964, 4–5.

22. Evan Marshall, in discussion with the author, July 26, 2019.

23. James Hall and Heather Hathaway, "The Art and Politics of Paule Marshall: An Interview," in *Conversations with Paule Marshall,* ed. James C. Hall and Heather Hathaway (Jackson: University Press of Mississippi, 2010), 181.

24. Hall and Hathaway, "The Art and Politics of Paule Marshall," 181.

25. Hall and Hathaway, "The Art and Politics of Paule Marshall," 181.

26. Paule Marshall, "Some Get Wasted," in *Harlem Voices from the Soul of Black America,* ed. John Henrik Clarke (New York: New American Library, 1970), 141.

27. The transcript of these speeches by Paule Marshall, Alice Childress, and Sarah E. Wright was reprinted in *Freedomways: A Quarterly Review of the Negro Freedom Movement* (First Quarter, 1966): 8–25. Sterling Brown also spoke, but his comments were not included in the written accounts.

28. Wright introduced each of the women on the panel through their "extraordinary" work, beginning with the "singer-extraordinary" Abbey Lincoln, noting her albums and the film she was starring in, *Nothing but a Man.* In her introduction of Alice Childress, she named the boards she served on and her novel *Like One of the Family* and then plugged Childress's current dramatic production *Wedding Band.*

29. Sarah Wright's introduction of Marshall on the panel at "The Negro Writer's Vision of America," organized by John O. Killens at the New School for Social Research in April 1965. "Reena" was reprinted in John Henrik Clarke's *American Negro Short Stories.*

30. Marshall, "The Negro Writer's Vision of America," in *Freedomways.*

31. *Freedomways,* a left-wing journal, was founded by W.E.B. Du Bois, Louis Burnham, Edward Strong, Shirley Graham, W. Alphaeus Hunton, Margaret Burroughs, and Esther Jackson in 1961.

32. Ponchitta Pierce, "Problems of the Negro Woman Intellectual: Liberated from Pall of Mediocrity," *Ebony,* August 1966, 148.

33. Pierce, "Problems of the Negro Woman Intellectual," 149.

34. In chapter 4, "The Problems and Possibilities of the Negro Woman Intellectual," in *Beyond Respectability: The Intellectual Thought of Race Women* (Urbana: University of Illinois Press, 2017), Brittney C. Cooper provides an excellent incisive and historicized analysis of Pierce's article that traces the idea of black women as intellectuals from the nineteenth to the twenty-first century.

35. Barbara Smith, "Toward a Black Feminist Criticism," *Conditions* 1, no. 2 (October 1977): 25–44.

36. Mary Helen Washington, ed., *Black-Eyed Susans: Classic Stories by and about Black Women* (New York: Doubleday, 1975); Mary Helen Washington, ed., *Midnight Birds: Stories of Contemporary Black Women Writers* (New York: Doubleday, 1980)

37. Paule Marshall, *Triangular Road: A Memoir* (New York: Basic Civitas Books, 2009), 7.

38. On March 7, 1965, a civil rights march in Selma, Alabama, led by twenty-five-year-old activist leader John Lewis, was attacked by state troopers and sheriff's deputies as the marchers attempted to cross the city's Edmund Pettus Bridge. Coverage of the marchers being beaten, tear-gassed, and trampled by police horses prompted outrage across the nation, and activists, religious leaders, and everyday citizens flooded into Selma to lend their support. On March 9, a second group of marchers, led by Dr. Martin Luther King, Jr., approached the bridge, prayed there, and returned to church. On March 21, thousands of marchers crossed the bridge, this time protected by federalized National Guard troops, and headed to Montgomery.

39. Paule Marshall, *Triangular Road: A Memoir* (New York: Basic/Civitas Books, 2009), *Triangular Road,* 8.

40. Marshall, *Triangular Road,* 23.

41. The State Department tour is described in detail in Arnold Rampersad, *The Life of Langston Hughes,* vol. 2: *1941–1967: I Dream a World* (Oxford: Oxford University Press, 1988), 389–91.

42. Department of State, Educational and Cultural Exchange: Annual Report for the Period July 1964–June 1965, A-173, September 8, 1965, 5. Courtesy of Special Collections, University of Arkansas Library, Fayetteville.

43. Department of State, Educational Exchange Circular, no. 17, no. 466, December 15, 1955, 4. Courtesy of Special Collections, University of Arkansas Library, Fayetteville.

44. Department of State, Educational and Cultural Exchange: Annual Report for the Period July 1964–June 1965, A-173, September 8, 1965, 5. Courtesy of Special Collections, University of Arkansas Library, Fayetteville.

45. Department of State, Educational and Cultural Exchange: Annual Report for the Period July 1964–June 1965, A-173. September 8, 1965, 5. Courtesy of Special Collections, University of Arkansas Library, Fayetteville.

46. "Langston Hughes Column," *Pittsburgh Courier,* July 31, 1965, 11.

47. Molara Ogundipe-Leslie, "Re-creating Ourselves All over the World: A Conversation with Paule Marshall," in Hall and Hathaway, *Conversations with Paule Marshall,* 32.

48. Paule Marshall, *The Chosen Place, the Timeless People* (New York: Random House Vintage Books, 1969), 80, 82.

49. Ogundipe-Leslie, "Re-creating Ourselves All over the World," 33.

50. Marshall, *The Chosen Place, the Timeless People,* 154.

51. Marshall, *The Chosen Place, the Timeless People,* 53.

52. Marshall, *The Chosen Place, the Timeless People,* 211.

53. Marshall, *The Chosen Place, the Timeless People,* 208.

54. Frantz Fanon, *Wretched of the Earth* (London: McGibbon and Kee, 1961), 125.

55. Marshall, *The Chosen Place, the Timeless People,* 138

56. Marshall, *The Chosen Place, the Timeless People,* 109.

57. Marshall, *The Chosen Place, the Timeless People,* 289.

58. Marshall, *The Chosen Place, the Timeless People,* 463.

59. Marshall, *The Chosen Place, the Timeless People,* 469.

60. Marshall, *The Chosen Place, the Timeless People,* 471.

61. Thomas Lask, "Promise and Fulfillment: A Review of *The Chosen Place, the Timeless People,*" *New York Times,* November 8, 1969, 31.

62. Robert Bone, "Merle Kinbona Was Part Saint, Part Revolutionary, Part Obeahwoman: A Review of *The Chosen Place, the Timeless People,*" *New York Times Book Review,* November 30, 1969, 4, 54.

63. Bone, "Merle," 4, 54.

64. James Smethurst, "Artists Imagine the Nation, the Nation Imagines Art: The Black Arts Movement and Popular Culture, History, Gender, Performance, and Textuality," chapter 2 in *The Black Arts Movement: Literary Nationalism in the 1960s and 1970s* (Chapel Hill: University of North Carolina Press,) 2005. Smethurst's study is the most comprehensive and incisive history of the BAM.

65. Larry Neal, "The Black Arts Movement," *Drama Review* 12, no. 4 (Summer 1968): 28–39. See GerShun Avilez, *Radical Aesthetics and Modern Black Nationalism* (Urbana: University of Illinois Press, 2016), which brings the Black Arts Movement into contemporary relevance and complexity, showing its relationship to experimental cultural forms and the way it is manifest in film, plays, and visual culture as well as in literature.

66. Jean Carey Bond, "*Brown Girl, Brownstones:* A Review," *Freedomways* 2, no. 2 (1982): 110–12.

67. Bond, "*Brown Girl, Brownstones:* A Review."

68. Bond, "*Brown Girl, Brownstones:* A Review."

69. Bond, "*Brown Girl, Brownstones:* A Review."

70. Cultural historian Ann duCille (along with scholars Deborah McDowell, Hazel Carby, and E. Patrick Johnson, to name a few), viewed the idea of racial or vernacular authenticity as an attempt to standardize blackness and erase difference, allowing certain writers and artists a stamp of approval. See duCille, *The Coupling Convention: Sex, Text, and Tradition in Black Women's Fiction* (Oxford: Oxford University Press, 1993), 80–81.

71. Alexis De Veaux, "In Celebration of Our Triumph," in Hall and Hathaway, *Conversations with Paule Marshall,* 47.

72. Hall and Hathaway, "The Art and Politics of Paule Marshall," 180.

73. Nikki Giovanni, review of *Chosen Place, Negro Digest,* January 1970, 52, 84. In her essay "Troubling Place, Troubling Time: Paule Marshall, Archipelagic Form and the Black Literary Tradition" (American Studies Association, Montreal, November 4, 2021), Randi Gill-Sadler challenged Giovanni on multiple grounds: "Perhaps most importantly, Giovanni foregoes an opportunity to tether Bourne Island to any other Black diasporic spaces or settings and effectively alienates the archipelagic setting of the novel, and Marshall by extension, from the Black literary culture of the day." Gill-Sadler notes Giovanni's "specific invocation of the West Indies is not connected to a wider, Black, diasporic, literary community. Instead, it is associated with foreignness, strangeness, and mystery. Even the suggestion that Marshall is the 'mysterious West Indian Princess' is quite jarring given the fact that Marshall was born and raised in Brooklyn, New York, and participated in Black American cultural groups like the Association of Artists for Freedom alongside figures like James Baldwin, Ruby Dee, and Amiri Baraka. Marking Marshall as a 'mysterious West Indian princess' and a 'Rembrandt in blackface,' both Giovanni and Bond make a case for Marshall's outsiderness in relation to the Black literary tradition on archipelagic grounds."

74. Giovanni, review of *Chosen Place,* 84.

75. Giovanni, review of *Chosen Place*, 84.

76. Barbara Christian, "The Race for Theory," *Cultural Critique*, no. 6 (Spring 1987): 51–63.

77. Marshall, *The Chosen Place, the Timeless People*, 328.

78. Marshall, *The Chosen Place, the Timeless People*, 380.

79. Marshall, *The Chosen Place, the Timeless People*, 381; my emphasis.

80. In 1968, when she was asked by the *New York Times* to contribute to a symposium, "Great Books We Never Finished Reading," she named William Styron's *Confessions of Nat Turner*, accusing him of such "blatant racism, she could not complete the novel." She resented Styron's reduction of Nat Turner, "the great 19th-century religious rebel, the revolutionary, . . . to a cowardly, irresolute, neurasthenic celibate obsessed with the thought of white female flesh," a clear contradiction of established historical fact: "I saw blood." Paule also objected to Nat Turner speaking in the voice of "an Emersonian schoolmaster" and to the novel being written in the formal tone of an essay rather than "the excitement and sense of lived experience of fiction," and, when Nat and his male friend Will were depicted tumbling amorously in the grass, "I called it quits."

81. James C. Hall, *Mercy, Mercy Me: African-American Culture and the American Sixties* (Oxford: Oxford University Press, 2001), 88.

82. Kimberly Benston, "Architectural Imagery and Unity in Paule Marshall's *Brown Girl, Brownstones*," *Black American Literature Forum* 9, no. 3 (Fall 1975): 67–70.

83. Margo Natalie Crawford, *Black Post-Blackness: The Black Arts Movement and Twenty-First-Century Aesthetics* (Urbana: University of Illinois Press, 2017).

84. For a perspective on how Paule Marshall's novel challenges Black Arts aesthetic manifestoes of the 1970s, see Williamenia Miranda Walker Freeman, " 'Their Past in My Blood': Paule Marshall, Gayl Jones, and Octavia Butler's Response to the Black Aesthetic," Aquila Digital Community, Dissertations, 458, University of Southern Mississippi, December 2010. In a 1988 introduction to *Soul Clap Hands and Sing*, literary historian Darwin Turner encapsulates Marshall's role in the 1960s as unheralded leader of [the Black Arts] age: "Paule Marshall inhales the spirit of the times . . . she has grown with the spirit of her era and often has anticipated literary themes that would gain greater popularity after her early treatment of them." Although some critics tried to identify a Black Arts novel, many decided it did not exist. In "And Shine Swam On" (in LeRoi Jones and Larry Neal, eds., *Black Fire: An Anthology of Afro-American Writing* [New York: William Morrow, 1968], 653–54), Larry Neal claimed that there could be no Black Arts novel because the performative arts—poetry, music, and theater—were the carriers of black radical activism, the truly liberating forms; the literary text, he wrote, was irrelevant, a bourgeois form of "one elite addressing another." In *Black Women Novelists and the Nationalist Aesthetic* (Bloomington: Indiana University Press, 1994), Madhu Dubey makes the case that the free-floating idea of

a black nationalist position could possibly be identified by its focus on overturning black stereotypes, presenting "positive" images of black life, employing black vernacular, or by its privileging of conventional social realism; but Dubey does not name any novel that meets these terms. In *Mercy, Mercy Me,* James C. Hall concludes, "No one felt confident enough to speak in any kind of extended fashion about the 'new Black novel,' the 'Black Arts novel,' or the 'Black Power novel' "(92).

85. James Baldwin, letter to Paule Marshall, December 1, 1969, in possession of the author.

86. June Jordan, letter to Paule Marshall, May 29, 1981, in possession of the author.

CHAPTER 7. In-Betweenness

1. Evan Marshall, in discussion with the author, June 19, 2020.

2. Paule wrote more extensively about Nourry's view of the Duvalier government in her unpublished notes: "The man's obvious love for his country's heroic past was matched only by his rage and despair at what had befallen it since that time. This I discovered one evening when, perhaps unwisely, I asked him about the present government. 'Ils ont *tous* ruine le pays! They have all ruined the country,' he cried, his almost ironclad composure suddenly gone. His clenched voice, the 'j'accuse!' emphasis of his outthrust forefinger held not only the despot of the moment responsible, but everyone and everything, all the powers and principalities that over time had conspired to bring (brought) about the ruin."

3. Evan Marshall, in discussion with the author, June 19, 2020.

4. Rosemonde Menard-Webb, in discussion with the author, June 30, 2019.

5. Rosemonde Menard-Webb, in discussion with the author, June 30, 2019.

6. Chantal Numa, in discussion with the author, July 17, 2020.

7. Evan Marshall, in discussion with the author, June 19, 2020.

8. Toni Morrison, letter to Paule Marshall, May 12, 1972, in Thorsson, *The Sisterhood,* 238n105.

9. Houston A. Baker, Jr., "Arna Bontemps: A Memoir," *Black World* 22, no. 11 (September 1973): 5.

10. Molara Ogundipe-Leslie, "Re-creating Ourselves All over the World: A Conversation with Paule Marshall," in *Conversations with Paule Marshall,* ed. James C. Hall and Heather Hathaway (Jackson: University Press of Mississippi, 2010), 39.

11. Paule Marshall, "Shaping the World of My Art," *New Letters* 40, no. 1 (Autumn 1973): 97–112.

12. Esther Jackson, "Shaping the World of My Art," *New Letters* (1973): 104.

13. James C. Hall, *Mercy, Mercy Me: African-American Culture and the American Sixties* (Oxford: Oxford University Press, 2001), 86–87.

14. Richard Dean So, *Redlining Culture: A Data History of Racial Inequality and Postwar Fiction* (New York: Columbia University Press, 2021). So uses quantitative models to study the persistence of racial inequality in the American publishing industry.

15. Margo Natalie Crawford, *Black Post-Blackness: The Black Arts Movement and Twentieth-Century Aesthetics* (Urbana: University of Illinois Press, 2017), 11.

16. Hall, *Mercy, Mercy Me,* 89.

17. Mel Watkins, "Sexism, Racism, and Black Women Writers," (*New York Times,* June 15, 1986, 35.

18. A private school with a tuition in the 1970s of around $8,000, Riverdale sits on twenty-seven and a half acres in the Bronx.

19. Jessica B. Harris, *My Soul Looks Back: A Memoir* (New York: Scribner, 2017).

20. Harris, *My Soul Looks Back,* 84.

21. Harris, *My Soul Looks Back,* 84.

22. Chantal Numa, in discussion with the author, July 17, 2020.

23. Chantal Numa, in discussion with the author, July 17, 2020.

24. Chantal Numa, in discussion with the author, July 17, 2020.

25. Courtney Thorsson, *The Sisterhood: How a Network of Black Women Writers Changed American Culture* (New York: Columbia University Press, 2023). Starting with the iconic photo of the women in the Sisterhood, Thorsson's excellent archival work establishes the importance of this cultural and literary history of U.S. black women in the 1980s.

26. Evelyn C. White, *Alice Walker: A Life* (New York: Norton, 2004).

27. Hortense J. Spillers, "Afterword: Cross-Currents, Discontinuities: Black Women's Fiction," in *Conjuring: Black Women, Fiction, and Literary Tradition,* ed. Marjorie Pryse and Hortense J. Spillers (Bloomington: Indiana University Press, 1985).

28. Alexis De Veaux, *Warrior Poet: A Biography of Audre Lorde* (New York: Norton, 2004). Lorde was another FESTAC participant, although Paule does not mention her and she may have come at a different time.

29. De Veaux, *Warrior Poet,* 170–74.

30. Paule Marshall, *Triangular Road: A Memoir* (New York: Basic Civitas Books, 2009), 151.

31. Evan Marshall, in discussion with the author, December 6, 2019.

32. Marshall, *Triangular Road,* 155.

33. Marshall, *Triangular Road,* 157.

34. Marshall, *Triangular Road,* 158.

35. Marshall, *Triangular Road,* 159.

36. Marshall, *Brown Girl, Brownstones,* 224.

37. Saidiya Hartman, *Lose Your Mother: A Journey along the Atlantic Slave Route* (New York: Farrar, Straus and Giroux, 2007).

38. Marshall, *Triangular Road,* 162.

39. Evan Marshall, in discussion with the author, June 19, 2020.

CHAPTER 8. A Journey Backward to Find Her Own Tribe

1. Alexis De Veaux, "In Celebration of Our Triumph," in *Conversations with Paule Marshall*, ed. James C. Hall and Heather Hathaway (Jackson: University Press of Mississippi, 2010), 50.

2. Sylvia Baer, "Holding onto the Vision: Sylvia Baer Interviews Paule Marshall," in Hall and Hathaway, *Conversations with Paule Marshall*, 123, 119.

3. Hortense J. Spillers, "Afterword: Cross-Currents, Discontinuities: Black Women's Fiction," in *Conjuring: Black Women, Fiction, and Literary Tradition*, ed. Marjorie Pryse and Hortense J. Spillers (Bloomington: Indiana University Press, 1985), 245.

4. Deborah McDowell, "New Directions for Black Feminist Criticism," in *The New Feminist Criticism*, ed. Elaine Showalter (New York: Pantheon, 1985), 190.

5. Cheryl Wall, in *Norton Anthology of African American Literature*, ed. Henry Louis Gates and Valerie A. Smith, 3rd ed., vol. 2 (New York: Norton, 2014), 957.

6. Florence Howe, director, the Feminist Press at the City University of New York, letter to Faith Childs, February 20, 1991, in the author's possession.

7. Joyce Pettis, "A MELUS Interview: Paule Marshall," in Hall and Hathaway, *Conversations with Paule Marshall*, 94.

8. Daryl Cumber Dance, "An Interview with Paule Marshall," in Hall and Hathaway, *Conversations with Paule Marshall*, 99.

9. Paule Marshall, "Shaping the World of my Art," *New Letters* 40, no. 1 (Autumn 1973): 107.

10. Dance, "An Interview with Paule Marshall," 111.

11. Cheryl A. Wall, "Bare Bones and Silken Threads: Lineage and Literary Tradition in *Praisesong for the Widow*," in *Worrying the Line: Black Women Writers, Lineage, and Literary Tradition* (Chapel Hill: University of North Carolina Press, 2005), 184.

12. Paule Marshall, *Praisesong for the Widow* (New York, Penguin Books, 1983), 16.

13. Marshall, *Praisesong*, 89.

14. Carriacou became the site of Audre Lorde's discovery of the name she chose for herself: "Zami." She heard her relatives use the word to describe female friends, the *zami* of Carriacou: these women who "were left on the island by seafaring men" and shaped a maternal heritage born of the friendships they formed. See Alexis De Veaux, *Warrior Poet: A Biography of Audre Lorde* (Norton, 2004), 300.

15. Marshall, *Praisesong*, 218.

16. Baer, "Holding onto the Vision," 119.

17. Paule Marshall, "Avey and Olaudah: Traditional Black Themes in Modern Dress" (talk given at the Fourth National Black Writers Conference [NBWC], Medgar Evers College, City University of New York, 1996).

18. Marshall, *Praisesong*, 249.

19. Marshall, *Praisesong*, 240.

20. Marshall, *Praisesong*, 244.

21. Marshall, *Praisesong*, 245.

22. Christopher Lehmann-Haupt, in *New York Times*, February 1, 1983, section C, 13.

23. Mary Kathleen Benet, "The White Death," *Times Literary Supplement*, September 16, 1983, 1002.

24. Carol Ascher, "Caught in the Middle: A Review of *Praisesong for the Widow*," *Village Voice*, March 28, 1983.

25. Marian K. Borenstein, "*Praisesong for the Widow*: A Review," *Freedomways* 24, no. 1 (1984): 56–57.

26. Anne Tyler, "A Widow's Tale," *New York Times*, February 20, 1983, section 7, 7, 34.

27. Joyce Pettis, *Toward Wholeness in Paule Marshall's Fiction* (Charlottesville: University of Virginia Press, 1995).

28. I am hesitant about language such as "she reclaims her own selfhood," or "achieves spiritual healing" or "spiritual transcendence" because the complexity of Marshall's work requires the reader to live with uncertainty, inconclusiveness, in spiritual yearning, not completeness, whatever that means. Pettis alerts us to Marshall's entire corpus, which continues to raise questions about the impacts of slavery, colonialism, capitalism, and community, noting that Marshall moves toward completeness in all her work.

29. Marshall, *Praisesong*, 254.

30. Susan Sontag, in Marshall, *Praisesong*, 212.

31. Courtney Thorsson, "Dancing Up a Nation: Paule Marshall's *Praisesong for the Widow*," *Callaloo* 30, no. 2 (Spring 2007): 644–52.

32. Wall, "Bare Bones and Silken Threads," 181.

33. Marshall, *Praisesong for the Widow*, 212.

34. Graulich and Sisco, "Meditations on Language and the Self," 149.

35. Alice Walker, letter to Paule Marshall, n.d., in the author's possession.

36. John Killens, letter to Paule Marshall, n.d., in the author's possession.

37. John O. Killens, in *Crisis*, 90, August-September 1983, 49–50, 49.

38. Vinson Cunningham, *Great Expectations* (London: Hogarth, 2024), 50–51.

39. Valerie Miner, in discussion with the author, January 22, 2019.

40. "Lucy" is the name given to the several hundred pieces of fossilized bone that represented a female body discovered in 1974 in Ethiopia and considered the earliest human. The name was taken from the Beatles' song "Lucy in the Sky with Diamonds," which was playing repeatedly at the exhibition camp after the excavation.

41. Like Selina in *Brown Girl, Brownstones*, the stunning sense of "the impact of my black face" produced what cultural historian Nicole Fleetwood labels a "Fanonian moment," an experience of objectification that Afro-Caribbean psychiatrist and philosopher Frantz Fanon describes in *Black Skin, White Masks* when a white child is alarmed by the sight of Fanon's dark face. Nicole Fleetwood,

"Introduction," *Troubling Vision: Performance, Visuality, and Blackness* (Chicago: University of Chicago Press, 2010), 23.

42. Alice Walker, "A Thousand Words: A Writer's Picture of China," in *Living by the Word: Selected Writings, 1973–1987* (New York: Harcourt, Brace, Jovanovich, 1988).

43. Walker, "A Thousand Words," 110.

44. Walker, "A Thousand Words," 110.

45. Valerie Miner, in discussion with the author, January 22, 2019.

46. Tillie Olsen and Paule were the oldest members of the group. The rest, born between 1934 and 1944 (Alice was the youngest at thirty-nine), came of age in the era of the feminist and the gay rights movements. Paule may not have felt as open as the younger women, who were clearly more comfortable in this discussion and freer to express their queer sexuality.

47. Valerie Miner, in discussion with the author, January 22, 2019.

48. Tess Gallagher, email to the author, January 24, 2019.

49. Paule Marshall, "Ties That Bind," *Essence,* May 1985, 64, 86.

50. "Great Books We Never Finished Reading," *New York Times,* June 3, 1984, section 7, 3, 47.

51. "An Exchange on 'Nat Turner': Anna Mary Wells, Vincent Harding, and Mike Thelwell Reply to Eugene D. Genovese," *New York Review of Books,* November 7, 1968. In the volume *William Styron's Nat Turner: Ten Black Writers Respond* (Boston: Beacon, 1968), ten black intellectuals—all men, Vincent Harding, John O. Killens, Mike Thelwell, John Henrik Clarke, Lerone Bennett, Alvin F. Poussaint, John A. Williams, Charles V. Hamilton, Ernest Kaiser, and Loyle Hairston—voiced their objections on many grounds to Styron's portrayal of Nat Turner.

52. Darlene Clark Hine, "Rape and the Inner Lives of Black Women in the Middle West," *Signs* 14, no. 4, Common Grounds and Crossroads: Race, Ethnicity, and Class in Women's Lives (Summer 1989): 912–20.

CHAPTER 9. I'm Taking More Risks

1. Martha Collins, in discussion with the author, April 20, 2022.

2. Virginia Woolf, *A Room of One's Own* (New York: Penguin Classics, 2000), 62.

3. Woolf, *A Room of One's Own,* 79.

4. Alexis De Veaux recounted this heated discussion between Cliff and Lorde in *Warrior Poet: A Biography of Audre Lorde* (New York: Norton, 2006), 182–84.

5. Joyce Pettis, "A MELUS Interview: Paule Marshall," in *Conversations with Paule Marshall,* ed. James C. Hall and Heather Hathaway (Jackson: University Press of Mississippi, 2010), 84–95, 94.

6. Daryl Cumber Dance, "An Interview with Paule Marshall," in Hall and Hathaway, *Conversations with Paule Marshall,* 103.

7. Sylvia Baer, "Holding onto the Vision: Sylvia Baer Interviews Paule Marshall," in Hall and Hathaway, *Conversations with Paule Marshall,* 122.

8. Pettis, "A MELUS Interview," 94.

9. Baer, "Holding onto the Vision," 122.

10. CBS *Today Show,* January 26,1992.

11. Daryl Cumber Dance, *Remembering Paule: A Photo Memoir of Her Richmond Years* (Jacksonville: Adducent, 2023), 20.

12. Melody Graulich and Lisa Sisco, "Meditations on Language and the Self: A Conversation with Paule Marshall," in Hall and Hathaway, *Conversations with Paule Marshall,* 145.

13. Paule Marshall, *Daughters* (New York: Atheneum, 1991), 13.

14. Jane Smiley, "Caribbean Voices," *Chicago Tribune,* October 6, 1991, 3.

15. See Erica Edwards's use of the term "charismatic leadership" in *Charisma and the Fictions of Black Leadership* (Minneapolis: University of Minnesota Press, 2012).

16. Merle Collins, "A Caribbean Story: Grenada's Journey: Possibilities, Contradictions, Lessons," *Caribbean Quarterly* 60 (March 2014): 23–41.

17. Marshall, *Daughters,* 295.

18. Marshall, *Daughters,* 273.

19. Marshall, *Daughters,* 285.

20. Marshall, *Daughters,* 353; see also Shirley Parry, "Shadows of Resistance: Ambivalence towards Community in the Novels of Paule Marshall" (PhD diss., University of Maryland, College Park, 1993). The Amazon was "one of the group of fierce women warriors who, according to Greek legend, cut off one breast in order to be more accurate archers. Their strength and their alleged refusal to mate with men has made them especially important symbolic ancestral figures to lesbians" (303).

21. Marshall, *Daughters,* 312.

22. Marshall, *Daughters,* 312.

23. Marshall, *Daughters,* 138.

24. Marshall, *Daughters,* 10.

25. Marshall, *Daughters,* 111.

26. Marshall, *Daughters,* 355.

27. Marshall, *Daughters,* 404.

28. Marshall, *Brown Girl, Brownstones,* 59.

29. Marshall, *Daughters,* 354.

30. Dance, "An Interview with Paule Marshall," 115.

31. Ursa recalls her feelings of complicity in the erotic pleasure her father evokes. Ursa's eventual emancipation from her father's seductions remains in the margins, overwritten by the story of his election defeat.

32. Francine Prose, " 'Another Country': A Review of *Daughters,*" *Washington Post Book World,* September 22, 1991, 1, 4.

33. Nancy Forbes Romano, "Suns and Lovers," *Los Angeles Times,* October 6, 1991, 1, 8.

34. Carol Ascher, "Compromised Lives," *Women's Review of Books* 9, no. 2 (November 1991): 7.

35. Susan Fromberg Schaeffer, "Cutting Herself Free," *New York Times,* October 27, 1991, 3, 29.

36. Evan Marshall, in discussion with the author, 2023.

37. Letter from Dean Smith, January 18, 1984, in Daryl Cumber Dance, *Remembering Paule: A Photo Memoir of Her Richmond Years* (Jacksonville: Adducent, 2023), 2.

38. John T. Kneebone and Eugene P. Trani, *Fulfilling the Promise: Virginia Commonwealth University and the City of Richmond, 1968–2009* (Charlottesville: University of Virginia Press, 2020), 118.

39. Kneebone and Trani, *Fulfilling the Promise.*

40. Richard Fine, email to the author, September 15, 2023.

41. Norrece T. Jones, in discussion with the author, July 7, 2019.

42. Richard Fine, email to the author, September 15, 2023.

43. Kneebone and Trani, *Fulfilling the Promise.*

44. Paule Marshall, *Triangular Road: A Memoir* (New York: Basic Civitas Books, 2009), 40.

45. Mary Lou Hall, phone interview with the author, June 18, 2024.

46. Alvin Schexnider, in discussion with the author, December 29, 2023.

47. Bert Ashe, email to the author, June 16, 2024. Bertram D. Ashe published an essay, "About Paule Marshall," in *Platform, New Virginia Review,* in 2001.

48. Bert Ashe, email to the author, June 16, 2024.

49. Erica Vital-Lazare, in discussion with the author, June 18, 2024.

50. Mary Lou Hall, email to the author, June 18, 2024.

51. Bert Ashe, email to the author, June 16, 2024.

52. Dance, "An Interview with Paule Marshall," 111.

53. In 2023, Daryl Dance was appointed the Sterling Brown Professor at Howard University.

54. Daryl Cumber Dance, *Remembering Paule: A Photo Memoir of Her Richmond Years* (Jacksonville: Adducent, 2023), 13.

55. Norrece T. Jones, in discussion with the author, July 27, 2019.

56. Toni Cooper, in discussion with the author, July 9, 2023.

57. Carmen R. Gillespie, "Wintergreen and Alaga Syrup: A Writer's Reflections on Memory, Writing, and Place," in *Shaping Memories: Reflections of African American Women Writers,* ed. Joanne Veal Gabbin (Jackson: University Press of Mississippi, 2009), 10.

58. Joanne Gabbin, in discussion with the author, August 17, 2023.

59. Trudier Harris, in discussion with the author, April 8, 2024.

60. Joanne Gabbin, in discussion with the author, August 17, 2023.

61. Opal Moore, in discussion with the author, August 15, 2023.

62. Joanne Gabbin, in discussion with the author, August 15, 2023.

63. Joanne Gabbin, in discussion with the author, August 15, 2023.

64. Evan Marshall in discussion with the author, August 8, 2023.

65. David E. Sutton, *Bigger Fish to Fry: A Theory of Cooking as Risk, with Greek Examples,* New Anthropologies of Europe: Perspectives and Provocations 3 (Oxford: Berghahn, 2021).

66. David Sutton, in discussion with the author, May 2024.

CHAPTER 10. The New Generation

1. Edwidge Danticat, "The Ancestral Blessings of Toni Morrison and Paule Marshall," *New Yorker,* August 17, 2019, https://www.newyorker.com/books/page-turner/the-ancestral-blessings-of-toni-morrison-and-paule-marshall.

2. Danticat, "The Ancestral Blessings of Toni Morrison and Paule Marshall."

3. Melody Graulich and Lisa Sisco, "Meditations on Language and the Self: A Conversation with Paule Marshall," in *Conversations with Paule Marshall,* ed. James C. Hall and Heather Hathaway (Jackson: University Press of Mississippi, 2010), 140.

4. Sharon Olds, in discussion with the author, New York City, June 2023.

5. Shamar Hill, in discussion with the author, January 29, 2023.

6. Shamar Hill, in discussion with the author, January 29, 2023.

7. John Keene, " 'You Have Permission to Do This': John Keene Reflects on Paule Marshall's Influence," *Anthurium: A Caribbean Studies Journal* 14, no. 1 (June 2017).

8. Keene, " 'You Have Permission to Do This.' " Keene is one of the few writers who notes what is daring and experimental in Paule's art.

9. "Brazil" gets revived in Keene's story "Cold" in *Counternarratives* (New York: New Directions, 2015), pointing the way to a new perspective on Paule's writing.

10. Oasis of Love was the name of a Texas mega-church.

11. Ben Rhodes, in discussion with the author, August 24, 2023.

12. Ben Rhodes, in discussion with the author, August 24, 2023.

13. Shay Youngblood, in discussion with the author, November 9, 2021.

14. Shay Youngblood, in discussion with the author, November 9, 2021.

15. Shay Youngblood, in discussion with the author, November 9, 2021.

16. Mel Tapley, in the *New York Amsterdam News,* November 25, 1995.

17. Shay Youngblood, in discussion with the author, November 9, 2021.

18. Paule Marshall, *The Fisher King* (New York: Simon & Schuster, 2000), 59.

19. Several scholars recognize Hattie's central role in *The Fisher King.* In her chapter, "*The Fisher King* and the Women of Jazz," Patricia G. Lespinasse calls attention to the way the promotional material for the novel excludes women, but she writes that a feminist reading reveals their importance. See *The Drum Is a Wild Woman: Jazz and Gender in African Diaspora Literature* (Jackson: University Press of Mississippi, 2022), 110–25. An essay by Daphne Lamothe argues that it is "the dialogue and recollections of female characters that convey the communal dynamics, family relations, personal memories and collective histories of the

community" and that the narrative privileges Hattie's perspective. See "The City-Child's Quest: Spatiality and Sociality in Paule Marshall's *The Fisher King*," *Meridians: Feminism, Race, Transnationalism* 15, no. 2 (2017): 494. In his " 'A New Kind of Music': Paule Marshall, *The Fisher King*, and the Dissonance of Diaspora," John Lowney identifies *The Fisher King* as part of the new jazz studies, with "an increasing emphasis on transnational and diasporic approaches to jazz which have enhanced our understanding of the history and cultural politics of jazz." He is also attentive to Hattie's role in the novel: "Sonny-Rhett's legacy is represented through multiple narrative memories of his music, and, most importantly, his most notable performances are conveyed through the consciousness of a woman whose relationship to him is both domestic and professional." *Jazz International: Literary Afro-Modernism and the Cultural Politics of Black Music* (Urbana: University of Illinois Press, 2007), 178, 162. Farah Jasmine Griffin also alerts us to the role of jazz in the fiction of women writers in " 'It Takes Two People to Confirm the Truth': The Jazz Fiction of Sherley Anne Williams, Toni Cade Bambara, and Ntozake Shange," in *Big Ears: Listening for Gender in Jazz Studies*, ed. Nichole T. Rustin and Sherrie Tucker (Durham: Duke University Press, 2008).

20. Marshall, *The Fisher King*, 143.

21. Marshall, *The Fisher King*, 18.

22. Marshall, *The Fisher King*, 183.

23. Marshall, *The Fisher King*, 183.

24. Marshall, *The Fisher King*, 188.

25. Marshall, *The Fisher King*, 184.

26. Harold Bloom, introduction to *Caribbean Women Writers: Women Writers of English and Their Works*, ed. Harold Bloom (Philadelphia: Chelsea House, 1997), xviii.

27. Marshall, *The Fisher King*, 18.

28. Rosamond S. King, "The Flesh and Blood Triangle in Paule Marshall's *The Fisher King*," *Callaloo* 26, no. 2 (Spring 2003): 543–45. Brooklyn College professor King recognized that the boldest experiment of *The Fisher King* is its representation of a black sexual love triangle as normative and happy, as opposed to the lesbian relationship in *The Chosen Place, the Timeless People*, which portrays the white woman sexually exploiting Merle, the black woman: King calls the triangle in *The Fisher King* a rare site of happiness in the novel, arguing that the fact that all three lovers are black is particularly important; their love and behavior presented as natural, not as a result of white contamination.

29. Evan Marshall, in discussion with the author, July 26, 2019.

30. Virginia Woolf, *A Room of One's Own* (New York: Penguin Classics, 2000), 68.

31. The online site *The Weeksville Lost Jazz Shrines of Brooklyn Collection* (*WLJSB*) documents a little-known story of Brooklyn as a mecca for jazz beginning in the early twentieth century as migrants and immigrants poured into the borough. Of particular interest is the Putnam Central Jazz Club, headed by

Frederick Eversley. Paule changes the name to Putnam Royal, the scene of Sonny-Rhett's debut performance.

32. Abbey Lincoln, "The Negro Woman in American Literature" panel at the New School for Social Research conference The Negro Writer's Vision of America, reprinted in *Freedomways* 6, no. 1 (1966): 11.

33. It's also likely that Paule was aware of fictional representations of jazz by black women. Years ahead of *The Fisher King,* in the 1970s, '80s, and '90s, black women writers published stories in which women were interpreters of jazz or muses for male musicians or jazz historians. They included Maya Angelou's short story "The Reunion," which first appeared in Amina and Amiri Baraka's anthology *Confirmations;* Toni Cade Bambara's "Medley," which was anthologized in Mary Helen Washington's 1980 collection *Midnight Birds;* Xam Cartier's novel *Muse-Echo Blues;* Gayl Jones's novel *Corregidora;* and Toni Morrison's *Jazz.*

34. Marshall, *The Fisher King,* 140.

35. Darryl Pinckney, "Roots," *New York Review of Books,* April 28, 1983, 26–30. Reprinted with permission from *The New York Review of Books*; copyright © 1983 Nyrev, Inc. Vol. XXX, No. 7, April 28, 1983, pp. 26–30.

36. Hanna Nowak, "The Wild Zone in Paule Marshall's Fiction," in *Opening Up Literary Criticism: Essays on American Prose and Poetry* (Bloomington: Indiana University Press, 1968), 70. Nowak indicates that she borrowed this term from Elaine Showalter, who borrowed it from anthropologists Shirley and Edwin Ardener.

37. James Hall and Heather Hathaway, "The Art and Politics of Paule Marshall: An Interview," in Hall and Hathaway, *Conversations with Paule Marshall,* 163.

CHAPTER 11. Portrait of the Artist

1. John Keene, " 'You Have Permission to Do This': John Keene Reflects on Paule Marshall's Influence," *Anthurium: A Caribbean Studies Journal* 14, no. 1 (2017).

2. The three April 2006 Harvard lectures are available on YouTube: "An Homage to Mr. Hughes" and "I've Known Rivers, Seas, Oceans," parts 1 and 2.

3. The final chapter, "Paule Marshall and Langston Hughes," in Shane Graham's critical study of Langston Hughes, *Cultural Entanglements: Langston Hughes and the Rise of African and Caribbean Literature* (Charlottesville: University of Virginia Press, 2020), points to the many ways Paule Marshall is "the perfect heir to Hughes's ethos and aesthetics of pan-African entanglement," 211.

4. Paule Marshall, *Triangular Road: A Memoir* (New York: Basic Civitas Books, 2009), 30.

5. Paule is referring to Hughes's apparent cooperation with Senator Joseph McCarthy's Senate Permanent Subcommittee on Investigations in 1953, although scholars with access to the declassified transcript of Hughes's testimony argue that Hughes did not simply capitulate to the committee but challenged McCarthy

and defended his pro-Communist work. See David E. Chintz, *Which Sin to Bear: Authenticity & Compromise in Langston Hughes* (Oxford: Oxford University Press, 2013) for the most illuminating discussion of identity, artistic goals, and political commitment in the life and work of Langston Hughes.

6. Paule Marshall, *Brown Girl, Brownstones* (Chatham, NJ: Chatham Bookseller, 1959), 210.

7. Shirley Parry, "Shadows of Resistance: Ambivalence toward Community in the Novels of Paule Marshall" (PhD diss., University of Maryland, College Park, 1994). Parry makes the astute observation that when Robeson is arrested, his mother Viney calls Sharon, an old friend and child psychologist, whose lover, Margaret, is also a friend from their college days at a woman's college that all four women attended, signaling obliquely that Viney and Ursa are a part of an "invisible" lesbian network (302).

8. James C. Hall and Heather Hathaway, eds., *Conversations with Paule Marshall* (Jackson: University Press of Mississippi, 2010), 103.

9. Marshall, *Triangular Road,* 98.

10. Marshall, *Triangular Road,* 102.

11. Marshall, *Triangular Road,* 103.

12. Marshall, *Triangular Road,* 124.

13. Marshall, *Triangular Road,* 152.

14. She dismisses the invitation to question herself or her work. It is the third and last day of the lecture series. She is ready for a glass of wine and has no intention of engaging in an academic debate. She is the authority, who has just ordered her life from her point of view. She writes in the memoir, "*I'm a fiction writer,* after all."

15. Marshall, *Brown Girl, Brownstones,* 293.

16. Marshall, *The Fisher King,* 36.

17. Paule thought Nourry was being deceived and she continued to warn him not to believe the government's flattery: "All their talk and suggestions struck me as a vial of hemlock they poured, drop by drop, into his ear each time they met. NM, though, dismissed my worries, blaming them on my being an American, a foreigner, an intellectual, an idealist, a writer, *un blan.* As such I couldn't possibly understand Haitian politics. Why, if he were president, he might also be forced to deal harshly with his enemies in order to preserve the state. Politics! Haitian politics! It has its own rules, some of them outright ridiculous. As president, for example, he would be expected, required even, to have a mulatto mistress. That had long been the custom. Now a sensible Haitian First Lady would accept the situation for what it was, a custom. But certainly not a feminist and writer wife from America . . . *Ca-ca rat!*"

18. Daryl Cumber Dance, "An Interview with Paul Marshall," in *Conversations with Paule Marshall,* ed. James C. Hall and Heather Hathaway (Jackson: University Press of Mississippi, 2010), 195. James Hall thought that Paule's reticence to publicly acknowledge gender bias was generational: "In a pre-Me-Too universe,

I think the sexism and worse she encountered left her confused . . . she really wasn't sure how to talk about men's bad behavior." Email to the author, September 24, 2024.

19. Dance, "An Interview with Paule Marshall," 104.

20. Melody Graulich and Lisa Sisco, "Meditations on Language and the Self: A Conversation with Paule Marshall," in Hall and Hathaway, 145.

21. Dance, "An Interview with Paule Marshall," 115.

22. Kevin Quashie, *The Sovereignty of Quiet: Beyond Resistance in Black Culture* (New Brunswick: Rutgers University Press, 2012), 21.

23. Quashie, *The Sovereignty of Quiet*, 17.

24. Darlene Clark Hine, "Rape and the Inner Lives of Black Women in the Middle West," *Signs* 14 (Summer 1989): 915. See also Elizabeth Alexander, *The Black Interior* (Minneapolis: Graywolf, 2004); Hortense Spillers, *Black, White and in Color: Essays on American Literature and Culture* (Chicago: University of Chicago Press, 2003); Candace M. Jenkins, *Private Lives, Proper Relations (Regulating Black Intimacy)* (Minneapolis: University of Minnesota Press, 2007); Deborah McDowell, "Reading Family Matters, in *Changing Our Own Words: Essays on Criticism, Theory, and Writing by Black Women,* ed. Cheryl A. Wall (New Brunswick: Rutgers University Press, 1989); *Shaping Memories: Reflections of African American Women Writers,* ed. Joanne V. Gabbin (Jackson: University Press of Mississippi, 2009).

CHAPTER 12. In the Presence of the Ancestors

1. Evan Marshall, in discussion with the author, July 27, 2019.

2. Evan Marshall, in discussion with the author, February 29, 2024.

3. Norrece T. Jones, in discussion with the author, July 27, 2019.

4. Evan Marshall, in discussion with the author, February 29, 2024.

5. Evan Marshall, in discussion with the author, February 29, 2024.

6. Interviews with Valerie Robinson, Norrece T. Jones, Daryl Dance, colleagues at NYU, including Sharon Olds, and colleagues at VCU, 2023.

7. Paule Marshall, *Triangular Road: A Memoir* (New York: Basic Civitas Books, 2009), 108.

8. Evan Marshall, in discussion with the author, February 29, 2024.

9. James C. Hall, *Mercy, Mercy Me: African-American Culture and the American Sixties* (New York: Oxford University Press, 2001), 86.

10. Mari Evans, ed., *Black Women Writers: A Critical Evaluation (1950–1980)* (New York: Anchor Books/ Doubleday, 1984).

11. Evans, *Black Women Writers*, 342–43.

12. Edwidge Danticat, "The Ancestral Blessings of Toni Morrison and Paule Marshall," *New Yorker,* August 17, 2019.

ACKNOWLEDGMENTS

My deepest gratitude to Evan Marshall for preserving the Paule Marshall archive and generously sharing memories of his mother with me for the past six years. This biography is dedicated to my two workshop partners, colleagues, and friends: Shaun Myers and Shirley Moody-Turner, superb scholars of African American and diasporan literary history, and my constant guides through this biography. I thank Robert Crossley, brilliant scholar and extraordinary friend, whose imaginative studies of Jacob Lawrence, Octavia Butler, Olaf Stapledon, and Mars inspired me. More: Bob set aside his own writing to help shape this biography with his grace, wisdom, and skill. I am truly grateful for Tony Unger, excellent reader and friend, who was there at the beginning and the end. My thanks to Annemarie Mott Ewing, now Dr. Ewing, who organized all of Paule's papers and efficiently formatted, footnoted, revised, and advised, making this biography possible. Karen Olson got this project underway and used her narrative skills as a mystery writer to urge me to become a storyteller. Pat Herron, head librarian at the University of Maryland, College Park, introduced me to the technology of the archive. Professor Henry Louis (Skip) Gates gave his full support for this biography when the board was considering it. James C. Hall and Heather

Hathaway edited *Conversations with Paule Marshall*, without which no biography of Paule Marshall would be possible. Courtney Thorsson and Erica Edwards wrote readers' reports that gave me courage and illumination. Thanks to the technology skills of Shawn Saremi, I was able to retrieve all the material on Paule's old computer; Jason Jackson's technical skills produced drafts, scanned photos, and assembled PowerPoints for many years; Daniel Rosenberg, son-in-law of my friend and colleague Philip Bonosky, curated and sent me the entries from Bonosky's journal from 1950 to 1954; André Bernard, former head of the Guggenheim Foundation, went to the office during the pandemic to locate the Paule Marshall files, and took pains to see that his assistant scanned and sent me Paule's 1960 application.

Thanks to my colleagues at the University of Maryland, College Park, who helped me in so many ways to get this done: Tita Chico, Robert Levine, Amanda Bailey, Julius Fleming, Chad Infante, Karen Nelson, Bill Cohen GerShun Avilez, Bonnie Thornton Dill, Israel Augustus Durham, and all the colleagues I have worked with for over thirty years. My thanks to the Department of English and the College of Arts and Humanities for supporting five years of research with the Distinguished University Professor funds.

Thanks to my left-wing crew, who kept me on the politically righteous path: Jim Smethurst, Jim Hall, Bill Maxwell, Bill Mullen, Alan Wald, James C. Hall, Kevin Gaines, Paul Lauter, Penny Von Eschen, and the late and beloved Philip Bonosky.

I am grateful to all the friends, colleagues, and interviewees who helped create this portrait of Paule Marshall: Daniel Rosenberg, Joyce Slochower (for giving me the background on her father's life that opened up the reading of "Brooklyn"), Peter Nazareth, Martha Collins (who provided great memories of Paule), James Martone (superb translator and friend), Jean Sammon (for reading and commenting on early drafts), Arnold Rampersad (the biographer's model of excellence), Faith Childs (Paule's faithful agent), Harryette Mullen (poet-scholar and incisive commentator on my work), my friend Zita Nunes (for her archival eye that spotted Paule's computer and for her scholarly advice and example), Tita Chico (sharing writerly space and wisdom on Martha's Vineyard and beyond), GerShun Avilez (for great scholarly advice), Christopher Brown, Merle Collins, Janelle Wong, William Seraile (for notes on Paule's life in Manhattan), Andre Numa, Edgar Numa, Chantal Numa, and the entire Numa family for their support, Chantal Hippolyte, Antonio Lauria (for wisdom and historical knowledge), David Sutton, Sharon Marshall Monica McAlpine, Linda Dittmar (for making the connection between Malcolm X and André Gide), Philip Leventhal (for launching my first book and encouraging this one); Deborah McDowell (always available for consultations about black women's literature), Kate Rushin (for reading and commenting, Elizabeth (Ginger) Patterson (friend and constant supporter), Trudier Harris, Maryemma Graham, Thad Davis, Andrea Powe, Sebastian Doherty (for saving the contents of Paule's desk drawer in her NYU office), poet Sharon Olds (for a private tour of Paule Marshall's office and information about Paule as a teacher), Leroy Paltrow, Richard Yarborough, Kathy Lavezzo, Farah Jasmine Griffin, Dana Williams, Eleanor Traylor, Randi Gill-Sadler, Ben Rhodes, Daryl Dance (for Richmond hospitality and her book on Paule), Antonio Lauria-Perricelli, and Shirley Parry (whose dissertation on Paule Marshall was a forerunner of this work).

Thanks to all those scholars who helped to document Paule's time at VCU: Bert Ashe, Erica Vital-Lazare, Richard Fine, Les Harrison, and Alvin Schexnider. Thanks to Edwidge Danticat, for her love and respect for Paule. To the late Dorothy Denniston (who wrote the first literary biography of Paule). To Joanne Gabbin,

Toni Cooper (Paule's good friend), Hilbourne Watson, Rose Baptiste, and Shay Youngblood. To Norrece Jones (for interviews and for caring for Paule), Paule's stepdaughter Rosemonde Menard-Webb, and Paule's niece Sharon Marshall. To Paule's China travel partners: Lisa Alther, Tess Gallagher, Valerie Miner, and Alice Walker (my longtime supporter and ally). To Kimberley Benjamin and family, who put me up in Barbados and gave me a tour of the entire island. For Joyce Carol Oates, for writing the first review of my first book. Thanks also to my Books98 crew, reading together for more than twenty-five years: Ginger Patterson, Helen Langa, Tish Crawford, Kent Benjamin, Chuck Lawrence, Roberta Maguire, Dominique Raymond, Jim Miller, and Shirley Parry. To Ponchita Argieard, dearest friend and supporter.

I thank the outstanding editorial and production staff at Yale University Press: Tom Wolejko, Ash Lago, and Margaret Otzel, whose encouraging emails and skilled editing uplifted and supported me. I thank Robin DuBlanc for her meticulous and judicious copyediting and for her enormous patience. Thanks to my superb proofreader, Millie Piekos. My special thanks to my editor, Jessie Kindig. I could not have asked for a kinder, more thoughtful, more rigorous, or inspirational editor.

I am grateful for my community-family at Holy Redeemer Church in Washington, DC, and for my Cleveland family: sisters Betty, Bernadette, Myrna, and Beverly Washington; brothers David, Byron (Didi), and Tommy Washington; nephews Rodney Washington, David (DaDa) Washington, Steven and Darryl Washington, Michael Mitchell, Mark Wilson, and Jason Washington; cousins Terrie McElroy and Mercedes and Melissa MacMaster. And especially for my grand-nephews Denzel Washington, Rodney Washington, Jr., and Sean Washington—the ones who give me hope.

INDEX